HALAS
BY
HALAS

HALAS
BY
HALAS

THE AUTOBIOGRAPHY OF GEORGE HALAS

WITH GWEN MORGAN

AND ARTHUR VEYSEY

McGRAW-HILL BOOK COMPANY

New York   St. Louis   San Francisco   Düsseldorf

London   Mexico   Sydney   Toronto

1 2 3 4 5 6 7 8 9 D O D O 7 8 3 2 1 0 9

LIBRARY OF CONGRESS CATALOGING IN PUBLICATION DATA
Halas, George Stanley, 1895–
    Halas.
    1. Halas, George Stanley, 1895–   2. Chicago.
Football club (National League)   3. Sports team owners
—United States—Biography.   I. Morgan, Gwen, joint
author.   II. Veysey, Arthur, joint author.   III. Title.
GV939.H26A33   796.33'2'0924 [B]   79-13554
ISBN 0-07-025549-0

Book design by Andrew Roberts.

TO MIN

Acknowledgments

I thank all of the people, named and unnamed, who have made this book possible. Above all, I thank my Bears.

BEAR HONOR ROLL

Below and on the following pages is a listing of 758 players who have been on the Chicago Bears' active roster for one or more National Football League games from 1920 through the 1978 seasons. The asterisks indicate deceased players; ( ) indicates the number of seasons with the Bears; date indicates first Bear season.

A

Abbey, Joe (North Texas State)	E	(2)	1948
Adamle, Mike (Northwestern)	RB	(2)	1975
Adams, John (LA State)	B	(4)	1959
Adkins, Roy* (Millikin & Bethany)	G	(2)	1920
Akin, Len (Baylor)	G	(1)	1942
Albrecht, Ted (California)	T	(2)	1977
Allen, Duane (Santa Ana)	E	(2)	1966
Allen, Eddie (Pennsylvania)	FB	(1)	1947
Allman, Robert (Michigan St.)	E	(1)	1936
Amsler, Marty (Evansville)	DE	(2)	1967
Anderson, Art (Idaho)	T	(2)	1961
Anderson, Ed* (Notre Dame)	E	(1)	1923
Anderson, Henry (Northwestern)	G	(1)	1931
Anderson, Hunk* (Notre Dame)	G	(6)	1922
Anderson, Ralph* (Los Angeles St.)	E	(1)	1958
Anderson, William (Compton Jr.)	HB	(2)	1953
Antoine, Lionel (Southern Illinois)	T	(6)	1972
Apolskis, Charles* (DePaul)	E	(2)	1938
Arnett, Jon (Southern California)	HB	(3)	1964
Artoe, Lee (California)	T	(4)	1940
Ashburn, Clifford (Nebraska)	T	(1)	1930
Asher, Bob (Vanderbilt)	T	(4)	1972
Ashmore, M. Roger* (Gonzaga)	T	(1)	1927
Aspatore, Edward (Marquette)	T	(1)	1934
Atkins, Doug (Tennessee)	E	(12)	1955
Autrey, Billy (SF Austin)	C	(1)	1953
Avellini, Bob (Maryland)	QB	(4)	1975
Aveni, John (Indiana)	E	(2)	1959

B

Babartsky, Al (Fordham)	T	(3)	1943
Babinecz, John (Villanova)	LB	(1)	1975

Badaczewski, J. (Western Reserve)	G	(1)	1953
Baisi, Al (West Virginia)	G	(3)	1940
Barker, Richard* (Iowa State)	G	(1)	1921
Barnes, Erich (Purdue)	HB	(3)	1958
Barnes, Gary (Clemson)	E	(1)	1964
Barnes, Joe (Texas Tech)	QB	(1)	1974
Barnett, Steve (Oregon)	T	(1)	1963
Barwegan, Richard* (Purdue)	G	(3)	1950
Baschnagel, Brian (Ohio St.)	WR-KR	(3)	1976
Bassi, Dick* (Santa Clara)	G	(2)	1938
Battles, Bill (Brown)	E	(1)	1939
Bauman, Alf. (Northwestern)	T	(3)	1948
Bausch, Frank* (Kansas)	C	(4)	1937
Baynham, Craig (Georgia Tech)	RB	(1)	1970
Becker, Doug (Notre Dame)	LB	(1)	1978
Becker, Wayland (Marquette)	E	(1)	1934
Bell, Kay (Washington State)	T	(1)	1937
Benton, Jim (Arkansas)	E	(1)	1943
Bergerson, Gilbert (Oregon State)	G	(2)	1932
Berry, Connie M. (N. Carolina St.)	E	(5)	1942
Berry, Royce (Houston)	DE	(1)	1976
Best, Art (Kent State)	RB	(2)	1977
Bettis, Tom (Purdue)	LB	(1)	1963
Bettridge, John (Ohio State)	HB	(1)	1937
Bingham, Don (Sul Ross)	HB	(1)	1956
Bishop, Bill (North Texas)	T	(9)	1952
Bishop, Don (Los Angeles City)	E	(1)	1959
Bivins, Charles (Morris Brown)	HB	(7)	1960
Bjork, Del (Oregon)	T	(2)	1937
Blackburn, J. A.	T	(1)	1923
Blacklock, Hugh* (Michigan State)	T	(6)	1920
Blackman, Lennon (Tulsa)	HB	(1)	1930
Blanda, George (Kentucky)	QB	(10)	1949
Bolan, George* (Purdue)	FB	(4)	1921

Name	Pos	No.	Year
Bonderont, J. B.* (DePauw)	C	(1)	1922
Boone, J. R. (Tulsa U.)	HB	(4)	1948
Brackett, M. L. (Auburn)	T	(2)	1956
Bradley, Chuck (Oregon)	TE	(1)	1977
Bradley, Ed (Wake Forest)	G	(2)	1950
Braidwood, Charles* (Chattanooga)	E	(1)	1932
Bramhall, Art (De Paul)	HB	(1)	1931
Bratkowski, Zeke (Georgia)	QB	(6)	1954
Bray, Ray (Western Michigan)	G	(10)	1939
Brink, Larry (Northern Illinois)	E	(1)	1954
Britton, Earl* (Illinois)	FB	(1)	1925
Brockman, Edward (Oklahoma)	B	(1)	1930
Brown, Charley (Syracuse)	DB	(2)	1966
Brown, Ed (San Francisco)	QB	(8)	1954
Brown, William (Illinois)	FB	(1)	1961
Bruer, Bob (Mankato State)	TE	(1)	1976
Brumbaugh, Carl* (Florida)	QB	(8)	1930
Brupbacher, Ross (Tex A&M)	LB	(4)	1970
Bryan, Johnny* (Chicago)	HB	(4)	1922
Bryant, Waymond (Tennessee St.)	LB	(4)	1974
Buck, Arthur (John Carroll)	HB	(1)	1941
Buckler, William "Bill" (Alabama)	G	(6)	1926
Buffone, Doug (Louisville)	LB	(13)	1966
Buivid, Ray* (Marquette)	QB-HB	(2)	1937
Bukich, Rudy (Southern Cal)	QB	(9)	1958
Bull, Ronnie (Baylor)	B	(9)	1962
Burdick, Lloyd* (Illinois)	T	(2)	1931
Burgeis, Glenn (Tulsa)	T	(1)	1945
Burks, Randy (SE Oklahoma St.)	WR	(1)	1976
Burman, George (Northwestern)	T	(1)	1964
Burnell, Max (Norte Dame)	B	(1)	1944
Buss, Arthur (Michigan State)	T	(2)	1934
Bussey, Young* (Louisiana State)	QB	(2)	1940
Butkus, Dick (Illinois)	LB	(9)	1965
Butler, Gary (Rice)	TE	(1)	1975
Buzin, Rich (Penn State)	T	(1)	1972

C

Name	Pos	No.	Year
Cadile, James (San Jose State)	G	(11)	1962
Caffey, Lee Roy (Texas A&M)	LB	(1)	1970
Calland, Lee (Louisville)	CB	(1)	1969
Campana, Al (Youngstown)	HB	(4)	1950
Campbell, Gary (Colorado)	LB	(2)	1977
Campbell, Leon (Arkansas)	FB	(3)	1952
Canady, James (Texas)	HB	(2)	1948
Carey, Bob (Michigan State)	E	(1)	1958
Carl, Harland (Wisconsin)	HB	(1)	1956
Carlson, Jules "Zuck" (Oregon St.)	G	(8)	1929
Caroline, J. C. (Illinois)	HB	(10)	1956
Carter, Virgil (Brigham Young)	QB	(4)	1968
Casares, Rick (Florida)	FB	(10)	1955
Casey, Tim (Oregon)	LB	(1)	1969
Castete, Jesse (McNeese State)	HB	(1)	1956
Chamberlin, Guy* (Nebraska)	E	(2)	1920
Chambers, Wally (E. Kentucky)	DT	(5)	1973
Chesney, Chester "Chet" (De Paul)	C	(2)	1939
Childs, Clarence (Fla. A&M)	DB	(1)	1968
Cifers, Ed (Tennessee)	E	(2)	1947
Clark, Gail (Michigan State)	LB	(1)	1973
Clark, Harry (West Virginia)	HB	(4)	1940
Clark, Herman (Oregon State)	G	(5)	1952
Clark, Phil (Northwestern)	DB	(1)	1970
Clarkson, Stuart* (Texas A&I)	G	(7)	1942
Clemons, Craig (Iowa)	S	(6)	1972
Coady, Rich (Memphis State)	C/E	(5)	1970
Cobb, Mike (Michigan State)	TE	(1)	1978
Cody, Ed (Purdue)	FB	(2)	1949
Coia, Angelo (Southern California)	HB	(4)	1960
Cole, Emerson (Toledo)	FB	(1)	1952
Cole, Linzy (T.C.U.)	WR	(1)	1970
Concannon, Jack (Boston College)	QB	(5)	1967
Conkright, Bill* (Oklahoma)	C	(2)	1937
Connor, George (Notre Dame)	T	(8)	1948
Conzelman, Jim* (Washington)	HB	(1)	1920
Cooke, Ed (Maryland)	E	(1)	1958
Copeland, Ron* (UCLA)	WR	(1)	1969
Corbett, George (Millikin)	HB	(7)	1932
Cornish, Frank (Grambling)	DT	(4)	1966
Corzine, Lester (Davis Elkins)	HB	(1)	1938
Cotton, Craig (Youngstown)	TE	(1)	1973
Cowan, Les (McMurry)	T	(1)	1951
Crawford, Fred (Duke)	T	(2)	1934
Crawford, James "Mush" (Illinois)	G	(1)	1925
Croft, Abe (Southern Methodist)	E	(2)	1944
Croftcheck, Don (Indiana)	G	(1)	1967
Cross, Bob (S. F. Austin State)	T	(2)	1952
Culver, Alvin (Notre Dame)	T	(1)	1932
Cunningham, Harold (Ohio State)	E	(1)	1929
Curchin, Jeff (Florida State)	T	(2)	1970

D

Name	Pos	No.	Year
Daffer, Ted (Tennessee)	E	(1)	1954
Damore, John (Northwestern)	C	(2)	1957
Daniell, Jim (Ohio State)	T	(1)	1945
Daniels, Dick (Pacific-Oregon)	S	(2)	1969
Davis, Art (Alabama State)	T	(2)	1953
Davis, Fred (Alabama)	T	(6)	1946
Davis, Harper (Mississippi State)	HB	(1)	1950
Davis, John (Missouri)	DB	(1)	1970
Davis, Roger (Syracuse)	G	(4)	1960
Dean, Fred (Texas Southern)	G	(1)	1977
DeCorrevont, Bill (Northwestern)	HB	(2)	1948
DeLong, Steve (Tennessee)	DE	(1)	1972
Dempsey, Frank (Florida)	G	(4)	1950
Denney, Austin (Tennessee)	E	(3)	1967
Devlin, Chris (Penn State)	LB	(1)	1978
Dewveall, Willard (So. Methodist)	E	(2)	1959
Digris, Bernie (Holy Cross)	T	(1)	1943
Dimancheff, Boris "Babe" (Purdue)	HB	(1)	1952
Ditka, Mike (Pittsburgh)	TE	(6)	1961
Dodd, Al (N. W. Lousiana)	DB	(1)	1967
Doehring, John "Bull"	FB	(6)	1932
Donchez, Tom (Penn State)	RB	(1)	1975
Dooley, Jim (Miami U.)	E	(9)	1952

viii

Dottley, John (Mississippi) FB (3) 1951
Douglas, Merrill (Utah) FB (3) 1958
Douglass, Bobby (Kansas) QB (7) 1969
Douthitt, Earl (Iowa) S (1) 1975
Dreher, Fred (Denver) E (1) 1938
Dressen, Charley* QB (1) 1920
Drews, Ted (Princeton) E (1) 1928
Dreyer, Wally (Wisconsin) HB (1) 1949
Driscoll, Paddy* (Northwestern) HB (5) 1926
Drulis, Chuck* (Temple) G (6) 1942
Drury, Lyle (St. Louis) E (2) 1930
Drzewiecki, Ron (Marquette) HB (2) 1955
Dugger, Jack (Ohio State) E (1) 1949
Dunlap, Bob (Oklahoma) QB (1) 1935

E

Earl, Robin (Washington) RB (2) 1977
Ecker, Ed (John Carroll) T (1) 1947
Edwards, Cid (Tennessee State) RB (1) 1975
Ellis, Allan (UCLA) CB (5) 1973
Elnes, Leland* (Bradley) QB (1) 1929
Ely, Harold (Iowa) G (1) 1932
Ely, Larry (Iowa) LB (1) 1975
Engebretsen, Paul (Northwestern) G (1) 1932
Englund, Harry E (4) 1920
Erickson, Harold* (Wash. & Jeff.) HB (1) 1925
Evans, Earl (Harvard) T (4) 1926
Evans, Fred (Notre Dame) HB (1) 1948
Evans, Vince (USC) QB-KR (2) 1977
Evey, Dick (Tennessee) T (6) 1964

F

Falkenberg, Herb (Trinity) FB (1) 1951
Famiglietti, Gary (Boston U.) FB (8) 1938
Fanning, Stan (Idaho) T (3) 1960
Farmer, George (U.C.L.A.) WR (6) 1970
Farrington, John* (Prairie View) E (4) 1960
Farris, Tom (Wisconsin) QB (2) 1946
Feathers, Beattie (Tennessee) HB (4) 1934
Febel, Fritz* (Purdue) G (1) 1935
Federovich, John (Davis & Elkins) T (2) 1941
Feichtinger, Andy* E (2) 1920
Fencik, Gary (Yale) S (3) 1976
Fenimore, Bob (Oklahoma A&M) HB (1) 1947
Ferguson, J. B. T (1) 1932
Ferguson, Jim (So. California) C/LB (1) 1969
Fetz, Gus* FB (1) 1923
Figner, George (Colorado) HB (1) 1953
Flaherty, Pat* (Princeton) E (1) 1923
Flanagan, Dick (Ohio State) G (2) 1948
Flanagan, Latham (Carnegie Tech) E (1) 1931
Fleckenstein, Bill (Iowa) G (6) 1925
Floyd, Bobby Jack (TCU) FB (1) 1953
Ford, Charlie (Houston) CB (3) 1971
Fordham, Jim* (Georgia) FB (2) 1944
Forrest, Tom (Cincinnati) G (1) 1974
Forte, Aldo (Montana) G (4) 1939

Fortmann, Dan (Colgate) G (8) 1936
Fortunato, Joe (Mississippi St.) LB (12) 1955
Francis, Sam (Nebraska) FB (2) 1937
Franklin, Paul* (Franklin) E (5) 1930
Frump, Milton (Ohio Wesleyan) G (1) 1930

G

Gagnon, Dave (Ferris St.) RB (1) 1974
Gaines, Wentford (Cincinnati) CB (1) 1978
Galimore, Willie* (Florida A&M) HB (7) 1957
Gallagher, Dave (Michigan) DE (1) 1974
Gallarneau, Hugh (Stanford) HB (5) 1941
Garrett, Carl (N. Mex. Highlands) RB (2) 1973
Garrett, T. (Oklahoma A&M) C (2) 1947
Garrett, W. D. (Mississippi State) T (1) 1950
Garvey, A. "Hec" (Notre Dame) E (4) 1922
Garvey, Ed (Notre Dame) HB (1) 1925
Gentry, Curtiss (Maryland State) DB (3) 1966
George, Bill (Wake Forest) G/LB (14) 1952
Gepford, Sid* (Millikin & Bethany) B (1) 1919
Gersbach, Carl (West Chester St.) LB (1) 1975
Geyer, Bill (Colgate) HB (3) 1942
Gibron, Abe (Purdue) G (2) 1958
Gilbert, Kline (Mississippi) T (5) 1953
Gilliam, John (S. Carolina St.) WR (1) 1977
Glenn, Bill (Eastern Illinois) QB (2) 1941
Glueck, Larry (Villanova) B (3) 1963
Goebel, Paul (Michigan) E (1) 1925
Goodnight, Owen* (Hardin-Sims) QB (1) 1946
Gordon, Dick (Michigan State) HB (7) 1965
Gordon, Lou* (Illinois) T (1) 1938
Gorgal, Ken (Purdue) HB (2) 1955
Grabowski, Jim (Illinois) RB (1) 1971
Graham, Conrad (Tennessee) DB (1) 1973
Grandberry, Ken (Wash. St.) RB (1) 1974
Grange, Garland "Gardie" (Illinois) E (3) 1929
Grange, Harold "Red" (Illinois) HB (8) 1925
Green, Bobby Joe (Florida) P (12) 1962
Greenwood, Glen* (Iowa) HB (1) 1924
Grim, Bob (Oregon State) WR (1) 1975
Grosvenor, George (Colorado) HB (2) 1935
Grygo, Al* (South Carolina) HB (2) 1944
Gudauskas, Pete (Murray State) G (2) 1943
Gulyanics, George (Ellisville JC) HB (6) 1947
Gunn, Jimmy (USC) LB (6) 1970
Gunner, Harry (Oregon State) DE (1) 1970

H

Haddon, Aldous (Wash. & Jeff.) B (1) 1928
Halas, George (Illinois) E (10) 1920
Hale, Dave (Ottawa) DE (3) 1969
Haluska, Jim (Wisconsin) HB (1) 1956
Hamity, Lewis (Chicago) HB (1) 1941
Hamlin, Gene (West Michigan) C (1) 1971
Hammond, Henry (Southwestern) E (1) 1937
Hanke, Carl* (Minnesota) G (1) 1922
Hanny, Frank* (Indiana) E (5) 1922

ix

Acknowledgments

Ronzani, Gene* (Marquette) QB (8) 1933
Rosequist, Ted (Ohio State) T (3) 1934
Rowden, Larry (Houston) LB (1) 1971
Rowland, Brad (McMurry) HB (1) 1951
Rowland, Justin (T.C.U.) HB (1) 1960
Rupp, Nelson* (Dennison) QB (1) 1921
Russell, Reginald (Northwestern) E (1) 1928
Ryan, John (Detroit) T (1) 1929
Ryan, Rocky (Illinois) E (1) 1958
Rydalch, Ron (Utah) DT (4) 1975
Rydzewski, Frank (Notre Dame) C (1) 1923
Rykovich, Julie* (Illinois) HB (3) 1949

S

Sacrinty, Nick (Wake Forest) QB (1) 1947
Sanderson, Reggie (Stanford) RB (1) 1973
Savoldi, Joe* (Notre Dame) FB (1) 1930
Sayers, Gale (Kansas) HB (7) 1965
Schiechl, John* (Santa Clara) C (2) 1945
Schmidt, Terry (Ball State) S (3) 1976
Schreiber, Larry (Tenn. Tech.) RB (1) 1976
Schroeder, Gene (Virginia) E (6) 1951
Schubert, Steve (U Mass.) PR-WR (4) 1975
Schuette, Paul* (Wisconsin) G (3) 1930
Schweda, Brian (Kansas) DE (1) 1966
Schweidler, Dick (St. Louis) HB (3) 1938
Scott, James (Henderson J.C.) WR (3) 1976
Scott, Ralph* (Wisconsin) T (5) 1921
Sears, George (Missouri) G (7) 1965
Seibering, Gerald (Drake) FB (1) 1932
Senn, Bill* (Knox) HB (6) 1926
Serini, Washington (Kentucky) G (4) 1948
Sevy, Jeff (California) T-DE (4) 1975
Seymour, Jim (Notre Dame) WR (3) 1970
Shank, J. L. HB (1) 1920
Shanklin, Ron (No. Texas St.) WR (2) 1975
Shaw, Glenn (Kentucky) HB (1) 1960
Shearer, Brad (Texas) DT (1) 1978
Shellog, Alec* (Notre Dame) T (1) 1939
Sherman, Saul (Chicago) QB (2) 1939
Shipkey, Jerry (U.C.L.A.) FB (1) 1953
Shoemake, Hub (Illinois) G (2) 1920
Shy, Don (San Diego State) RB (3) 1970
Siegal, John (Columbia) E (5) 1939
Sigillo, Dom* (Xavier) T (2) 1943
Sigmund, Arthur W. G (1) 1923
Simmons, J. (Bethane-C'km'n) WR (1) 1969
Sisk, John (Marquette) HB (5) 1932
Sisk, John Jr. (Miami) B (1) 1964
Skibinski, John (Purdue) RB (1) 1978
Smeja, Rudy (Michigan) E (2) 1944
Smith, Clarence (Georgia) E (1) 1942
Smith, Eugene (Georgia Tech) G (1) 1930
Smith, H. Allen* (Mississippi) E (2) 1947
Smith, J. D. (N. Car. A&T) FB (1) 1956
Smith, James (Compton J.C.) HB (1) 1961
Smith, Ray Gene (Midwestern) HB (4) 1954
Smith, Ron (Wisconsin) S (4) 1965

Smith, Russell* (Illinois) T (3) 1921
Snyder, Bob (Ohio U.) QB (5) 1939
Sorey, Revie (Illinois) G (4) 1975
Spivey, Mike (Colorado) CB (2) 1977
Sprinkle, Ed (Hardin-Simmons) E (12) 1944
Stahlman, Dick* (DePaul) T (1) 1933
Standlee, Norm (Stanford) FB (1) 1941
Stautberg, Gerald (Cincinnati) G (1) 1951
Staley, Bill (Utah State) DT (2) 1970
Steinbach, Larry* (St. Thomas) G (2) 1930
Steinkemper, Bill* (Notre Dame) T (2) 1942
Sternaman, Edward* HB (10) 1920
Sternaman, Joe (Illinois) HB (8) 1922
Stenn, Paul (Villanova) G (4) 1948
Steuber, Bob (Missouri) HB (2) 1942
Stickel, Walt (Pennsylvania) T (4) 1946
Stillwell, Roger (Stanford) DE-DT (3) 1975
Stinchcomb, Pete* (Ohio State) QB (2) 1921
Stoepel, Terry (Tulsa) G (1) 1967
Stolfa, Anton* (Luther) HB (1) 1939
Stone, Billy (Bradley) HB (4) 1951
Strickland, Larry (North Texas) C (6) 1954
Sturtridge, Dick (DePaul) HB (2) 1928
Stydahar, Joe* (West Virginia) T (9) 1936
Sullivan, Frank* (Loyola, N.O.) C (5) 1935
Sumner, Charles (Wm. & Mary) HB (4) 1955
Sweeney, Jake (Cincinnati) T (1) 1944
Swisher, Bob (Northwestern) HB (5) 1938
Szymanski, Frank (Notre Dame) C (1) 1949

T

Tackwell, C. O.* (Kansas State) E (3) 1931
Taft, Merrill (Wisconsin) FB (1) 1924
Taylor, Clifton (Memphis St.) RB (1) 1974
Taylor, J. R. "Tarz"* (Ohio State) G (2) 1921
Taylor, Joe (No. Carolina A&T) DB (8) 1967
Taylor, Lionel (Highland U.) E (1) 1959
Taylor, Roosevelt (Grambling) DB (8) 1961
Thomas, Bob (Notre Dame) K (4) 1975
Thomas, Earl (Houston) WR (3) 1971
Thompson, Russ (Nebraska) T (4) 1936
Thrower, Willie (Michigan State) QB (1) 1953
Tom, Mel (San Jose State) DE (3) 1973
Torrance, Jack* (Louisiana State) T (2) 1939
Trafton, George* (Notre Dame) C (13) 1920
Trost, Milt (Marquette) T (5) 1935
Tucker, Bill (Tennessee State) RB (1) 1971
Turner, Cecil (California Poly) FL (6) 1968
Turner, Clyde (Hardin-Simmons) C (12) 1940

U

Usher, Lou* (Syracuse) T (1) 1920

V

Vactor, Ted (Nebraska) CB (1) 1975
Vallez, Emilo (New Mexico) TE (2) 1968
Van Valkenburg, Pete (BYU) RB (1) 1974
Veach, Walter* HB (1) 1920

xiii

Venturelli, Fred	T	(1)	1948	Whitsell, Dave (Indiana)	DB	(6)	1961
Vick, Ernie (Michigan)	C	(3)	1925	Whittenton, Jesse (West Texas)	HB	(1)	1958
Vick, Richard (Wash. & Jeff.)	QB	(1)	1925	Wightkin, Bill (Notre Dame)	DE	(8)	1950
Vodicka, Joe (Lewis Institute)	HB	(3)	1943	Williams, Bob (Notre Dame)	QB	(3)	1951
Voss, Walter "Tillie"* (Detroit U.)	E	(2)	1927	Williams, Broughton (Florida)	T	(1)	1947
Vucinich, Milt (Stanford)	G	(1)	1945	Williams, Fred (Arkansas)	T	(12)	1952
				Williams, Perry (Purdue)	RB	(1)	1974

W

				Wilson, George* (Northwestern)	E	(11)	1937
Wade, Charles (Tenn. St.)	WR	(1)	1974	Wilson, Nemiah (Grambling)	CB	(1)	1975
Wade, William (Vanderbilt)	QB	(6)	1961	Wright, Steve (Alabama)	T	(1)	1971
Wager, Clinton (St. Mary's)	E	(2)	1941	Wynne, Elmer (Notre Dame)	FB	(1)	1928
Wallace, Bob (Texas-El Paso)	E	(5)	1968				

Y

Wallace, Stan (Illinois)	HB	(4)	1954				
Walquist, Laurie (Illinois)	QB	(10)	1922	Youmans, Maury (Syracuse)	T	(4)	1960
Walterscheid, Len (S. Utah)	S-KR	(2)	1977	Young, Adrian (So. Calif.)	LB	(1)	1973
Ward, John* (Oklahoma State)	C-G	(1)	1976	Young, Randolph (Millikin)	T	(1)	1920
Watkins, Bobby (Ohio State)	HB	(3)	1955	Youngblood, George (L. A. State)	S	(1)	1969
Weatherly, Gerald (Rice)	C	(3)	1956	Yourist, Abe	E	(1)	1923
Wetoska, Bob (Notre Dame)	T	(10)	1960				

Z

Wetzel, Damon (Ohio State)	HB	(1)	1935				
Wheeler, Ted (W. Texas State)	G	(1)	1970	Zarnas, Gust (Ohio State)	G	(1)	1938
Wheeler, Wayne (Alabama)	WR	(1)	1974	Zeller, Joe (Indiana)	G	(6)	1933
White, Roy (Valparaiso)	FB	(5)	1923	Zizak, Vince* (Villanova)	G	(1)	1934
White, Wilford (Ariz. St.)	HB	(2)	1951	Zorich, George* (Northwestern)	G	(3)	1944
Whitman, S. J. (Tulsa)	HB	(2)	1953	Zucco, Vic (Michigan State)	HB	(3)	1957

Head Coaches

Halas, George	1920-29, 1933-42, 1946-55, 1958-67	Driscoll, John L.	1956-57
		Dooley, Jim	1968-71
Jones, Ralph	1930-32	Gibron, Abe	1972-74
Anderson, Heartly, and Johnsos, Luke	1942-45	Pardee, Jack	1975-77
		Armstrong, Neill	1978-

Assistant Coaches

Allen, George	8	1958-65	Haupt, Dale	1	1978	
Anderson, Hunk*	8	1940-42, 1946-50	Hilton, John	3	1975-77	
Austin, Bill	1	1971	Jagade, Chick	1	1956	
Bratkowski, Zeke	3	1972-74	Johnsos, Luke	30	1935-39, 1941-42, 1946-68
Brumbaugh, Carl	3	1938, 1940, 1944				
Callahan, Ray	3	1975-77	Kuhlmann, Hank	1	1978	
Carr, Jim	3	1969, 1973-74	LaRue, Jim	1	1978	
Cherundolo, Chuck	6	1966-68, 1972-74	Lord, Bob	1	1974	
Cody, Ed	6	1965-70	Luckman, Sid	16	1954, 1956-70	
Conner, George	2	1956-57	Mather, Chuck	8	1958-65	
DeCorrevont, Bill	1	1949	Meyer, Ken	1	1978	
Dimancheff, Babe	3	1966-68	Moss, Perry	4	1970-73	
Dooley, Jim	5	1963-67	O'Connor, Fred	3	1975-77	
Dovell, Whitey	3	1972-74	Ringo, Jim	3	1969-71	
Driscoll, Paddy	20	1941-55, 1958-62	Ronzani, Gene	3	1947-49	
Ecklund, Brad	3	1975-77	Ryan, Buddy	1	1978	
Fichtner, Ross	3	1975-77	Scovil, Doug	1	1978	
Fortunato, Joe	2	1967-68	Shaughnessy, Clark	12	1951-62	
Frei, Jerry	1	1978	Shaw, Bob	3	1969-71	
George, Bill	1	1972	Shinnick, Don	2	1970-71	
Gibron, Abe	7	1965-71	Stoltz, Jerry	4	1973-76	
Gillman, Sid	1	1977	Stydahar, Joe	2	1963-64	
Goldston, Ralph	1	1974	Turner, Bulldog	4	1952-56	
Grange, Red	8	1933-40	Walquist, Laurie	2	1933-34	
Handler, Phil	17	1952-68	Wilson, George	2	1947-48	

Contents

XV

HALAS
BY
HALAS

Super Bowl XIII

THE GUSTING WIND bends the palm trees double and blows the rain in sheets across the beach. The water drums against the windows of the big hotel and cascades down the blue tinted glass.

George Halas lies in bed, searching for breaks in the clouds.

"I've seen better days for a game," he says.

A long pause.

"And a lot worse," he says. "A little water never hurt anyone. Ice, that's different."

He rubs his elbows, miniature battlefields scarred by crashing falls on frozen Wrigley Field. He swings his long, slim, straight legs over the side of the bed. He raises the left leg five times, then the right.

"Must get these gimpy legs going," he says. "They can't desert me on a day like this."

3

He reaches for his stout black ebony walking stick, pushes himself upright, and marches off to the bathroom.

He studies his face in the mirror. He raises his battleship jaw and breaks into song, loud and happy:

> Hail to the Orange,
> Hail to the Blue,
> Hail Alma Mater,
> Ever so true . . .
> Vic tor eee.

"Clears the lungs," he calls out. "And if there's anyone about, it clears the room too."

He steps on the scales: 182.

"Good," he says.

He would have been astounded at any other weight. He weighed 178 at the University of Illinois the day he tackled a runner and broke his own jaw. He weighed 182 on New Year's Day of 1919 when he was voted the Most Valuable Player in the Rose Bowl. He weighed 182 when he and Hugh Blacklock made Jim Thorpe, the mighty Jim Thorpe, fumble on the 2-yard line. Halas scooped up the ball and charged for the goal 98 yards away. His touchdown went into the record books and stayed there for forty-nine years.

Halas weighed 182 in 1925 when he played end (Red Grange was at halfback) on an unbelievable Chicago Bears' coast-to-coast winter tour. They played a record-breaking seventeen games in forty-seven days, drawing 73,000 in New York and 75,000 in Los Angeles. Halas weighed 182 when, after the last game of the 1929 season, he, now thirty-four years old, took off the uniform of his beloved Chicago Bears for the last time. "They ran around me," he told the press. "They ran over me. They

4

ran through me. They ran under me; I was no good to no one."

And he was still 182 when, on December 17, 1967, his Bears came off the field after beating the Atlanta Falcons 23–14. It was his final game as coach. He was seventy-two. He had coached for forty years. His teams had gone into action 716 times and won 480 games, almost seven out of ten. Only Amos Alonzo Stagg had more years of service. In fifty-seven years Stagg had sent college teams into 546 games and had won 314, about six out of ten.

Wearing a striped shirt, a rich blue tie, sharply ridged slacks, long black socks pulled up firmly from gleaming black shoes, Halas walks into the sitting room and settles into a chair near the windows.

His secretary, Ruth Hughes, a tall, trim woman with laughter in her blue eyes, enters.

"It's good you brought your umbrella to Miami Beach, Junior," Halas says.

"Mr. Halas, I brought the umbrella to make sure it won't rain this afternoon," Ruth says. "You know it never rains when I have my umbrella."

Halas waves at the water-coated windows.

"Well, Junior, see if you can turn it off by noon, would you please? I'm talking about noon today, January 21, 1979."

"I'll work on it, Mr. Halas," she says.

"It's good we went to Mass last night," Halas says.

"The important thing right now," Ruth says, "is do you have the coin?"

5

Halas works a big broken-fingered hand into a side trouser pocket and brings out a little plastic packet in which a gold coin glistens. He opens the packet and slides out a 1920 $20 gold piece, bright as the day it left the mint.

He jiggles the coin.

"I'd better practice," he says. "I don't want to goof it today."

He balances the big coin on a thumb—the way he did when matching pennies as a kid in the Chicago alley. The coin slides off.

"No good," he says.

He puts the coin flat into the palm and throws it upward. It wriggles and wobbles.

"That won't work either."

He holds the coin between thumb and first finger. He lifts his hand sharply, at the same time drawing back his elbow. The coin rises 3 or 4 feet, fast flipping side-over-side. It falls to the floor. Ruth picks it up.

"Higher. You will have 100 million people watching on television."

The coin hits the ceiling.

"Perfect," he says.

After a dozen tries, Halas pronounces himself an acceptable coin tosser. He works the coin back into its packet and puts the packet into the right-hand pocket, thrusting the coin deep to make sure it stays there until wanted.

"Just think," Halas says. "In 1920 that coin was twenty dollars. Do you know what I paid for it last week? three hundred thirty-one dollars. Now think of how rich people would be if they had bought a lot of gold coins in 1920—if they had had the money."

6

Halas takes up his stick, walks down the hall, rides the elevator to the top floor and walks along the hall to Pete Rozelle's penthouse suite.

"Good morning, Commissioner," Halas says.

"I hope the weather clears," Rozelle says.

"It will," Halas says.

Halas reaches into his left pocket and pulls out a packet. "Commissioner," he says, "you did me a great favor in asking me to toss the coin at Super Bowl XIII. I do appreciate it."

"You are the right man," Rozelle says. "Who else has been player, coach, manager and owner? Who else living today was at Ralph Hay's Hupmobile showroom that day in 1920 when the League was formed?"

"Commissioner, the class of 1920 needs new blood," Halas says. "I am authorized to induct you into our class."

Halas hands over the packet.

Rozelle is astonished. He slips from the packet a gold coin.

"Is this the one you are using for the game today?" he asks.

"Its brother. The game one is in my other pocket."

"Is it really mine?"

Ethel Kennedy comes in, quickly followed by Lamar Hunt, president of the American Conference—Halas is president of the National Conference—Lowell Perry, one-time Pittsburgh player now a Chrysler executive, Congressman Jack Kemp of New York, a one-time Buffalo Bills player, and David Mahoney, chairman of the board of Norton Simon Corporation.

7

"We are all here," Rozelle says. "Shall we begin the semi-annual meeting of the NFL Charities?"

Rozelle reports that since the clubs turned over to the charities their royalty rights, the charities had received $2.2 million. The committee discusses possible new products, contracts and recipients. Rozelle says the charities' gift to the Blind Athletes Association was especially appreciated. "More than 500 blind athletes took part in a competition at Macomb, Illinois, last summer. It was a great thing for everyone," Rozelle says.

The meeting ends.

Halas returns to his suite. The telephone is ringing. When he finishes his call, he explains:

"That was Shirley Cowell. She's the granddaughter of Mr. A.E. Staley. A great man, Mr. Staley. He brought me to Decatur, Illinois, to start the football team that became the Bears. He changed my life. Shirley told me something I had not heard before.

"She said one day when she was seven, her grandfather sat her down and told her: 'Stick-in-the-mud, I am going to tell you two things that you must never forget. First, you must remember that soybeans will become the most important crop in the United States and, second, professional football will become the biggest game in America and George Halas will be the greatest man in professional football.'

"Shirley said her grandfather told her he would not live to see either of these developments, but she must not forget," Halas adds softly.

There is a knock on the door. Sid Luckman, once one of the greatest quarterbacks in football, hurries in. He carries a basket of fruit. He sees his coach. "Can only stay a minute," he says. "I expect you know the Judge is giving your annual birthday party next month. How many years, Coach?"

"Eighty-four," Halas replies.

"I'm still sorry you wouldn't let us call the modern T-Formation with man-in-motion the Halas Formation," Sid says.

"It wouldn't have been right," Halas says. "I didn't want to handicap it. Professional football needed it, and I was sure it would change the game."

Sid bends over and kisses Halas. "I love you, Coach," he says. "You are like a father to me."

He hurries out.

"I do believe there were tears in his eyes," Ruth says.

"We've been very close," Halas says. "He was a pall-bearer for Min. He is like a second son."

The wind has gone down. It gently rattles the panes. The sheet of water on the glass has become a splatter.

"I swear I can see bits of blue sky," Halas says.

By 1:30, the rain has ceased. Clouds still fill the sky but they ride high. They have lost most of their water. Now and then, a gust whips the trees. Halas slips into a bright plaid sports coat.

"My three angels chose this for me at Phoenix last winter," he says. "I like it."

Ruth enters.

"I spoke to Art Rooney on the phone," Halas says. "We reminisced about the League meeting in 1969 when my Bears and his Steelers shared the cellar. Bradshaw was the top draft choice that year. We both wanted him. We both needed him. We flipped a coin and Art won."

9

"Bradshaw is going to be important in the game today," Ruth says.

Halas grips Ruth's right arm. Together they go from the room, down the hall, Halas stamping until the blood zings. He uses the walking stick as a balancer. "I hope this gimpy leg behaves itself," he says.

"It will, Mr. Halas," Ruth says.

"Thank you, Junior, for your support," Halas teases. "Hail to the . . ."

"Shush."

In the lobby Halas' daughter Virginia waits.

"Hi, Gin, where's Ed?"

"Holding the car, Dad."

The three pass through the lobby, chatting. At the steps a station wagon waits.

"NBC wants me there at three. Can we make it?"

"I know a back way that should be all right," the driver says. "It misses all the usual jams. I tried it this morning and made it in 30 minutes. We should do it in 40 this afternoon."

Forty minutes later to the second, the station wagon is 100 feet from the owner's gate to the Orange Bowl. A policeman recognizes Halas and opens a way into the stadium yard and right up to Gate 9 on the 50-yard line.

The 80,000 ticket holders move in slow waves toward the gates. Halas and Ed push through to the NBC tent. Halas' son Mugs is there. Halas sees Woody Hayes. The Ohio coach shows the strain of having had his long career ended abruptly.

"Hiya, Woody," Halas says. "Good to see you. How have you been?"

"It's been rough," Woody says.

"As to critics," Halas says, "@#$%¢&× to them!"

10

The old Woody Hayes suddenly comes to life. He beams.

"You've had a wonderful career," Halas says. "Is there anything I can do for you?"

"Thanks," Hayes says. "I'll be all right. But if you could help some of my assistants, I'd appreciate it."

"I'll do what I can," Halas says.

Halas watches the frenzied television activities. How different from 1947 when the Bears first went on television. Chicago had just one station, WBKB, and fewer than 10,000 sets. WBKB paid the Bears $900 per game, a total of $5,400 for the season, and Halas thought that generous. The next year he paid $19,000 to have Bears' games carried into Indianapolis via Louisville and subsequently he built the country's biggest independent sports network, reaching into Florida. He was hoping to draw people into Chicago for the Bears' games. Then networks discovered the pulling power of professional football. In the recently ended season, television paid $140 million to carry League games coast to coast.

An NBC man approaches. "The League couldn't find a Hupmobile but it did find a 1920 touring car," he says. "Incidentally, there is a bit of rain about."

"Better take my raincoat," Mugs says. Halas puts it on.

It's an hour before game time. More than half of the seats are filled. Hawkers cry their wares, peanuts, pennants, pompoms, programs, hotdogs, badges. The enthusiastic throng flows up the aisles and out into the rows. Gradually, one quarter takes on the blue-and-white hue of Dallas while Pittsburgh's black and gold

11

pervade the adjacent section. Raindrops spatter. Timid souls raise umbrellas.

Suddenly a roar rises from the blue-and-white section. Out of a tunnel trot the Dallas Cowboys. They form up on the crosslines. Five team captains face backwards, like teachers. Together players and captains go through limbering up exercises, twisting and stretching, bending, touching hand to toes, head to knees, slowly, methodically, pulling taut each muscle, holding it for seconds. Trainers and coaches walk through the military-like lines, watching for any laxity. Head Coach Tom Landry, in natty jacket and a snap-brim hat, watches coldly, restraining any sign of emotion.

Now a mighty roar comes from the black-and-gold section. Pittsburgh fans have seen their heroes. A garden of pompoms, chrysanthemum gold, flutters, dances. The Steelers run with long strides the length of the field, turn and come back onto the grass, spongy from the rain. They form small groups. Passers pass. Receivers receive. Kickers kick. Centers hand off. Offensive linemen spring ahead like clay pigeons freed from a trap. Head Coach Chuck Noll watches, emulating the pride of a successful father.

The high-stepping Cowgirls prance into the arena, white high-heeled boots enhancing American Beauty legs, tight white shorts, brief blue and white vests swinging open, long hair flowing, pompoms worn like gloves flouncing about in cadence. Now the entire stadium roars applause. Rock blares from the amplifiers, the volume turned so high the sound must carry halfway to Dallas.

The stadium clock hands move to four o'clock. Rock dies away. Everyone stands as amplifiers pick up a male chorus on the field singing "The Star-Spangled Banner."

12

Seven officials gather in midfield, yellow penalty flags hanging ready from their belts, whistles dangling on strings. Never again can a referee blow a whistle merely because he is panting. Halas stopped that some years ago.

Out of the tunnel chugs the 1920 car. Halas sits erect in the back seat. Beside him is Ed. The car curves onto the grass. It stops on the 50-yard line. Halas stands, the walking stick ignored. He wills steel into his legs.

The referee calls the team captains to the car. Halas holds out the coin. "The Liberty Lady is heads, the eagle is tails," he says.

He signals he is ready.

Over the amplifiers comes the voice of the field announcer.

"Ladies and gentlemen . . ."

Roar!

"For Super Bowl XIII . . ."

Roar!

". . . the coin will be tossed by George Halas . . ."

Roar!

". . . the most famous . . ."

CHAPTER ONE

The Kid

MY HAPPIEST EARLY MEMORIES are of playing softball on warm summer evenings in the street under the gas light. Manhole covers and sewer grills served as bases. My brothers and I would take on all comers, providing one of the others caught for us. Frank pitched. How he made the 17-inch ball zing across home plate! I looked upon him as the best pitcher of all time. Walter played between second and third bases and I spread myself between first and second. If seven or eight boys showed up, we would even up sides, two or three of them joining us. If no boys came, my brothers and I hit flies.

My brothers called me Kid. I was not only the youngest but small for my age. I had to try doubly hard to be acceptable to them.

Mother watched from the porch. If we won a game, she would have my sister Lil fetch ice cream from the ice cream parlor on the corner.

By the time I was ten, I was a roaring Cub baseball fan. My heroes were the infield double-play trio— Tinkers to Evers to Chance—assisted at times by Stein-felt at third base. Frank Chance played first base and was captain of the team.

At every opportunity, I would present myself at the entrance to the Cubs' Park, then at Polk and Wood Streets, about a mile and a quarter from home.

I often went with a pal, John Dubek, whose family lived in one of our flats. We had to pass through the notorious 14th Street gang. The youths would try to sur-round us. John and I worked out a successful strategy to gain comparatively safe passage. I would take a sock at the nearest punk and both of us would run. I believe that is how I acquired the speed that, later, was to be helpful to me in all sports.

At the park, we would hang about the pass-gate and call to our heroes as they entered. I was always very polite. I would say:

"Mr. Chance, I hope you win today. I wish I could see the game."

Or:

"Mr. Chance, I hear you were wonderful yesterday. I wish I had seen the game."

Or:

"Mr. Chance, are you going to hit a homer today? I wish I could see you hit a homer."

Sometimes he would reply:

"Come along, kids."

And he would take my friend and me through the pass-gate.

On unsuccessful days, we would watch through knotholes, or climb the fence.

15

I dreamed of the day when the big league star would be George Stanley Halas.

I grew up in the Bohemian community about two miles southwest of downtown Chicago. My parents had come from Bohemia, now part of Czechoslovakia. Mother, Barbara Poledna, came first, in 1863. Father, Frank J. Halas, came five years later. In Bohemian, Halas is pronounced as though it were spelled Halash, with the prolongation of the second syllable.

My parents, like most of the families in the neighborhood, were building new lives on the foundation of hope and faith. They were thrifty, hard-working people out to make a better life and convinced the way lay through education and effort. They were succeeding. They built solid houses, two and three story, of brick or limestone cut from the nearby quarry. Almost daily, Father would remark on his gratitude to his parents for coming to the new world. Mother would say, "I bless the day I came to America." My parents early adopted the English language and, as we children came along, made sure we were proficient in the language so we would be well equipped for American life. My ability to use the Bohemian tongue is limited to an occasional "*yak s mahsh?*"—how are you?—and a few other phrases picked up from neighborhood friends.

Father first earned his living as a reporter on a Bohemian-language newspaper published in a stout building, still standing, around the corner from the first family home at 1815 Ashland Avenue. The Halas family lived on the first floor of the house. The two upper floors of the three-story building, also still there, were rented to two families. Soon Father developed a flourishing tailoring business. He built a two-story structure behind the house. The first floor served as a tailoring workshop, and the second as an apartment rented out to increase the Halas income. Father's business centered on making up ready-cut suits for large clothiers. Tasks were assigned to the women employees. Mother did the buttonholes. One day, a customer doubled his order because, he said, "Halas buttonholes are best." "Halas buttonholes" became part of the family's everyday speech. The words always made Father beam with pride and Mother smile with happiness. "Halas buttonholes" taught me that a person must pay attention to the smallest details and joy comes with any task well done.

Father suffered a stroke. He sold the business, rented the ground-floor flat and the workshop and built a three-story substantial brick structure at 18th Place and Wood Street with an apartment on each floor and a large corner street-level shop in which Mother opened a grocery store and dairy. Father soon doubled the building, adding three apartments. We lived on the second floor. Rent from the apartments and profit from the shop maintained the growing family comfortably, with money left over for new investment.

I was born in this new 18th Place and Wood Street apartment on February 2, 1895. I was the eighth child but I knew only Frank, Lillian and Walter. The other four had died in infancy.

We were a tightly knit family. Father was frail but ran a strict household. He insisted we always be neat. Meals were prompt and we were expected to be in our chairs with clean hands and faces. Mother was an excellent cook. My favorite dish, provided on special occasions, was duck cooked Bohemian style. The bird, stuffed with apple and roasted crisply, was served with potato dumplings and sauerkraut. School evenings were devoted to study. Almost daily Mother or Father would speak of the importance of a good education. The family dream was a university degree.

"I want you to have the education I did not get," Father would say, adding, "and I expect you to make the most of it."

Mother and Father insisted we always arrive on time at Peter Cooper School, a large, impressive red brick building a block away. I liked school. My best subject was math. I did not miss a day all through grade school. I maintained the record at high school and university—if trips with athletic teams are omitted.

At times, my enthusiasm overcame my deportment. One day I entertained my classmates making faces while our teacher, Miss Gallagher, was writing a lesson on the blackboard. I thought I was safe, her back being toward us. However my antics were reflected in her glasses. She turned sharply. She ordered me to remain behind after school. It was my turn at the blackboard, writing "Good behavior maketh a man" one hundred times.

We all had chores. Lil was Mother's enthusiastic, dedicated taskmaster. How we boys tried to avoid her on Saturday mornings when she issued her assignments! I toted coal for the greedy nickel-plated stoves. We all helped in the store. Mother insisted on having fresh produce. She and Father bought a horse, Lucy, and wagon. Once a week I would hitch Lucy to the wagon and drive Father to the South Water Street market to buy fresh vegetables and fruits. Almost every morning someone went to the railroad station for milk fresh from sub-

18

urban farms. Later I had a paper route. Arising at 5:30, I made the deliveries on foot. I never owned a bicycle.

For helping in the store Father paid me 50 cents a week but made it plain that most of the money should be put into a savings account for university. Chores in the flats were unpaid, being considered part of my contribution to the well-being of the family. I became frugal. Later it was sometimes said of me that I threw dollars around as though they were manhole covers. That is correct. It is precisely what I did do. By being careful with money, I have been able to accomplish things I consider important.

Life centered on St. Vitus Church and the Pilsen Sokol. St. Vitus exhibited Bohemian rococo exuberance, with marbled pillars, rows of brightly painted statues, vivid windows and a magnificent altar. Every Sunday the family went there to Mass. The parish had a school but Father and Mother sent us to the public school to speed our development as Americans.

The Sokol was the social center. I looked upon the building as a palace. Tall stone pillars ran up its face and a balustrade across the top. The windows were ornately framed. There were three entrances. A double center door, up a flight of stone steps from the sidewalk, led to an upstairs hall that, to me, was vast. A door on the left led to a basement swimming pool, the one on the right to a branch of the public library.

In the hall, families held parties and banquets and lectures. On Sunday evenings, there were dances, featuring the two-step and the waltz and ending with a quadrille. Lil met her future husband at a Sokol dance. On winter afternoons the hall became an indoor baseball diamond, with first and third bases just inside the side walls and second tight against the rear wall. We became expert at caroming the big, soft ball off the side walls beyond first and third. A fly ball against the rear wall counted as a home run. To advance a base, the runner would take three or four giant strides, dive and slide the rest of the way on his stomach. It was a fast game. I loved it.

One day I decided to master swimming. I went to the pool. No attendant was there. Rules forbade anyone to enter the pool by himself. I dived in. I sank. I panicked. I beat my arms. I kicked. After perhaps ten seconds, each as long as a year, I grasped the lip of the pool. Huffing and puffing, I pulled myself from the water. I developed instant respect for rules and saw that behind each good rule is a good reason.

The librarian was a fine man who did his best to introduce me to great literature. I failed him. My favorite reading was the sporting adventures at Yale of Dick and Frank Merriwell as related in *Tip Top* magazine. Father came upon a copy and declared it to be rubbish and a waste of time and tore up the magazine. I became careful not to leave my precious future copies about.

The Pilsen brewery built a new plant. Father thought its stock would be a good investment but it was available only to beer retailers. Father and Mother converted the grocery store into a saloon. The stock did prove to be an excellent investment. The saloon itself produced a good income. It was a happy place. Men from the neighborhood gathered there in the evening to talk and play pool. Women and children came to a side door to collect buckets of beer. Huge draft horses brought kegs to be rolled into the cool basement.

On summer Sunday afternoons Mother would have Mr. Tirrug, our handyman, hitch Lucy to a buggy and she would go for a drive through Douglas or Garfield Parks, not far away.

Father would put on his old clothes and go to Lake Michigan to seek perch. One hot Sunday in July he sought to introduce me to the joy of fishing. Frank and Walter were off playing baseball. I would have preferred to be with them. The fish were really biting and we brought home eighteen. It had been fun until we reached home. Then Father decided I should learn to clean fish. I had to scale and gut every one of those eighteen damned perch. Just as I finished, Frank and Walter walked in, exhausted but exhilarated by their afternoon on the baseball diamond. Mother fried the perch and my two brothers ate almost all eighteen. The experience ended for all time my interest in fishing.

It was about this time I decided I should test the thrills of smoking. I chose a Sunday. We had feasted on Bohemian duck. The duck was marvelous, crisp and succulent. I ate heartily, preparing for my venture into adulthood. From the garbage can I took corn silk and from the bathroom some tissue paper. In the alley, I rolled a cigarette, lit it and puffed away, manfully. In almost no time, I wished I could die. Up came the duck. Up came the apple stuffing, the potato dumplings, the sauerkraut. I was finished with cigarettes, forever.

However, my latent interest in tobacco continued. A few weeks later, an older boy introduced me to chewing tobacco. I took a big bite from his plug of Climax. Under his guidance I chewed, matching chaw for chaw. I made a mistake. Instead of spitting out the juice, I swallowed it. The upset after the cornsilk cigarette was nothing compared to the malaise brought upon me by the tobacco juice. From that day to this I have accepted as totally true a comment by Rudyard Kipling or some one that tobacco is a dirty weed.

Some evenings the boys in the neighborhood would shoot dice in the alley for pennies with a 10-cent limit. I was lucky and usually came away enriched as much as a dollar or two. The fourth time, Father caught me and ordered me into the house. He said playing dice was evil and I must not do it. He reinforced the words with a switch. He drove every blow home effectively.

Charlie Pechous became a special pal. Our mothers had been classmates at St. Wenceslaus parish school. One day Charlie told me: "You can rent a canoe on the Des Plaines River for only 25 cents." We rode a streetcar to the river, paid our 25 cents, pushed the canoe into the river, climbed tenderly into it, and sat, afraid to move. Then we pretended to be Indians and tried to paddle the way we thought Indians did. We neared a pier. I asked Charlie to take my picture in the canoe. We pulled the canoe against the pier. Charlie clambered out with his camera. I shoved off. The canoe upset. As the water closed over me, I remembered I could not swim.

My feet touched bottom. I straightened up. My head popped up out of the water.

"How deep is it? George, how deep?" Charlie shouted.

"Right up to the chin," I yelled.

"Hold it, I want this picture," Charlie said.

"Don't take it!" I shouted and started splashing into

the river. Fortunately the river did not deepen. Charlie did get a picture but he double exposed it on shore after my clothes had dried and I was dressing.

I entered Crane Technical High School in 1909. I weighed 110 pounds. Four years later, when I was graduated, I had ballooned to a hefty 120. Weight had become an obsession. No matter how much I ate, gobbling everything Mother put before me and adding a few extra meals on my own, I did not acquire the brawn helpful to the athlete. To make the grade with my brothers, I had to enhance my speed.

Despite my parents' continuous advice, Frank elected to take a job in the post office. He spoke firmly about the security of the postal service with a pension at the end. In time Mother accepted his choice. The security sold her. Frank married a lovely girl named Mamie O'Connor who worked on behalf of the postal union to raise wages. They moved into our second-floor flat. Frank remained keen on sports and played semi-pro hardball and pitched for the A.G. Spaulding softball team.

Lillian was engaged for several years to a wonderful guy, Mart Lauterback, a Presbyterian. In June, 1910, the Catholic priest of nearby St. Procopius parish married them in his rectory. Mother was pleased with the marriage. She thought a great deal of Mart. Also, the marriage put an end to his spooning with Lillian in the parlor. During the courting days, Mother became very upset at the way Mart put his arm around Lillian as they sat on the sofa. Mart wore a big ring and cufflinks, which scratched the sofa's mahogany frame. Marriage eliminated this problem. Father gave them an apartment in the Ashland Street building in return for their managing that property.

Father died quite suddenly on Christmas Eve of 1910. In his will he wrote that if Mother remarried, his estate would be divided among the children. She did not remarry. She devoted herself toward our achieving the education she deemed so necessary.

The city of Chicago decided to create a park in our neighborhood and began buying up property. The city paid Mother a good price for our building. With the money, she bought a half-block–long three-story corner building at 23rd Place and Washtenaw, with six apartments and, on the corner, a large shop which she rented out as a saloon. The rents and Pilsen brewery dividends enabled the Halas family to live comfortably.

If I had any thoughts about a more liberal mode of life after Father's death, I was corrected quickly. Mother assumed command. All important developments were discussed at family meetings presided over by Mother. Mother raised my salary, dramatically, to 75 cents. She admonished me to save heavily for college.

At Crane, I went out for football, track and indoor baseball. I was too light for the first football team, but I did play tackle four years on the lightweight team. I did not once think of quitting football. That would not have gone down well with Frank and Walter. They encouraged me to play all sports.

Indoor baseball was my best game. I pitched and in the senior year I was captain. We won the championship by beating Lane Tech. By graduation I had compiled more individual records than any other student.

During a game against Harrison High, a Harrison girl harassed me unmercifully. Her constant, vehement abuse forcibly brought her to my attention. I was pitching. The catcher was Jack Hamm.

"Ham and eggs! Ham and eggs!" she kept calling out. "Ham can't catch and Eggs can't pitch!"

I had to admit she was pretty. Certainly she was spirited. I made it my business to find out who she was. She was Wilhelmina Bushing but everyone called her Min. She lived at 2139 South Western Avenue, three blocks away, in a beautiful house of cut stone with a Mansard roof and two richly carved circular windows that made the house resemble a miniature French château.

I decided I would rather have Min cheer for me than against me. A friend, Arthur Schneider, attended Harrison. He introduced me to her. I invited her occasionally to socials and ice cream parties. Her family was German Lutheran; mine was Bohemian Catholic. We didn't let that hinder our relationship. Nor did our families ever speak up one against the other. But I had a long, long road to travel before I could start thinking about girls, certainly not one girl.

In the summer when I was sixteen, we kids formed a baseball club, the Concords, named for a neighborhood piano factory. We met almost every Sunday. I played second base. We took on many semi-professional teams. Each Concord would contribute ten dollars or so to a kitty. The other team would match it. The winner took all. We won more than we lost. We amassed $200 for a game with Waukegan, our richest rival. They put up $225. We took our umpires with us. We won.

We did most of our practicing in Douglas Park and

played in one of the parks. In those days almost every park had several baseball diamonds. Four "Concords" today are still among my best friends—Dr. Charlie Pechous, Art Schneider, Bill Rohn and Jim Reedy.

I began jotting into a small notebook facts I wished to remember, such as dates and times of games and the names of players. Later I added quotations or words I wanted to make part of me. I continue this practice today. I have substituted single small sheets of paper for the notebook because the sheets are less bulky and can be kept in an inside pocket, then filed, or acted upon and thrown away the next morning. The habit has stood me in good stead.

Crane Tech provided a fine education. The school offered carpentry and foundry work designed to prepare youngsters for Chicago's burgeoning industry. I concentrated on subjects which would prepare me for college: mathematics, physics, English and history. In a trigonometry class I realized I was not a genius and would have to study hard to make marks good enough to enter college. I doubled my efforts. One of my classmates was Ralph Brizzolara, who later meant a lot to the Bears.

I regret Crane did not offer a course in public speaking. A man cannot be too good before a crowd. To this day, I study speakers and admire the good ones.

By the spring of my senior year, my thoughts were occupied with going to college. My choice was the University of Illinois. Walter was completing his second year there in architectural engineering, on his way to achieving the family dream.

During vacations he regaled the family with stories about baseball and life at the Tau Kappa Epsilon fraternity. There was no doubt in my mind that the star loom-

26

ing on the horizon of the campus at Champaign was one George Stanley Halas.

Walter came home for Easter. Mother scheduled a family meeting. I fully expected she would announce that I would enroll at Illinois in the fall. Throughout Holy Week I thought of nothing else.

Mother, Walter and Lil had been all for it, even Frank who had opted for the post office.

"The Kid is going to college," Frank always said.

Mother cooked duck, Bohemian style. Lil made apple pie. Frank and Mamie came. We feasted. The table was cleared.

Mother reported on the rents, the saloon, the brewery stock. It was, to me, a very, very long report. Then she asked the older children to report. Frank told about his progress at the post office. Mother approved.

Lil and Mart declared they were off to a fine start. Mart had a good job as office manager for the Thiele Detective Agency, a job he was to hold first in Chicago and after 1923 in St. Louis until he retired at the age of seventy-two.

Mother turned to me. My heart pounded.

"I think," she said, "that George should go to college this fall."

I could have shouted hooray.

But Frank spoke up first.

"No, Mother," he said, "it would be best if he worked for a year."

I was shocked. All I ever had heard from Frank had encouraged me and now Frank, my hero Frank, was recommending hard labor.

Everyone joined in a heated discussion. Frank prevailed.

"All right, George," Mother said with a finality I knew I had to accept. "You will work for a year and then go to Illinois."

Lil brought ice cream. It offered little solace.

That night I lay on my bed, hurt by Frank's betrayal. Walter came in and sat on the bed.

"How much do you weigh, Kid?" he asked.

"Over 120."

"Well, Kid, if you weigh over 120, you don't weigh over 122," he said. "You really should work and get some meat on that skinny frame. You can do all right at baseball. Your speed will see you through. But the speed will make you terrific at football if you can put on some weight."

I knew Walter was speaking sense. Anyway, I didn't have any options. The family had decided.

In June I was graduated from Crane Technical High School. I secured a job in the payroll department at Western Electric Company in Cicero, keeping attendance cards. I learned to be precise and to keep meticulous records. I rode the streetcar to and from work. I brought home the wages. Mother saw to it that most went into the college fund.

Charlie Pechous, Ralph Brizzolara and Min also went to work at Western Electric. I made it a point to pass Min's desk frequently and pause for a few words. I played with the Western Electric payroll department baseball team and also on the Logan Square team, a semi-pro club managed by John J. Callahan, who became a good friend. Now and then, after a game, I treated Min to a soda.

CHAPTER TWO

The Road
to the Rose Bowl

IN THE FALL OF 1914, I packed three shirts, three pairs of socks, three sets of underwear. In my pocket was $30 Mother had given me to see me through the month.

I also was carting 140 pounds of taut muscle which I yearned to unveil for the coaching staff at Champaign. Walter had done a thorough job as advance man. The Tau Kappa Epsilon house eagerly awaited its future star.

I enrolled in civil engineering. I signed up for twenty hours instead of the usual eighteen so, in my final year, I would have more time for sport and fun. The fraternity gave me a job waiting tables. Mother took note. The October check was cut to $25. There the figure stayed for the remainder of my college days.

I reported to freshman football coach Ralph Jones, a smallish man with a mammoth spirit. He was not enchanted with young Halas but he did make me a relief halfback.

Home for Christmas, Walter tried to explain away my unimpressive season:

"The Kid's too light."

Frank wouldn't settle for that. Neither, in my heart, would I. Frank produced as a Christmas present a can of food supplement he guaranteed would add 40 pounds to my frame before the next football season.

In the spring I made the freshman baseball team and the Varsity coach, G. Huff, said he wanted me the following year. I ate Frank's guck every day but when we went home the scales still showed 140. I threw the can into the garbage.

Frank looked me over when I came home for summer vacation. "Well, Kid, I see the stuff didn't work," he said. "Throw it away."

After a family dinner of roast duck, Bohemian style, I gave Mother $21 I had saved from the money she had sent me. During the school year I had not gone on one date nor seen one show.

"Good boy, George," she said. "I think we should have some ice cream."

All was well.

I went back to my job at Western Electric and played outfield on the payroll department's baseball team. I was hitting well and had picked up a lot of speed. I even had a few dates. Min seemed to enjoy my company but there was nothing exclusive, nor promising, about our relationship. She was singing with a Swedish choral club that went on a tour of Europe and performed for the King of Sweden.

On July 24, Western Electric held its annual picnic at Michigan City, around the end of Lake Michigan in Indiana. The company teams scheduled a doubleheader.

Charlie Pechous, Ralph Brizzolara and I bought tickets on a popular lake excursion ship, the *Eastland*.

As I was about to leave the house, Frank said, "Come on, Kid, I'll weigh you."

I never won an argument with Frank, so off came the clothes. I stepped onto the scale. I couldn't believe its report—163!

"Just do everything I tell you and you'll be okay, Kid," he said. "Now get dressed and catch that boat."

"And hit a homer," he shouted, as I ran out the door.

When I came to the river where the *Eastland* was docked, an appalling sight awaited. The *Eastland* had turned onto its side. Only a few passengers had escaped. Ralph Brizzolara and his brother had been pulled through a porthole. The final toll was 812 dead. Charlie was saved by his sisters. They were slow dressers, delaying their brother from getting off to the picnic.

Going to work Monday was a strange experience. Everyone asked, "Who went down?" That evening two fraternity brothers, Elmer Stumpf and Walter Straub, came to the house to commiserate with Mother. They were astounded to see me. A reporter had obtained a list of Western Electric employees signed up for the picnic. My name was on it. I was thought to be dead.

The magnitude of my good fortune overwhelmed me.

Mother suggested I say a rosary. I found the advice sound. Luck was with me that day.

During the summer I added another 15 pounds. By September I felt I was ready to join the best. Robert C. Zuppke, the great Zuppke, had an excellent team. The star was Harold Poague, All-American halfback. I decided to replace Poague.

Zuppke was a tremendous coach. He was a careful

teacher. He knew how to get the best out of young men. He was an innovator. He started the spiral pass from center and the huddle.

After my first scrimmage Zuppke ordered: "Get the Kid out of there before he gets killed!"

So ended my career as halfback. Poague was safe.

Assistant Coach Justa Lindgren, working with the line, made me an end. We scrimmaged against the Varsity. One afternoon Poague started around my end. I tried to tackle him. He drove those piston-like legs into my chest and kept right on going. He did so a second time. On his third attempt, luck came to me. I was off balance and instead of getting him by the legs in the approved fashion, I hit him in the chest. Down he went. From then on, I nailed him time and time again, always hitting him high. No one seemed to notice how I did it. Word got around that Poague was a fearsome runner who would punish all tacklers except young Halas.

That established me, although I remained on the scrubs. Late in the season, during a scrimmage, a Varsity player intercepted a pass. I chased him 60 yards. I dived for him and brought him down on the 3. His heel came up against my chin, breaking the jaw. That ended the season but Zuppke told me: "Next year, Halas, you'll play end for me." He told others: "I heard the Kid's mother was worried about his getting hurt. So I had Lindgren make him an end. And the first thing he breaks his jaw."

Our star quarterback, Potsy Clark, also broke his jaw. An enterprising young photographer took our picture and used it for a postcard with the caption: "The Order of the Broken Jaw." Students bought postcards, out of respect for Potsy, and mailed them to families and friends.

"Halas" did not become a household word but when I went home for Christmas, several people did ask me about my jaw. Years later, when seeking publicity for the Bears, I recalled the postcards and did everything to bring the Bears to the attention of potential supporters.

Suddenly it was spring and baseball time. Walter was the star and Coach Huff welcomed me to the first practice. I played all outfield positions and batted about .350. The team won the championship.

Western Electric again filled my summer with work. Now and then I went out with Min. I learned she spent most of her earnings on clothes, hats and shoes, after contributing to her mother for room and board. Her father had died.

Min's only sport was tennis. She tried to entice me into it. I never yielded. She had plenty of company. The Bushings were a big, active family. Mrs. Bushing would say with a laugh, "I really don't like children but I have had eight!" She couldn't have been kinder to the children, to their friends and, in time, to their spouses.

In almost no time Walter and I were back at Champaign. Coach Zuppke started me as end. The workouts were intense. One afternoon I limped from the field. I thought I had merely pulled a muscle or had been awarded a bruise. So did the trainer.

The next day the pain increased. I reported for practice but, although I tried to ignore the hurting, I did not put total vigor into my blocking and tackling.

Coach Zuppke called the team together to explain the practice for the next day. As he ended, he pointed at me and said:

33

"Halas, stop loafing! Get in there and hit!"

I blew up. That is the only way to put it. My temper is always near the surface. That afternoon it went up like an explosion.

I pulled off my helmet and threw it at Coach Zuppke. I was so angry I couldn't even throw straight. I missed him.

"I'm not loafing," I said. "If I am not getting in there and hitting, it's because I have a painful leg!"

"Leave the field," Coach Zuppke ordered.

I don't remember the limping walk to the locker room. My mind was taken over by the fit of temper. Looking back, I know there is truth in the old saying: "Anger doth a bonehead make!"

The trainer sent me to the hospital. An x-ray showed the leg bone was broken. The doctor put the leg in a cast. After five days, I pleaded for permission to return to my classes. The doctor admired my academic ambitions and released me. With cast and crutches I watched the master, Robert C. Zuppke, prepare his team.

Zuppke put me in charge of the supply room at $300 a semester. Suddenly I found myself affluent. I also found myself short of time. I paid another student $150 to substitute, earning myself a nice profit and free hours.

Late in the season Coach Zuppke paid me an honor I always shall cherish. As I hobbled on crutches from the practice field, Coach Zuppke said, "Halas, tomorrow you will go to Minnesota with us."

I was too surprised to say "thank you."

The Minnesota Gophers were expected to beat us by 50 points, but we upset them 19–14. I threw my crutches into the air. Our locker room was joyous, the ride home was pleasurable to the ultimate. Victory is sweet, especially if unexpected and deserved!

The team had its annual banquet. Coach Zuppke spoke. His message was short:

"Just when I teach you fellows how to play football, you graduate and I lose you."

His words were to govern the rest of my life.

At the family Christmas dinner I told Mother I no longer needed the monthly check, but she said my education was her responsibility. She continued sending checks.

Early in January Ralph Jones came to the fraternity.

"George," he said, "I want you at basketball practice tomorrow."

I said I had broken my leg and I had exams coming up.

"I saw you throw the crutches into the air when we beat Minnesota," he said. "You can manage. Be there."

"Yes, sir," I said.

Jones made me a back guard. My duties were to keep players away from the basket and, when a throw missed, get the ball off the backboard.

I discovered basketball is a contact sport. I enjoyed it. In the first game I lasted two minutes and a half. By then I had accumulated four fouls, a record for speed in this activity, I believe, and was sent off for being too eager. "Too rough," was the way the referee put it.

Ralph Jones taught me finesse. My staying time extended. We reached the championship game against the Wisconsin Badgers. With 30 seconds to play, Wisconsin went ahead by 1 point. The centers jumped. The ball came into our court. I grabbed it. Everyone headed into the Wisconsin end. I dribbled slowly up court. I saw Jones waving a towel furiously. I didn't know what he meant. Just past mid-court I stopped, measured the distance carefully and made a two-handed shot at the basket. The ball seemed to hang in the air forever. With fascination, I watched it go through the hoop just as the whistle sounded. We were Big Ten Champions! The team elected me captain for the 1917–1918 season. Two fraternity brothers, Ralph and Ray Wood, were responsible. I learned something of the value of having political arrangers.

Coach Huff sent out the baseball call. Walter and I were first to report. Again Illinois won the championship.

Frank, Walter and I found an opportunity to play indoor softball at night in Chicago with the Commodore Barry team. G. Huff learned of our exploits and ordered us to end such extracurricular activities.

In June Walter collected his diploma. I took home $178. Mother called a family meeting. She cooked roast duck, Bohemian style. Walter was the star. He had achieved the family dream—a university degree, the first in our family. Mother was close to tears. All evening she sat with her arm on the back of his chair. After everyone had gone, I offered the $178. She said I should open a savings account. She said her next great joy would come when I brought home the second Halas diploma. Mother was a saint.

Ralph and I double dated. He took Florence Hurley, who had been going with his brother. I took Min. We'd go to the movies and then have an ice cream sundae or we'd go dancing in a Loop restaurant. We thought we were some diggity dogs when we ordered a drink of ginger ale and a twist of lemon. We did the two-step and a new dance, the bunny hop. Ralph would borrow the family Hudson tourer. We'd put the top down. I'd sing "Alice Blue Gown" until Florence threatened to choke me. We'd drive up to Channel Lake, where Min's mother and Uncle Billy had cottages. We swam. Florence and Ralph assumed that some day Min and I would marry. We had the same feeling about them. The summer passed quickly between Western Electric and baseball. I settled down at 178. Every pound was hard and strong and crying out for competition.

That autumn Coach Zuppke, because of my speed, used me to return kickoffs and punts. One day Wisconsin kicked off. Suddenly the ball lost speed and took on an unusual shape. It came down to me flat as a wet rag. I caught it and stood there. The episode caused considerable consternation among officials. The referee, J.J. Schommer, called for a new ball and told Wisconsin to kick again. I demote myself every time I think about that event. I should have run for a touchdown while everyone was scratching his head.

Basketball followed almost immediately. I needed only six credit hours to graduate. I had achieved a 70 in Spanish, thanks to a very pretty blonde coed. The fact that the teacher was a football nut may have helped.

For several months the United States had been at war with Germany. Gradually the events in Europe began to crowd sport from my mind. I talked to Mother about enlisting but she asked would I please first get my degree. But in January of 1918 I decided the time had come for me to serve the country which had been so good to the Halas family. I would soon be 23. I must add that the draft was getting close to students such as myself. I went to Great Lakes Training Station, volunteered for the navy and asked to be sent to sea on a submarine chaser. The university promised to forgive the six remaining hours and in June to mail the degree to me wherever I was. The offer mollified Mother but Coach Jones was upset at losing his basketball captain.

The navy made me a carpenter's mate second class. Instead of sending me to sea or even giving me a hammer, the navy assigned me to the sports program at Great Lakes. I protested to Mother but she advised me not to make a fuss.

"Son," she said, "the navy knows much better how to win the war than you do, so be a good boy and do as they say."

Ralph also joined the navy. Min and Florence got together with other girls whose fellows had gone to Great Lakes and put out a little newspaper. Min moved to a grain brokerage firm in the Loop.

We were joined by Paddy Driscoll, the Northwestern University star and one of the greatest of collegiate quarterbacks, and Charlie Bachman, top center from Michigan State.

Paddy, Charlie and I signed up for officers' training school. Charlie helped me with seamanship and I helped him with mathematics. After three tough months we were commissioned as ensigns. We expected to go to sea and clear the Atlantic of submarines. No orders came.

Great Lakes was heavy on sports. Soon after arriving I had joined the basketball team. Then came baseball and football. Oh, the players available in that ocean of navy blue—Driscoll, Reichle, Ecklund, Keefe, Jones, Hugh Blacklock, the terrific tackle. Erickson, Eilson,

Blondy, Reeves, a running back, the Barnard brothers, Knight, Abrahamson, Willaman, Jimmy Conzelman, all stars in college!

The officer training school commander, Lt. C.J. McReavy, was also the football coach. The school left him little time for football so after our first tied game, Paddy, Charlie and I suggested we coach the team. He agreed, but said he would be in charge on Saturdays.

Driscoll, our star, had been a star in high school at Evanston, Illinois, and at Northwestern, class of 1917. For a summer he had played professional baseball. Some purists claimed that ruled him out of amateur sport but a war was on and the critics muted their voices against a man wearing the uniform of his country. We beat Illinois, Purdue and Iowa. Northwestern and Notre Dame escaped with ties. We were champions of the Midwest.

In the East, Rutgers was unbeaten. Their star was an All-American named Paul Robeson. A game was arranged at Ebbets Field in Brooklyn. Twenty thousand people came. The stands were golden with officers' braid. The Easterners boasted Rutgers would sweep through Great Lakes like a dreadnought. Rutgers did score in eleven plays and again in the second quarter. Then, according to some memories, Rutgers started playing rough. We gave up our naval gentlemanly manners. We opened routes for Paddy. He took a punt and ran it 80 yards for a touchdown. He added short run to short run for four, yes, four, more touchdowns. Each time he kicked a conversion. Thirty-five points he scored. Others added nineteen. We won 54–14.

After the game I asked Robeson if he planned to continue in football. No, he said, he had had enough. He found greater pleasure singing with a quartet. He thought he might go to New York and have a crack at the stage. He did, after another year. *Show Boat* came along and overnight Paul became an international singing star.

Three trainloads of sailors went with us to Annapolis for a game with the Naval Academy. The Academy scored a touchdown but missed the conversion. Their great fullback, Bill Ingram, was about to go over for a second touchdown when he was hit on the 1-yard line. He fumbled. The ball bounced right into the arms of our Dizzy Eilson. Conzelman and I broke a path for him. Eilson twisted free. When he reached midfield, no one was in front. Conzelman and I dropped back to protect him from the rear.

"Get him, go get him!" the Academy coach shouted from the bench.

Lo and behold, a substitute who had been resting there got up, ran onto the field, intercepted Eilson and brought him down.

There followed quite a ruckus involving both teams, coaches, officials, midshipmen and gobs.

The Academy superintendent, Captain Edward Walter Eberle, marched onto the field and demanded order. It has been said he pulled his sword but Admiral Bill Gallery insists that was an inter-service canard spread by the army.

The officials decided the Academy should be penalized halfway to the goal line but Captain Eberle decreed we should be awarded a touchdown. The officials said that was contrary to the rules. The captain replied he didn't care a whistle about the rules.

"I said it was a touchdown," he stated. "I run this place and a touchdown it is."

On such men the American navy has built its great-

ness. In time the captain became an admiral and chief of
naval operations. Because of him, we won 7–6. The train
ride back to Chicago was a party.

We were invited to Pasadena, California, to play in
the Tournament of Roses New Year's Day game in the
Rose Bowl. For the first and only time, the 1918 post-
season game would be played by service teams.

The Mare Island Marines, led by Biff Bangs and a
great center, Jake Risley, had emerged as the best team
in the West.

On January 1, 1919, 27,000 fans gathered. The
Marines fumbled early. We recovered. Paddy drop-
kicked to put us ahead 3–0. A pass interception by
Lawrence Ecklund set up a touchdown by Blondy
Reeves, 215-pound plunger. Blacklock kicked for
the extra point. After a second interception Driscoll
threw to me on the 10 and I zipped my way to the goal.
Later I intercepted a pass and returned it 77 yards. A
determined marine, Jim Blewitt, caught me on the 3. I
should have scored. After I took up coaching, I told the
carriers that when they reach the 3-yard line, they should
dive across the goal. Anyone who can't dive 3 yards
should play Parcheesi.

Later Paddy threw a pass to me in the end zone. It
was short. I ran for it, bending low. My hands were only
an inch off the ground. The ball came in and I held it. But
the referee, Walter Eckersall, ruled the ball had touched
the ground. It had not. He cheated me out of a
touchdown. And Walter came from Chicago! I would
have expected a little more civic cooperation. The incident taught me officials are human and can make mis-
takes. Later, when victory meant the Bears ate well, I
concerned myself vitally with official decisions. Since

that New Year's Day in the Rose Bowl I have always tried to assist officials to make correct calls. Over the years I have achieved some success in this pursuit.

The final score was Great Lakes 17, Mare Island 0. The game brought Great Lakes the National Service Championship, and an extra day in Hollywood. I was named Most Valuable Player. Walter Camp named Driscoll, Bachman and Blacklock on his 1919 All-Service eleven, and Driscoll to his All-American team. Paddy fully deserved the honor. He was an all-around athlete and a perfect teammate. I hoped our paths would follow a mutual course. Camp put me on his second team.

We returned to Chicago. I went home on leave. The papers had been full of the Rose Bowl game. Mother was concerned I might be seriously injured. I assured her that I played end and was apart from the rough stuff.

"Well, if that is so, how did you happen to break your jaw and a leg at Illinois?" Mother asked.

I told her football was over for me. I said I still loved the sport but would devote my athletic efforts henceforth to baseball. That mollified her somewhat. Frank and Walter had played baseball for years without being hurt.

During the final weeks in service, I played basketball and functioned as base recreation officer. My discharge came in March. I went home. Mother had framed my diploma and hung it on the wall beside Walter's.

I felt uneasy about not having made a more serious contribution to the war effort. Mother said I had participated fully in all I was told to do and the games had been good for the sailors. She did not convince me. I resolved that if ever again my country went to war, I would make a more military contribution.

CHAPTER THREE

I Learn to Direct My Energies Positively

IN MY JUNIOR YEAR AT ILLINOIS, a New York Yankee Baseball Club scout, Bob Connery, had asked me to come to their spring training camp at Jacksonville, Florida. I said I would come after I finished college. The navy service brought a further postponement. One year late, I rode the train to Florida. I considered myself in perfect condition, ready to astound baseball fans with my speed and desire.

The Yankees accepted me but did not kill a fatted calf. Servicemen were flooding home, and athletes were everywhere, seeking berths.

Miller Huggins was the manager. I think he was impressed with my speed and my eagerness. I had a good eye and could be in the right place in the field to catch the ball. I had a good arm. I could throw to home from right field unless the hit was too deep. I could hit a fast ball, but I couldn't hit a curve.

A veteran, Ping Bodie, taught me how to camp under a fly ball, how to position my body for a quick throw to home plate, how to play a grounder so the ball would never get past me.

We met the Brooklyn Dodgers in a spring game. Their left-handed pitcher, Rube Marquard, was famous for his curve. I figured he wouldn't risk his arm throwing me a fancy pitch in a pre-season game, so I prepared to welcome a fast ball. It came, right down the middle. I swung. The ball sped out between left and center field. As I rounded second I could see the ball rolling. I went for third. I slid in hard. I was safe but when I stood, my hip was painful. I managed to get home on a long drive, but every step hurt.

The trainer thought I had a charley horse. Miller Huggins must have agreed because when we moved North he took me along, gave me a contract for $400 a month and said I would, on arrival in New York, receive a $500 bonus for signing from Mr. Jake Ruppert, the owner, who liked to hand out such bonuses personally.

We opened in Boston. Bodie was missing. His place had been given to me. I felt guilty. It took me a long time to accept the blows that come in professional sport as veterans are set aside for youth.

When we came into New York, Miller Huggins introduced me to Mr. Ruppert, who handed me a check for $500 and asked, "Young man, what are you going to do with the money?"

"I intend to invest it wisely," I said.

He beamed and suggested Miller Huggins ask his friend, Harry Sinclair of the Sinclair Oil Company, for financial guidance for the new Yankee athlete and financial wizard. Some days later Miller Huggins said Mr. Sinclair was starting oil exploration in Central America and thought I would prosper by backing the venture. My fortune consisted of the $500 plus $200 in savings. I put it all into Sinclair Oil of Central America. Sinclair hit it big in South America but found nothing in Central America. Only the Panama Canal prevented me from becoming a millionaire. I still have the Central American stock and if ever Sinclair finds oil there they will hear from me.

We played the Washington Senators. The famous Walter Johnson threw a straight ball, I hit it into the right-field stands. It was foul by a foot. He threw a second straight ball and I hit it again into the right-field stands. It too was foul. He threw a curve. I struck out.

I was in and out of the lineup. Every two or three days my hip would bother me, but Miller Huggins continued his interest in me. I was a switch hitter; that may have attracted him. Switch hitters were not common in those days.

When we played the Detroit Tigers I was on the bench in the dugout. I was a pretty fresh kid and when Ty Cobb came to bat for Detroit, Ernie Shore, a pitcher, and Truck Hannah, a catcher, encouraged me to bait him.

How foolish I was! Cobb was my idol, but I shouted nonsense at him, using some gutter terms. He dropped his bat, strode to the dugout and said:

"Punk, I'll see you after the game. Don't forget, punk."

I told him brashly, "I will look for you."

45

After the game I took a long shower. The other players departed. I was alone. I loitered, hoping Ty Cobb would depart. When I finally stepped from the dressing room, out of the Detroit dressing room opposite came Ty Cobb.

I grew taut, ready to defend myself and hit back.

Ty Cobb, the great Ty Cobb, put out his hand and said:

"I like your spirit, kid, but don't overdo it when you don't have to."

He turned and went away.

Our trainer suggested I take long walks to ease the hip. One day while walking down Broadway from 145th Street to 42nd, I ran into Ty Cobb. He walked a half-mile with me and gave me very sound advice.

"Direct your energy positively," he said. "Don't waste yourself being negative."

Cobb and I became good friends. Much later, after he left baseball, he would come to the Commodore Hotel for a talk whenever the Bears played in Los Angeles. To think such a friendship could have started because I was a fresh kid!

I should have changed my ways, but no, it was not the last time I made a chump of myself.

One day Home Run Baker asked to borrow my bat, a Louisville Slugger with my name on it, just like bats used by the stars. My bat was an ounce lighter and a half-inch shorter. Baker hit four doubles but did not use my bat again.

We traveled to Cleveland. My hip was really bothering me. I asked Miller Huggins if I could go to

Youngstown, Ohio, to see Bonesetter Reese, a man with no formal training but a genius in treating injuries. Twice at Illinois Coach Huff had sent me to him. The first time I had banged my bat hard against the ground in anger when a colleague tried to steal home and was out by a mile. Bonesetter said a tendon in my elbow had snapped out of place. In two seconds he snapped it back. The second time I hurt my knee while playing football. Bonesetter felt my ankle.

"Bonesetter, it's the knee," I said.

"Quiet," Bonesetter said.

He continued feeling my ankle and suddenly applied a lot of pressure to one spot. Instantly the pain in the knee ceased.

Coach Huff had tried to get Bonesetter to come to Illinois but Bonesetter preferred to stay in Youngstown. He said he wanted to pass on his skills to his daughter.

Miller Huggins approved another visit to this marvelous man. I caught the 5:30 A.M. electric train to Youngstown, an hour and a half away. I found a line of people stretching down the block but Bonesetter had a soft spot in his heart for athletes and took me right in.

I told him my story.

"Get on the table," he said. "Lie on your face."

He felt my derrière. "When you slid into third base," he said, "you twisted your hip bone. It is pressing on a nerve."

He pushed his steely fingers deep into my hip, clasped the bone and gave it a sharp twist. The pain vanished.

I danced out of his office, down the street to the station and, in Cleveland, back to the ball park. In the afternoon I raced around like a wild horse.

47

We came to Chicago, my home town. A newspaper headline announced my arrival. The writer, Warren Brown, did quite an account of the rising young Yankee baseball star, George Halas.

The game began with me on the bench. Late in the game Miller Huggins sent me in as a pinch hitter against a great right-hander, Dash Cicotte. I batted lefty. The first two throws seemed to break away from the plate early. I let them go by. The umpire called them strikes. The third pitch seemed to be coming through. I swung at it mightily. I missed.

Some homecoming! Some rising young star!

I was mortified. I had played in eleven games. My batting average was .091.

That night Miller Huggins told me I needed more experience and he was sending me to St. Paul, in the American Association. I was heartbroken but, looking back, I am grateful for the manner in which Miller Huggins told me my big league career was over. Through the years, whenever I have had to cut a player, I have tried to emulate his grace and consideration.

I rode the train to St. Paul. I was depressed, but a few hours with Mike Kelly, the wonderful coach there, restored my confidence. He was a teacher. Miller Huggins was a great manager but he wasn't a teacher. He didn't have to be. When a player came to the Yankees, Miller Huggins expected him to be the finished product.

Mike Kelly watched me bat. He saw the cause of my trouble. I had grown up on softball where the pitcher is only 27 feet from the plate. The ball is big, 17 inches, and soft, but a good pitcher can throw it very fast. To be

48

successful in softball, the batter must stand in the center of the batter's box and choke the bat several inches from the end. He must start to swing when the ball leaves the pitcher's hand and swing hard to get distance. In hardball, the pitcher's box is 60.5 feet from home plate. The pitcher has much more control over the smooth, small ball. He can make it break just as it approaches the plate. The good batter must stand in the middle or back in the box and watch the ball come. He must clasp the bat at or near the end of the handle. He must start the swing only as the ball nears the plate after it has revealed its true course. Mike Kelly taught me how to hit a curve ball.

One day an umpire called a strike when I was certain the ball passed above my shoulder. I was furious and jawed the umpire. He turned away and strolled toward first base. I ran after him and grabbed his coat sleeve.

"Listen to me!" I shouted. "Listen to me!"

I must have been rather upset because I found myself standing there holding an empty sleeve. I had pulled it out of his coat. He threw me out of the game. You would think Mike Kelly would have become angry with me. But no, from then on I was his boy. I had spirit, the great desire.

Mike Kelly wanted to keep me, but at a reduced salary. I objected. By then the Yanks had a new man in right field, Babe Ruth.

After the baseball season, I found a job in the bridge design department of the Chicago, Burlington and

49

Quincy Railroad. The pay was $55 a week. Mother was delighted.

"A railroad job," she said, "is secure." It was also safe.

I figured stresses and strains on bridges, but in my ears echoed Coach Zuppke's words: "Just when I teach you fellows how to play football, you graduate and I lose you." I ached for the excitement of a good game, for the competition, for the challenge to the muscles, for the joy of victory.

At Hammond, just across the line in Indiana, a doctor, A.A. Young, operated a semi-professional football team as a hobby. He paid his players $100 a game, a most attractive sum. The contests were played on Sunday afternoon. Practice was held Thursday evening. Hammond was an hour away by electric train. If I made the team, I could continue to live at home and work on railroad bridge designs.

I went to Hammond and found Paddy Driscoll there; also Jimmy Conzelman; Shorty DesJardien, All-American center from Chicago; Hugh Blacklock, right tackle, Michigan State; Bert Basten, the greatest end in football; Doc Hauser, All-American tackle from Minnesota; Gil Falcon, 230-pound fullback, and a good one. The coach, Richard Stewart King, had been at Harvard. With me, the squad numbered fourteen, all with much experience.

We took on the Canton Bulldogs, a formidable team built that year, 1919, around the great, great Jim Thorpe. I had long been a Thorpe fan. Thorpe was a tremendous man, a giant with a vast chest, broad shoulders and tree-trunk arms, capped with a shock of black hair. He was perfectly coordinated, faster than the wind, as sure-

50

footed as Indians are reputed to be. One of his grand-
fathers was Chief Blackhawk. The other was Irish. A
great-grandmother was French. Thorpe called himself an
American Airedale. He loved to feel the crunch of flesh
against flesh. He loved to win. When he threw himself
against a runner, it was better to be hit by a falling tree.

In the 1912 Olympics in Stockholm, he had won the
decathlon and the pentathlon and King Gustav said,
"You, sir, are the greatest athlete in the world." New
York welcomed him with a parade up Broadway but
small-minded people recalled he had accepted $15 a
game playing summer baseball. The Olympic committee
took back the medals. Thorpe signed with the New York
Giants to play baseball. The experience was miserable.
He was traded here and there. No team wanted him as a
player; they wanted him only as a name. He found his
home in football.

Big Gil Falcon was not intimidated by Thorpe's muscle or reputation. As Thorpe ran along the sidelines in
midfield, Gil threw himself, all 230 pounds, at Thorpe.
The Indian crashed into the bench. Blood spurted from
his forehead. The trainer patched the cut. Soon Thorpe
saw a need to stop Falcon. He did halt him so effectively
that, I swear, Falcon sailed 3 feet into the air, all 230
pounds, and came down with a thud. He just lay there,
gasping. Our trainer needed quite a little time to get the
air back into him.

Late in our game we reached the Canton 1-yard line.
It was fourth and one. Falcon was given the task of
plunging over for the score. He started through a hole.
Up came Thorpe and down went Falcon on the 2-yard
line. The ball went to Canton. Thorpe dropped back.
Paddy took up a receiving position in midfield. Thorpe

51

kicked. The ball sailed over Paddy's head and didn't stop until it came to our 20, an 80-yard kick.

Later I caught a pass. Thorpe knocked me to my knees. Today the referee would whistle the ball dead, but in those days a carrier could keep on crawling. There I was, on hands and knees, scrambling along like a crab, trying to get an extra yard or two.

Jim threw a leg over me and sat down on me.

"All right," he said, "if you are a horse, I'll ride you."

His weight bore me to the ground.

After the game I thanked him. He could have thrown both his knees into my ribs, practically ruining me.

Many other players would have done that.

Jim brushed off my gratitude.

We watched the happy fans leave.

"That's a great crowd today, Jim," I said. "How about another game?"

"It is okay with me if it's okay with the manager," he said.

We went to the manager, Ralph Hay. He agreed to another game.

We played six games and claimed the championship. A good autumn.

The season deepened my love for football, but I assumed my future rested with the railroad. Now and then, I would look at some of the other engineers, doing the same thing day after day for thirty years. The prospect did not excite me as on cold winter days I rode the streetcar to and from the CB&Q offices.

My real love was football.

CHAPTER FOUR

Opportunity Knocks

IN MARCH OF 1920 a man telephoned me at the railroad office and asked if I would meet him at the Sherman Hotel. He said his name was George Chamberlain and he was general superintendent of the A.E. Staley Company at Decatur, 172 miles southwest of Chicago in the tall corn country.

I found Mr. Chamberlain to be a very determined man, about fifty, well muscled—he had played football and baseball in his younger days. He was bald, wore steel-rimmed round spectacles and had a Teddy Roosevelt mustache.

Mr. Chamberlain told me the president of the company, Mr. A.E. Staley, was dedicated to company athletics. Three years earlier the company's Fellowship Club had formed a baseball team around the great "Iron Man" Joe McGinnity, who had been the Most Valuable Player in the 1900 World Series. In 1919 the Fellowship

Club had formed a football team. It had done well against other local teams but Mr. Staley wanted to build it into a team that could compete successfully with the best semi-professional and industrial teams in the country. He was willing to put money into the enterprise. He had two objects, to stimulate employee morale and fitness and to spread the Staley name through the nation.

Mr. Chamberlain asked if I would like to move to Decatur to work for the Staley Company, play on the baseball team and manage and coach the football team as well as play on it. I might start a basketball team. In between times I would learn how to make starch, putting my engineering and chemical training to use and starting a lifetime career in the fast-growing concern.

I don't remember how much money he offered. It may have been a little less than the $55 the railroad paid me. The magnet for me was the opportunity to build a winning football team.

I asked Mr. Chamberlain if I could recruit players who had made their name in college, at Great Lakes or on semi-pro teams.

Certainly, he said. In fact, it was because of my knowledge of and acquaintanceship with such players that Mr. Staley wanted me. Mr. Staley knew good products could be made only from good material. Mr. Chamberlain said I could offer the players steady year-round work, the pleasure of playing football on a good team and a share of any profits from gate receipts.

Could we practice daily?

Of course, Mr. Chamberlain said. Mr. Staley was a firm believer in solid preparation for any task. How much time would be needed?

"Two hours each day," I said, speaking the words as a flat statement of proven fact.

Mr. Chamberlain wondered if we really needed that long.

"Absolutely."

"All right," Mr. Chamberlain said, "you are the expert. You will be the boss."

"One more thing," I asked. "May we practice on company time?"

I presume Mr. Chamberlain ran some figures through his mental calculator.

"Yes," he said.

I was elated. I saw the offer as an exciting opportunity but did not suspect the tremendous future Mr. Staley was opening for me.

On March 28, 1920, I ceased being a railroadman, packed a small bag, said goodbye to Mother and took the train to Decatur. Mother was delighted. In her mind, I had decided to settle down in a good job with a good company leading to a career that would be both prosperous and safe.

I rented a small room on the second floor of a downtown boarding house near the streetcar line that led to the factory at the edge of town.

The playing field, located at Eldorado and 22nd Streets, adjoined the factory. The field had been built for baseball but was large enough for a football field. We would have to level the mound but we didn't consider sodding the infield. After playing on cinders, I considered this field as soft as a mattress.

55

The team accommodations were comfortable, with good showers, lockers for each man and a room for blackboard sessions which I was certain would be the place where we would win the games. The grandstand could accommodate about 1,500. Other fans could watch from the sidelines.

I was assigned to the factory weighing room, checking deliveries of corn. Decatur called itself "The Greatest Little City on Earth." The Staley Company had just completed a plant described as the biggest engineering project in central Illinois that year.

Mr. Staley had grown up on a low-producing farm in North Carolina. He had taught himself to read and write—the small school was open only two months or so each winter. The only farm task the boy enjoyed was taking produce into town and selling it door to door. He got on well with people. He could sell.

When he was sixteen, his father died. The boy convinced his mother he could earn more money for the family—there were three younger children—if he went to Greensboro, 20 miles away. He took a job in a hardware store but was fired in a week. Next, he began peddling tobacco on commission and made so much money that when he brought home his profits, his mother hurried into town to make certain he had come by the money honestly. He added other products. Gradually, he concentrated on grocery stores in small towns off the path of most salesmen.

For fourteen years he was on the move. At thirty, he proposed marriage. She said yes, but on condition he settle down. He decided to go into business for himself. He had noted that starch was a steady item with all grocers. He rented a small loft in Baltimore, bought starch in bulk from makers, packed it by night and peddled it by day to his old customers. He hired a boy, then a girl. By the fourth year profits were good. A fire wiped him out. A banker staked him to a new start. His business grew fast. In time starch makers realized he was cutting into their retail sales, the end of the business which produced the biggest profits. Makers became reluctant to sell him large quantities. The way out of the squeeze, he decided, was to make his own starch.

He learned of an idle, bankrupt mill in Decatur, but lacked money to buy it. He went to the people he knew best, the small grocers. Twenty-six hundred agreed to buy stock. The A.E. Staley Company was born. The year was 1912. To run the plant, Mr. Staley brought in a most experienced engineer, the very same Mr. Chamberlain who came to Chicago to hire me. He had built some of the largest corn products mills in the country.

The editor of the Staley *Journal* wrote:

> Decatur is coming out of its small town shell. It is like a butterfly emerging from its chrysalis, like a rough block of stone emerging under the keen chisel of the sculptor into a work of beauty and strength. Decatur today is a City of Great Promise. Within a few years it will be known as the City of Wonderful Fulfillment.

I was glad to note the enthusiasm spread to sport. The football and baseball teams had been built around employees who had played in high school, at Millikin or at the University of Illinois. The football coach was the plant's construction superintendent, Mr. James Cook, a quarterback at Illinois a quarter-century earlier. The manager was a pipe fitter, Fritz Wassem. The quarterback was a local boy, Charley Dressen, who later went into baseball and managed the Washington Senators.

The Fellowship Club had voted to spend $1,000 on football during the 1919 season. It had brought in six players. Examining the vague records, I suspected all six were collegians playing under assumed names, a common practice in those days. One group of collegians had on six Sundays worn six different uniforms in six towns. The Sunday game was an easy way for collegians to pick up pocket money. Playing for money was against college rules. However, I find it hard to condemn the deed when compared to the practice of offering scholarships and jobs to players, and sometimes compounding the felony by faking or ignoring scholastic attainments.

The most formidable foe had been a club in Taylorville, 20 miles away, which had won six semi-pro championships in a row. Taylorville was regularly serviced by players from Ohio State University, a powerhouse. The 1919 stars were two gentlemen who, despite abundant application of facial adhesive tape, were recognized as being Chic Harley and Pete Stinchcomb, on their way to All-American greatness.

During the summer, I played baseball and worked out veterans of the 1919 football club, tested other employees and listed players I hoped to draw to Decatur. In August I set off on probably the first professional football recruiting journey.

At Madison, Wisconsin, I signed Ralph Scott, All-American tackle; I got Guy Chamberlin, 6-foot 3-inch, 220-pound All-American end at Nebraska; Hugh Blacklock, who had made his name with the Michigan Aggies and Great Lakes; and Jimmy Conzelman, from

58

Washington University at St. Louis and Great Lakes. I wanted Paddy Driscoll but he had joined the Chicago Cardinals.

From former University of Illinois teams I drew Burt Ingwerson, Ross Petty, and the star scorer, Edward Sternaman, once known as the Dutchman but later as just Dutch. I acquired three former Notre Dame men, Jerry Jones, who had been with me on the Hammond team, Emmett Keefe and a great center, George Trafton.

I added tackle Randy Young and guard Roy Adkins, both of Millikin, and three backs, Kile MacWherter, of Bethany, "Pard" Pearce from the University of Pennsylvania and Bob Koehler, Northwestern's captain. From the 1919 Staley Fellowship team we had only quarterback Charley Dressen, center Jack Mintun and halfback Walter Veach.

All summer I worked out plays learned at Illinois from Robert C. Zuppke. He used the T-Formation, the oldest in football, although most colleges had gone over to the single wing or the double wing. Notre Dame and Minnesota had their own formations. In a little clothbound notebook, I diagrammed plays, one to a page, properly numbered and coded. I still have that book. Over the years, play books have been a prized possession.

Paid football was pretty much of a catch-as-catch-can affair. Teams appeared one week and disappeared the next. Players came and went, drawn by the pleasure of playing. If others came to watch, that was fine. If they bought tickets or tossed coins into a helmet passed by the most popular player, that was helpful.

59

I thought the Staleys had gone beyond this mobile situation. I wrote various teams suggesting games. Replies were indifferent and vague. We needed an organization.

I wrote to Ralph Hay, the manager of the Canton Bulldogs, one of the best run and most prominent teams. I mentioned our need for a league. He had already discussed the idea with Stan Cofall, a former Notre Dame star who was running the Massillon Tigers. They met with Frank Nied and A.F. Ranney of Akron and representatives from Cleveland and Dayton on August 20 in Akron. Hay was appointed temporary chairman. He called a meeting on September 17, 1920, at his automobile showroom in Canton.

Morgan O'Brien, a Staley engineer and a football fan who was being very helpful in administrative matters, and I went to Canton on the train. Twelve teams were represented. They were the Canton Bulldogs; Cleveland Indians; Dayton Triangles; Akron Professionals; Massillon Tigers; Rochester, New York; Rock Island, Illinois; Muncie, Indiana; Staleys of Decatur, Illinois; Chicago Cardinals; Racine, Wisconsin; and Hammond, Indiana. The showroom, big enough for four cars—Hupmobiles and Jordans—occupied the ground floor of the three-story brick Odd Fellows building. Chairs were few. I sat on a runningboard.

We all agreed on the need for a league. In two hours we created the American Professional Football Association.

To give the Association some financial standing, we voted to issue franchises on payment of $100. Twelve teams were awarded franchises on the spot—Akron, Canton, Cleveland, Dayton, Decatur Staleys, Hammond,

Massillon, Muncie, Chicago Cardinals, Racine (Wisconsin), Rochester and Rock Island. Massillon withdrew for the 1920 season.

The Association needed someone with a name. Our minds turned to Jim Thorpe, absent but the biggest name in sport. Unanimously, we elected him our president.

When I told other managers about the top players I had lined up, there was great eagerness to meet us on the field.

CHAPTER FIVE

Zuppke Was Right

OUR TEAM WAS READY for my first season. Our hometown sportswriter, Howard Millard, commented modestly: "It looks like the best bit of material ever gathered in Illinois. The fellows will meet some of the greatest football machines in the country. They are expected to hold their own with the best of them."

"Hold our own!" No, I thought when I read the article, we would win! We had the men, the skill, the daily practice and the desire. Blocking was the essential task. I was an eager blocker but I was too light. I tended to hold a bigger opponent whenever the umpire wasn't looking. In those days we had just three game officials—the referee, the umpire and the head linesman. Passing played little part in the game. We had a fat ball, hard to pass.

Fans bet heavily, but I forbade my players to gamble on any of our games. Betting on one's own team to win may not be harmful, because one player cannot make a team win.

One player can make a team lose, however, by fumbling or missing a pass or failing a tackle. Although players have a sixth sense for detecting when a teammate is not doing his best, there is a terrible temptation to bet against the team. No gambler has ever approached me. Perhaps the word got around that gamblers would, at best, be wasting their time.

We breezed past Moline Tractors, 20–0, and Kewanee Walworths 27–0. I quickly drafted to the Staleys an ex-Illinois linesman and kicker, Hubbard Shoemake, who had almost made a touchdown for Kewanee. The games drew a couple of thousand, too few to pay expenses.

We came against the Rock Island Independents, considered by everyone except Staley fans to have replaced Taylorville as the strongest team in the region. Staley fans chartered a train. The game drew more than 5,000, one of the biggest pro-football crowds up to that time. Conzelman ran 40 yards for a touchdown. We won 10–0. Our starting eleven played the entire game and our betting fans cleaned up.

We beat the Chicago Tigers, 10–0, and massacred Rockford, 29–0. After Conzelman made the third of our four touchdowns, I suggested we go easy. I did not want to destroy all local pride in Rockford. We beat Champaign 20–0 and Hammond 28–0.

We returned to Rock Island. Local feelings were running high against us there because of the money Staley backers had made on the last game. Being cautious—off the field—I made our overnight headquarters at Hotel Davenport in Davenport, Iowa, across the

Mississippi River from Rock Island. Several gamblers appeared in the hotel and offered substantial sums that the Independents would win. They boasted that George Trafton, our best defensive man, would be knocked out of the game in the first quarter. Some even mentioned the name of the Rock Island player, a Mr. Chicken, who would put Trafton on the bench, or worse.

Early in the game, the Rock Island hit man was carried from the field, knocked out by Trafton, accidentally, of course. The Rock Island doctor revived the unfortunate Mr. Chicken, put nineteen stitches in his scalp and a plaster cast around a broken wrist.

The Rock Island fans were extremely upset by the disappearance of Mr. Chicken and the continued aggressive tackling by our George. It was a tough game and neither side could score. Again, our starting eleven played every minute.

We foresaw trouble for our George. Fortunately, as the end neared we had the ball. We devised a play that had George running toward the exit. As the gun fired with the score still 0–0, George went out the gate. We threw him a sweatshirt to hide his numerals. He headed for the bridge and Iowa. A car stopped and carried him to safety across the river and the state line.

Our share of the gate was $3,000, in cash. At the hotel I gave it to Trafton to bring to the train. I knew if we did encounter obstreperous Rock Island fans, I would run for the money but Trafton would run for his life. Trafton returned the money to me on the train.

Our next game was with Minneapolis. On the way there some of the older men gathered in the large

Pullman washroom and started a dice game. Here was my first personnel problem. I was against gambling, even as a pastime among friends. And I favored early bed before a game.

What should I do? Had I gone in and said, "None of this, we've got a hard game tomorrow," they would have said, "This is a real jerk."

Or I could have said, "All right, get the books out. Let's study strategy." That would not have earned me a gold star.

I joined the men. When midnight came, I said: "All right, let's go to bed."

I was down $12 so I was in a good position to propose a halt. Off to bed they went, those oldtimers. I didn't mind losing the $12. I think the lesson I learned that night in handling men was worth much more than $12.

We won the game, on a frozen field, 3–0. We had played nine games and no team had scored against us. Four days after that, on Thanksgiving Day, we were back in Chicago and again beat the Tigers, 6–0. The following Sunday, a very cold day, we lost to the Chicago Cardinals on a fumble, 7–6. The gate was encouraging—5,400. Capacity! Latecomers climbed trees and watched from nearby houses. I proposed a replay in the bigger Wrigley Field. The gate was 8,500. The Cardinals brought in some well-known college players. We won 10–0 although we were constantly put in trouble by the punting of Paddy Driscoll, my old Great Lakes friend. How I wished I could get him on my team!

We declared ourselves champions of the West. The Akron Indians, unbeaten, proclaimed themselves champions of the East. We arranged a match for the national championship.

65

Twelve thousand well-wrapped people came to Wrigley Field. Of these 10,800 actually bought tickets at 50 cents each. We won the toss but fumbled the kickoff. That's the kind of game it was. Neither side could move on the slippery, muddy ground and the game became, as a sportswriter said, a duel of punters. Once I intercepted a pass. I was in the clear and should have scored, but slipped. Several times I managed to bring down the Akron star, a Black named Fritz Pollard who had been chosen by Walter Camp for his All-American team several years earlier. It was a hard, clean game—scoreless. We made just one substitution. The enthusiasm was so great I proposed a replay but Akron declined. I am certain 15,000 people would have come. What drew them? Fine players, tight teamwork and a great desire. We had won ten, lost one, and tied two. In all thirteen games our opponents had scored just once. We proclaimed ourselves World Champions.

The 1920 season confirmed my belief that professional football had a great future. It confirmed the correctness of Coach Zuppke's statement that college football players are only reaching their peak when they are graduated.

But professional football was expensive. The thirteen games we played brought in $38,762.49, an astronomical sum compared to the previous year's $1,950.41. Travel, park upkeep, insurance, equipment and other things cost $13,228. Had we been amateurs, the team would have earned $25,000. But we were professionals and Mr. A.E. Staley had agreed that gate earnings would be split among the players. The shareout averaged about $125 per man for each game played. Chamberlin got the most, $1,650; Sternaman and Trafton $1,618 each. I, as coach, player and manager, was voted an extra share. My take was $2,322.77. Our trainer, Andy Lotshaw, got $175 for the season and our praiseworthy sportswriter $100. In addition, each player received his full salary of $50 a week as a Staley employee. I had little trouble persuading them to stay.

The team gave a victory dinner for Mr. Staley. He said he was delighted with our performance; our success had spread the Staley name far and wide; he personally had enjoyed the season very much; he desired to have an even better team in 1921 and was already talking with the Cubs about our using Wrigley Field again the next year.

Mr. Staley was a good businessman. I assume he went over the accounts carefully. One glance must have shown him the way to the future did not lie in Decatur. The three games played there brought in $1,982.49 while our first game in Chicago brought $10 more than the three Decatur games together. Then, as word spread, the fans grew steadily until the fifth game in Chicago drew $6,594.14. The five Chicago games produced $20,162.06. The only good earner outside the big city was Rock Island.

Mr. Staley appointed me athletic director. Through the winter we all made starch. Then it was baseball time again.

We played eighty-three baseball games and won fifty-two. Five men hit over .300. Ray Demmit was steadfast at .383. I was third at .320, including seven home runs. When we played the Missouri Valley White Sox, the game was so one-sided that in the ninth inning we gave up the bat even though only two men were out. The score was 29–0.

One day there was no umpire. Andy Lotshaw was drafted. The game was with Lincoln, I think. We were behind 1–0. It was the ninth, two men on, two out. I was at bat. The count was three and two. I got a curve. It broke perfectly over the plate. I didn't even swing at it. I was out, the game lost.

Lo and behold, from behind the catcher I heard Lotshaw bellow:

"Ball four! Take your base!"

The next man singled. Two men came home.

We won 2–1 and Andy knew that his job as trainer for the football team was secure.

More important, the time had come when I could propose marriage to my most enthusiastic fan—Min. A friend who was an expert on diamonds and I toured Chicago's best pawnshops. For $250, my friend found a 1¼-carat diamond that met his high requirements for cut, brilliance and color.

A few evenings later Min and I had the comfortable Bushing sitting room to ourselves.

I asked her if she would like to spend a lifetime rooting for me.

"I would," she replied.

When she recovered from my bear-like embrace, I put the ring on her finger.

The Bushing and Oetting girls and friends admired the diamond. One asked, "How many carats?"

Min was indignant: "You don't think I'd ask George a question like that!"

I rejoiced that I purchased a good ring at the start. I didn't know how, for many years to come, football would absorb all our extra cash. Nor did I realize the changes occurring in the nation's economy and in that of the A.E. Staley Company—changes that, once again, would alter the course of my life.

The new man I sought most for the football team was Chic Harley, a 165-pound All-American back at Ohio State. He could pass, kick, run. His brother Bill offered to supply the team with Chic, Pete Stinchcomb, also an All-American, and John R. Taylor, an aggressive guard known as Tarzan, in return for a percentage of the profit.

I accepted. I had no idea of the problem I was creating for myself.

A 35–0 opener against a Waukegan American Legion team served as a workout for another meeting with the Rock Island Independents in Decatur. The American Legion was holding a state convention there. We doubled the stands to 3,000. Scalpers were busy.

Meanwhile something wonderful happened to me, although at the time I did not appreciate how it would change my life.

Mr. Staley asked me to come to his office. I had no idea what he wanted. We had talked only on the field. But there was no question in my mind that the sports program would continue and I would make a good career in the engineering and chemistry departments of the company.

Mr. Staley greeted me warmly.

"George," he said, "I know you are more interested in football than starch. As you know, there is a slight

recession in the country. Time lost practicing and playing costs a huge amount of money. I feel we can no
longer underwrite the team's losses."

I was flabbergasted. I didn't know what to say.

After a very long half-minute or so, Mr. Staley said:

"George, why don't you take the team to Chicago? I
think football will go over big there."

I was dumbfounded.

Mr. Staley continued talking. He said the previous
season had indicated very clearly that towns the size of
Decatur never could support a professional football
team. The parks were too small; there would never be
enough fans.

"Professional teams," he said, "need a big city base.
Chicago is a good sports city. Look at the way the
baseball games in Chicago draw profitable crowds."

I agreed with everything he said but there was still
an immediate problem—ready cash.

Before I could ask, Mr. Staley went on:

"I'll give you $5,000 seed money to pay costs until
the gate receipts start coming in. I ask only that you
continue to call the team the Staleys for one season."

Five thousand dollars! Out of the goodness of his
heart! A team of my own! Chicago! I could not believe
such good fortune had come upon me. I was elated.

"I will do it," I said. "Thank you, thank you, thank
you very much."

We shook hands.

A written agreement, presented to me by Mr. Staley
some days later on October 6, filled in details (see p. 72).
It said $3,000 was being given in return for two pages of
advertising in our program, plus pictures and 100-word
biographies of the chief Staley company officials. We

70

would print 50,000 programs and any not sold would be given away. The other $2,000 would be paid at the rate of $25 a week per player up to a total of nineteen players.

I promised to obtain the "utmost publicity" for the Staley company. Of course, Mr. Staley made it clear that I could not incur any obligation on behalf of the company.

There was another provision that I liked very much. Mr. Staley demanded the team conduct itself, on and off the field, in a manner that would reflect credit upon the A.E. Staley Company.

From that day on, I have made it a team rule that my players behave as gentlemen and dress as gentlemen. I wanted to end a popular conception that professional athletes were a bunch of roughnecks.

I signed the letter of agreement. (See next page.) A whole new life opened to me.

Immediately after my conversation with Mr. Staley, I telephoned Mr. William Veeck, Senior, president of the Chicago Cubs Baseball Club, and asked if I could come to see him. He said yes. I hopped a train.

"I am bringing the Staley team to Chicago and I would like to use Cubs Park as our home, for practice as well as for our home games," I told Mr. Veeck.

He welcomed the idea. After the baseball season, the park was empty. With football it could have a second season of earnings.

"On what terms?" I asked.

"Fifteen percent of the gate and concessions," he said.

I considered that very fair. I rejoiced silently that he did not ask for a fixed rent, which might incur early obli-

A.E. Staley Manufacturing Company

CORN PRODUCTS

Decatur, Ill. October 6,1921.

The Staley Football Team,
Decatur, Illinois.

Gentlemen:

Confirming our verbal agreement with you, we agree to place the names of all your football players (Total number not to exceed nineteen) on our payrolls at a salary of $25.00 per week with the exception of those already being taken care of in that manner on regular jobs.

We also agree to enter into an advertising contract with you whereby we undertake to pay you Three Thousand ($3,000.00) Dollars for such advertising in your score book as you have suggested.

It is our wish and plan that when the football team goes to Chicago on October 15th, it remain there until the end of the season.

In this event while the team is in Chicago we will maintain on the payroll the entire nineteen men on the team at $25.00 per week until this Company shall have paid you in total, including both advertising and salary amounts, the sum of Five Thousand ($5,000.00) Dollars.

In consideration of these various payments, it is agreed that the team is to operate under the name of "The Staley Football Club" That you are to use your best efforts to disseminate information regarding, and to facilitate the business of the A.E.Staley Manufacturing Company; that you are to secure the utmost publicity in the newspapers for the team and the Company; that you are to so conduct the team, its playing and management as to reflect credit upon the A.E.Staley Manufacturing Company; that you will enter into no contracts or obligations in any way binding upon the A.E.Staley Manufacturing Company with this present exception.

It is understood that this arrangement shall terminate at the end of the present football season.

Please indicate your acception of the provisions of this agreement. I remain

Accepted by
Staley Football Club
Geo.S.Halas

Yours very truly,
A.E.STALEY MANUFACTURING CO.

President.

gations I could not meet, but I always had heard that in negotiations a person never should accept the first offer. So I said:

"All right, providing I can keep the program rights."

Programs sold for 10 cents in those days.

"Done," he said.

I left the park a happy man.

This verbal agreement stood firm without change for fifty years. It is a pleasure to do business with people like the Veecks and the Wrigleys.

I rented ten rooms at Blackwood Apartment Hotel at 4414 Clarendon, for $2 a week a player. The hotel was cheap, clean, decent and within walking distance of the field.

When I returned to Decatur, and told the team we were moving to Chicago, only John Mintun declined to come. He explained that he had been born and reared in Decatur and intended to make a career at Staley's. He became night superintendent.

The essentials attended to, I telephoned Min. "Coming to Chicago! How wonderful," she said.

Our first task was to deal with Rock Island in Decatur. Staley people, Decatur fans and Rock Island supporters who came seeking revenge more than filled the doubled stadium. Never before did 3,600 people see a football game in Decatur. Nor did they ever again. We won 14–0.

I packed the Staley uniforms, orange and blue, the University of Illinois colors. Orange and blue are still the Bears' colors. Jerseys for carriers and receivers had broad vertical stripes of rough material to help players hold on to the ball.

73

The problems of running the team seemed endless. I decided to take a partner. I wanted Paddy Driscoll, but he wasn't available. So I looked around the team and settled on Dutch Sternaman. He was our most successful scorer. I offered him a 50–50 partnership. He would have taken less. Had I made it 51–49, I would have saved myself a lot of heartaches and difficulties. He and I agreed to take $100 each a game, same as the players—if any money were still in the bank.

I scheduled daily workouts at 9 A.M. and imposed fines on late players. The system made sure the players were in bed each night at a decent hour, although players were rarely distracted by the revelries of the big city. They were too interested in making good as professionals.

We beat Rock Island 14–0. The Jeffersons came from Rochester. George Trafton blocked a punt, the ball rolled behind the goal and Ralph Scott fell upon it, making his first score in all of his years as a tackle. We won 16–13. The 7,500 fans went home happy and I walked to the hotel very, very content.

The Dayton Triangles followed. Neither of us could score. In the final minutes we were on their 4-yard line. It was fourth down. We did a hide-and-seek play within the backfield. Sternaman tossed the ball to me across the goal. Dayton protested the play was illegal but the referee ruled for us. We won 7–0. The gate reported 7,239 paid admissions. I felt almost financially secure.

So it went.

Staley 20, Detroit Tigers 9; Chic out with injured ribs, gate 6,500.

Staley 3, Rock Island 0, played in snow; gate 3,000.

Staley 22, the great Jim Thorpe's Cleveland Tigers 7. Ten thousand fans howling as Stinchcomb ran 80 yards. Thorpe punted from behind his own goal line to our 10-yard line, the ball traveling more than 100 yards. Thorpe said in his eighteen years he never had met a team that hit harder. We had desire.

On Thanksgiving Day, the Buffalo All-Americans squeezed us out 7–6. Ten days later we met them again. Guy Chamberlin took a Buffalo pass on our 10-yard line and ran 90 yards to score. The Buffalo team got even by blocking a punt, recovering it and scoring. A Chamberlin placekick gave us a 10–7 victory.

Between the two Buffalo games, we met a new team formed by the Indian Meat Packing Company in Green Bay, Wisconsin. The manager was Curly Lambeau. We won 20–0 and began what was to be our longest rivalry and, for me, the happiest series of games.

We ran through the Canton Bulldogs 10–0. A week before Christmas with the temperatures near zero and fans fewer than 3,000, we played the Chicago Cardinals. We slid around scorelessly. There was just one substitute. Players were hardy. They loved to play. To take one out during a game was almost worth my life.

Our season ended with nine won, one lost, one tied. The League proclaimed us World Champions.

When the Hall of Fame was established at Canton, four Staley players were named—Chamberlin, Conzelman, Trafton and me.

Wonder of wonders, we paid all our bills and still had $7 in the bank. But the players had to seek jobs to carry them through to next fall, and Dutch and I had to find a way to finance the new season. Meanwhile, Min and I set our wedding for February 18, 1922.

My obligation to the A.E. Staley Company ceased. I

75

considered naming the team the Chicago Cubs out of respect for Mr. William Veeck, Senior, and Mr. William Wrigley, who had been such a great help. But I noted football players are bigger than baseball players; so if baseball players are cubs, then certainly football players must be bears!

Sternaman and I established The Chicago Bears Football Club with capital stock of $15,000. Dutch and I put up $2,500 each and another $2,500 jointly. We locked the remainder of the stock in a safe. The $7,500 cash would see the new club through the winter and pay training costs in the autumn.

I asked the Association at our January meeting to transfer the franchise from the A.E. Staley Company to The Chicago Bears Football Club.

Unexpectedly Bill Harley produced a startling demand for one-third ownership because of our agreement the past year. He obtained a lawyer and went to court. He came to the Association meeting and asked that the Staley franchise be given to him.

The executive committee telephoned Mr. A.E. Staley. He said he had transferred the team to me the previous fall. The company, he said, was quitting all paid athletics.

The members debated all day and into the evening. In the end, they decided to vote on whether the franchise should be given to Sternaman and me or to Bill Harley. Eight voted for us, two for Harley.

The Chicago Bears were born!

The sequel occurred in court two years later. Never having had any business with lawyers, I had told Mr. William Veeck, Senior, about Harley's suit. I asked him what to do.

"Why don't you use our lawyers, Mayer, Meyer, Austrian and Platt?" he said. I went to them. A partner, Mr. Albert Austrian, said Harley's case could not stand up in court. He said the case would take two years but would be decided for me on this point, this point and this point. I do not recall the points, but the case came out just as Mr. Austrian said.

CHAPTER SIX

My Bears
Come Out Roaring

MIN WAS A LUTHERAN and sang with a Swedish chorus. I was Catholic and went to Mass every Sunday. The difference did not disturb us, nor our mothers. But the churches took a different view. When Min told her minister she planned to marry a Catholic, he tried to stop her. I called on him. He was most courteous. The question of any children's religious upbringing did not come up. My parish priest told me the wedding ceremony could not be performed in the church.

Min and I were married on February 18, 1922, by a Catholic priest in the rectory of Old St. Mary's, Wabash Avenue at Ninth Street. His kindness encouraged Min to pledge that children would be brought up in the Catholic faith.

Min wore a white dress. She was beautiful. I had a carnation in my buttonhole. Ralph Brizzolara was best man and Min's sister, Lil, was maid of honor. No one else was present. Afterward Min's mother gave a dinner at her home for the family and Ralph and Florence. The talk was of football. Then all escorted us to the railroad station and threw rice. I had enough money for round-trip Pullman tickets as far as Tampa, Florida. The Florida weather was good, warm enough for swimming. We went sightseeing but our conversations always included football.

When we came home, Min's eldest sister, Laura, and her husband, Herman Oetting, had gone to Europe. They let us use their apartment until we found a small first-floor apartment in Oak Park on Humphrey Avenue, just south of the Douglas Park elevated station. I made sure the landlord tended the furnace. As a boy I had toted enough coal.

Herman and his brother, William, owned an ice business. For years they had cut ice in Channel Lake, stored it and in the summer brought it, covered with hay, to Chicago and sold it door to door. By 1922 William—we called him Uncle Billy—had constructed an artificial ice plant in Chicago. The machinery was complex. He needed an engineer, and I was an engineer with services to offer. I enrolled in a three-month correspondence course with the University of Wisconsin and, to gain practical experience, offered myself to a meat packing company as a refrigeration engineer, free of charge. When Uncle Billy considered my expertise sufficiently widened, he put me on the midnight-to-eight shift to leave days free for my Bears, and, in summer, to play with the semi-pro Logan Square baseball team, from which I gained much pleasure and a little cash.

Min quit the grain brokerage firm and plunged into Bears' administrative affairs. She wrote letters and helped with accounts. She read all the papers, clipped everything she saw about the Bears and popped the clippings into a big breadbox. When the box was full, she pasted the clippings into scrapbooks. In time they filled an entire wall. How they bring alive those days when the Bears set out to conquer the world.

During the summer J.B. Bonderant came from De-Pauw to understudy our great center George Trafton. Halfback Johnny Bryan came from the University of Chicago; Guard Carl Hanke from Minnesota; End Frank Hanny from Indiana; and from Notre Dame a veritable master of football, Hunk Anderson, who was to have a major role in the Bears, and to become the greatest line coach in football.

Anderson, christened Heartly, had grown up in the copper-mining town of Calumet at the top of Michigan. The favorite game was ice hockey, played on the frozen lakes. Heartly was big for his age so the kids called him Unk. In high school he made the All-State football team. His father worked on the railroad and had only enough money to send a daughter to a teachers' college. Unk assumed he would have to go to work. But World War I was on and colleges had lost many of their best athletes to the army. An older Calumet boy, George Gipp, was doing well at Notre Dame and told Knute Rockne about Unk. Rockne arranged for a tryout. He said he would run and Unk should try to stop him. Unk brought him down once, twice, three times, four times. "You're on," Rockne said, and arranged for a scholarship to pay board, room, tuition and books.

Notre Dame was at its peak. With Unk as guard, Notre Dame won twenty-six games, lost two, and tied our 1918 Great Lakes team. The unmovable Unk became Hunk—as in granite. He developed the tactic of rushing

80

through a hole in the line to get at the passer. Now everybody blitzes. He was All-American.

During his last two college years, he coached a semi-pro team, the South Bend Arrows. On graduation, he came to the Bears, for $100 a game. Hunk was so special that I was glad to have him for only Saturday night and Sunday. From Monday through Friday, he coached the Notre Dame line for Rockne—without pay—replacing my brother, Walter, who had moved on to Davenport where the money was better. One day Fielding Yost and Amos Alonzo Stagg went to South Bend and told Rockne he should get rid of Hunk unless Hunk left the Bears. Rockne refused.

The Chicago Bears' first opponent was an American Legion team in Racine, Wisconsin. We won 6–0. We went to Rock Island for another contest with the Independents. They had a great Black tackle from Iowa State, Duke Slater. He took out the entire left side of our line on one play, but we won 10–6.

The end of the baseball season let us move into our new home, Wrigley Field. Our first guests were the Rochester, N.Y., Jeffersons. The two lines shoved back and forth. We finally won 7–0. I ordered double practice. The following week fumbles, punts and plunges led us to another inauspicious 7–0 victory over the Buffalo All-Americans.

Then we came up against the unbeaten Canton Bulldogs. They scored within three minutes. We pulled ourselves together. In the final quarter Pete Stinchcomb threw several good passes. I got to the 12 and Sternaman ran around end to score but his placekick failed. We passed down the field and reached the 25. We tried to beat the gun with a field goal. The kick was wide. We lost

7–6, but the sight of 10,000 fans in the stands softened the loss.

A fine Yale former captain, Nelson Talbott, had brought to the Dayton Triangles the captains from Indiana, Miami and Dennison and the newest strategy developed in the Ivy League. I was eager to test it against our tried and true T-Formation. We beat Dayton 9–0, confirming my belief in the superiority of the T. Sportswriter Frank Smith of the *Tribune* reported:

"The contest provided some of the cleanest football it has been our fortune to witness for many years."

One of the most popular teams that year was Jim Thorpe's Oorang Indians. The players had fascinating names such as Running Deer, Thunder War Eagle, Long Time Sleep, White Cloud, Eagle Feather and Down Wind. There were two really good men, Joe Guyon and Pete Calac. And later there was Little Twig!

The Oorang team was organized by a man named Walter Lingo who raised Airedale dogs in LaRue, Ohio, a little town about 50 miles north of Columbus. His primary avocation was Indian lore. He spoke several Indian tongues. His secondary avocation was football. He recruited Indians, mostly from Carlisle and Haskell Indian schools. Most players were Chippewas from Wisconsin and Minnesota. I think he made up the name Oorang.

The field was deep in mud. A writer found the condition amusing: "They missed tackles and skidded yards on their faces, the mud cascading right and left off their helmets like water before the prow of a speedboat."

Thorpe was not billed to play—he was thirty-three years old. But when Guyon was hurt, Thorpe came in.

He made a touchdown. For expertise and competition the game does not rank very high. We won 33–6.

The Akron Tiremakers brought thirteen men with good college records. We won 20–10. The game produced one important invention. Paul Robeson had delayed his singing debut and was giving us trouble. Hunk Anderson, who feared no other football player, went at him, head lowered to make the standard shoulder block, but then planted a foot firmly and pivoted, swinging his hip into Robeson's side.

The contact deflected Robeson. By the end of the game Hunk was pivoting both to the left and right. Robeson was totally confused. The next week at Notre Dame, Hunk demonstrated his invention to Rockne. The great coach was delighted. He said the invention would let blockers handle any opponent regardless of size. Thus was born the reverse body block.

The Rock Island team came to Chicago for a replay. We won in the last two minutes 3–0.

I had long coveted a Rock Island player, Ed Healey, former Dartmouth star. The Rock Island owner, Walter Flanigan, owed me $100. I offered to cancel the debt if he would give me Healey. He agreed, completing professional football's first or second player trade.

There was one problem. I offered Ed $75 a game. He wanted $100. I could not resist his charm. I rejoice that I succumbed. I received a great player for my Bears and a firm lifetime friend.

On Thanksgiving Day we met the Cardinals.

Healey often recalled:

A situation came up in which Halas and Joe Sternaman were engaged in trying to hold Driscoll and he
was making every effort to break away. I figured it
was time for me to come in there with an effective
attack and sort of bring Driscoll to the ground in a
careful way. While I was meditating, a group of south
side thugs left the Cardinal area and approached me.
I came to a halt immediately. With my hands forward
and looking toward heaven, I said, "Jesus, Mary and
Joseph, here am I, playing on this field for a hundred
bucks after joining it just two days ago and, my God,
they want to kill me!"

In truth, Healey did not just stand there, hands and
eyes in prayer position. No indeed. He was punching
away with his teammates.

What happened was this: Paddy Driscoll made a
good run around end, reaching our 20. Joe Sternaman
and I thought that must not be allowed to happen again.
On the next play, Driscoll set off with the ball. Joey and I
brought him down with all the force we could muster,
which was considerable. Paddy was down but not out.
He pulled himself to his feet, wobbled toward Joey and
started pummeling him with both fists. That is when the
thugs came out. So did reserve players. So did fans from
both stands. The police came out, too, wielding sticks
and blowing whistles and shouting. In time, in quite a
time, order was restored.

The referee ordered Paddy to leave the field for slug-
ging Joey, and that started the disagreement all over
again.

Seeking peace, I announced the Bears would be
happy if the referee would withdraw Paddy's banish-
ment. I said I recognized that Paddy had hit out in a flash
of temper. My forgiveness seemed only to increase the

heat. I found myself on my back on the ground, felled by three simultaneous blows from three directions. A disgruntled Cardinal sat astride me.

The referee ordered Joey and me to join Paddy in the showers.

We lost 6–0. But everybody had a good time. I proposed a replay. Chris O'Brien accepted.

The tumult that Thanksgiving Day brought out the season's largest professional football crowd for the rematch—more than 10,000. Automobiles were parked in nearby streets and the elevated trains were packed as though on a rush hour.

Both teams turned up in red jerseys. We pulled on white T-shirts. Paddy beat us. Paddy and his educated toe beat us. One of his punts stopped on the 2-yard line, another on the 1-foot line. Two untimely fumbles and an intercepted lateral helped the Cardinals approach our end zone three times. Each time Paddy kicked a field goal. We lost, 9–0, but the sight of all those people in the stands on the tenth of December promised a healthy future for professional football.

As Bears, we ended our first season with nine wins and three losses, placing us second in the eighteen-team League. Canton took the championship, with ten wins and two ties. The Cardinals were third, with eight wins and three losses.

The time had come to have an All-American professional team. Boldly, I made the selection, the first ever.

The lineup:

Left end, CHAMBERLIN, Nebraska, Canton
Left tackle, HENRY, W-J, Canton
Left guard, STEIN, Pitt, Toledo
Center, ALEXANDER, Syracuse, Rochester
Right guard, HEALEY, Dartmouth, Bears

85

Right tackle, BLACKLOCK, Michigan State, Bears
Right end, URBAN, Boston, Buffalo
Quarterback, HUGHITT, Michigan, Buffalo
Left halfback, DRISCOLL, Northwestern, Cardinals
Right halfback, STINCHCOMB, Ohio State, Bears
Fullback, KING, West Virginia, Akron

Six had been on various All-American collegiate teams—Henry, Stein, Alexander, Urban, Stinchcomb and King.

In submitting my team to newspapers, I attached a note: "It might be amusing to wonder what would happen to college heroes if they had to smack up against this super eleven." More than a decade would pass until we could test relative abilities.

On the last day of 1922 I drew up the financial accounts. Ticket sales brought $73,979.20. The Cubs' 15 percent for use of the park came to $9,091.81. We paid visiting teams $22,160.95. Players received $18,315.00. We gave Stinchcomb a bonus of $1,635.00. We spent $3,026.64 for rain insurance and $2,908.60 for advertising and publicity. Traveling—first class—cost $1,197.00. Equipment was relatively cheap—$737.49, thanks partly to the use of the Staley uniforms. There were the costs of printing tickets, of telephone, of telegraph, of laundry and a host of other things. Add it all up and the outgo was precisely $72,502.28. Deduct that from our income, and we actually made a profit! A profit of $1,476.92!

We were offered $35,000 for our franchise. We turned it down.

With pride I showed the accounts to Mother. She looked at the bottom line, shook her head sadly and said, "George, go back to the railroad, dear. You'll have a steady income there."

86

In 1923 we won nine games, lost two and tied one, ending second to Canton, which won eleven and tied one. We drew larger crowds but finished with a loss of $366.72. I did not show the book to Mother. Min became resigned to waiting many years for a fur coat.

The game I remember that year was one with the Oorang Indians in Wrigley Field. Heavy rain supplied us abundantly with mud. We slipped and slid. The Indians reached our 2-yard line. We assumed that Jim Thorpe would try to take the ball over on the next play. He did try. He smacked into the line just outside our strong tackle, Hugh Blacklock, and the wet muddy ball squirted from Jim's hands into mine. I sidestepped and took off. I heard an angry roar. It was Thorpe, coming after me. I ran faster and faster but I sensed he was gaining. I could hear the squishing of his shoes in the mud. When I could almost feel his breath, I dug in a cleat and did a sharp zig. Thorpe's momentum carried him on and gave me a few feet of running room. He narrowed the gap. I zagged. Again he lost a stride. He turned and came on. I zigged. I zagged. Zig. Zag. Just short of the goal, Thorpe threw himself at me and down I went, into a pool of water. But at the same time I slid over the goal. No professional had run 98 yards for a touchdown. None did so again until 1972. For forty-nine years, the name of George Stanley Halas was in the book of records. You can look it up on page 229 in the 1978 yearbook.

You never forget plays like that, so when my ribs ache, I remember a game in 1924 against the New York Giants. Joe Guyon, who had played beside Jim Thorpe earlier, was in the Giants' backfield. He was tough. He was rough. I thought he needed a lesson in etiquette. I waited until his back was turned and threw myself at him. While I was in full flight, he turned and set his knees. My ribs hit them. I collapsed, flat on the ground, gasping and moaning. The big Indian bent over me and said: "Let that be a lesson to you, George. Never try to sneak up on an Indian." The trainer sent a stretcher to haul me to the locker room. The doctor found two broken ribs. Worse, the referee walked off 15 yards against the Bears. That was truly painful. In the future, I employed less noticeable ways to instruct opponents about proper behavior.

We won six games in 1924 and were beaten just once, by Green Bay. But we were tied four times. In those days, we ignored ties in figuring percentage so our .857 kept us in second place, this time to the Cleveland Bulldogs, who had played only nine games, winning seven, losing one and tying one. I thought this rating method had serious flaws. To ignore ties was not correct. The number of games played varied widely. A title-seeking manager could improve his chances by scheduling weak teams. Eventually, the League began to arrange schedules, and we began counting a tie as half win, half loss.

Our gate receipts fairly soared from $80,877.04 the previous year to $116,534. I increased players' salaries by 50 percent. For the first time I spent money on scouting—$264.50. We ended the 1924 season with $3,474.03 in the bank.

Despite this solvency, when fall came I always had to borrow money to see us through the training period and the first games. I used Foreman Brothers, now the American National Bank, which was then a small second-floor bank with a big reputation for helping small business. I would ask the loan officer, Ed Sullivan, for $1,000. This he granted. Then I'd come back and receive a second helping. The third time I walked through the door, he shouted, "No, no, no." After that, I called him "No No Sullivan," but he always made another loan. The secret was that each time I brought some money to repay part of earlier loans. In truth, the Bears lived hand-to-mouth.

At last the newspapers discovered the Bears. I kept writing articles about upcoming games, and by reading the papers I learned editors like superlatives. I blush when I think how many times I wrote that the next game was going to be the most difficult of the season, or how a new player was the fastest man in the West, or how our tackles were fierce giants. "Giants"—that word frequently found its way into my copy. And I tried to stress the quality of our players. I would write how fearless they were on the field, but what fine gentlemen they were at all other times. Despite my efforts, the sportswriters eventually found a favorite word for us— monsters!

I made several copies of each article I wrote. Dutch and I took them to newspaper offices. We offered complimentary tickets generously. It always hurt when I saw the previous week's tickets lying on a writer's desk, unused.

In time I decided the Bears deserved a professional reporter. I hired a writer with *The Chicago Evening Post* for $25 a game. He could be professional football's first paid public relations man, and his professional writing increased our exposure. One glorious Monday I awoke to find the *Chicago Tribune* had made our game its top sports story, with an inch-high headline running across the entire page! I went to the *Tribune* and thanked the young sports editor, Don Maxwell.

"You and the Bears have nothing to thank me for," Maxwell said. "The *Tribune* and I should thank you. Sunday in autumn is a dull sports day. We need something exciting for our Monday pages. The Bears are giving us that excitement. When I gave the Bears the banner, I wasn't doing it to help the Bears but to help the *Tribune*." As years passed Maxwell became city editor, managing editor and, after Colonel McCormick died, editor. He also became one of my very best friends.

Other sports editors were giving us serious consideration, too. One wrote: "Pro football is building a new class of sports fan, people who work hard on weekdays. The majority were deprived of a college education. The patronage of college sports is confined almost exclusively to students and alumni. Naturally, the uncollegiate element sought an outlet for its curiosity which has developed into enthusiasm."

Another editorialized: "Football is the coming game. It's almost as popular as baseball. It should be boosted for the benefit of young Americans. It should be played in neighborhoods so families living next door won't be strangers."

Meanwhile the American Professional Football Association had many weaknesses. The great Jim Thorpe had served us well gaining publicity but, as we knew, he was no administrator, nor did he pretend to be. With the sport growing, we needed a man who could direct the development of our organization, help design rules and enforce them. Such a man was Joe F. Carr of Columbus,

Ohio. He was a born organizer. He had organized employees in the Panhandle workshop of the Pennsylvania Railroad into powerful baseball and football teams. He had organized professional baseball in Ohio. He wrote sports for the Ohio State *Journal*. At the Association's annual meeting we unanimously elected him as our president.

I lacked enthusiasm for our name, the American Professional Football Association. In baseball, "association" was applied to second-class teams. We were first-class. The Chicago Cubs baseball club belonged to the National League, not the American League. "Professional" was superfluous. I proposed we change our name to the National Football League. My fellow members agreed.

The problem most on Carr's mind was the casual relationship between players and teams. A fellow would play for a team one week and against it the next. Ask him why and he would say: "They offered me five dollars more." Some teams would dump players at will, often owing them money. Not the Bears. We agreed no team would hire a player from another team until that team had declared him a free agent. The arrangement basically survives to this day.

At subsequent meetings, we considered establishing limits for the number of players and salaries. I thought sixteen players were sufficient and $100 a game a good average salary, with star players getting more and merely satisfactory players less. Some thought the figures high, others low. In time both figures were adopted.

The most difficult problem was the use by professional teams of players still attending college. From the very first, the League had declared its opposition to using collegians, but we did not enforce the rule. No wonder that when two rival Illinois county seats, Carlinville and Taylorville, met for their annual game in 1922, with perhaps $100,000 in side bets riding on the outcome, Carlinville brought in players from Notre Dame and Taylorville from Illinois. Taylorville won 16–0.

The players, when questioned by their coaches the following Monday, said they had played only for fun and to help raise money for the American Legion, the game's sponsor. But the colleges banned sixteen players, including Dutch's kid brother Joey, from further collegiate sport. Joey came to the Bears.

Our League decided to take parallel action against a member of Curly Lambeau's Green Bay Packers, which had used two collegians. We revoked the Green Bay franchise and demanded an apology from Curly. Fortunately for the League, Curly found another packing house sponsor and, with cash raised by a friend who sold his car, applied for a new franchise. We supplied it.

Even so, our reworded ban on using collegians remained vague. An ingenious manager could find loopholes in it. I did so in 1925, to the profit of the Bears and, I believe, to professional football.

We had hoped that our newly worded ban would reduce the opposition of certain collegiate coaches, among whom the great Amos Alonzo Stagg of the University of Chicago and Fielding Yost of Michigan were most bitter. Stagg announced that when the collegiate conference directors next met, he, as president, would bring up the "menace" of professional football. He said that college coaches had been trying to fight the evil individually but now the time had come for concerted action. He did not get that concerted action. G. Huff, director of athletics at

Illinois, a fine, wise gentleman, would not join in the denunciation. He said football is a great game and colleges should not consider it their monopoly. He said he thought players, after graduation, had a right to play wherever they chose and fans had a right to watch games on Sunday. But even G. Huff was not totally on our side. He said one should not think a college player did wrong in playing for a professional team after graduation but added he was rather sorry to see any college player do so. The road ahead of me had many frightful potholes and traps. And many years passed before I came to understand the reason for collegiate opposition.

I spoke out at every opportunity against the evils of gambling and its danger to sport. I persuaded the League to draw up a statement of principle: "Members are expected to behave as gentlemen and sportsmen. Any flagrant violation of the principle may subject the offender to fine and suspension."

At best, it was what I call a toothless bite. The truth was that other managers and owners did not see the dangers in gambling that I did.

The League took more positive action in other areas. It organized scheduling and, to improve officiating, authorized our president to appoint the referees and pay them, but not more than $35 a game. We also dealt with many small items—the color of socks and jerseys, cancellation, the ball to be used (the Spaulding), the number of passes a team could give away, admission prices, an open gate to kids.

We upgraded our championship by authorizing the League to present the champion club with a pennant and each of its players with a small golden football—to cost not more than $10. For winning Super Bowl XIII each Pittsburgh Steeler took home $18,000 and a ring heavy with diamonds.

The increased popularity of the sport was producing semi-pro and pro teams in many towns and cities. We required a $1,000 deposit with applications. One year we threw out eight teams that did not come up with the money. Membership stabilized between sixteen and eighteen. But there was one major lack—a team in New York City. We oldtimers thought this to be a severe hindrance to the development of professional football as a popular sport and as an economic proposition, so in the summer of 1925, we assigned President Carr the task of trying to plug the hole. He went to New York to call on a very active sports promoter, Billy Gibson. His prize property was Gene Tunney, the boxer. Tim Mara, a very successful bookmaker, happened to walk into the office while Carr was there. Gibson introduced them and said Carr had a proposition about a football franchise, which did not interest him but might interest Mara. Tim asked how much the franchise would cost. Carr said $2,500. "Any franchise in New York, even if only for an empty room with two chairs, is worth that kind of money," Mara replied. He offered to take the franchise if Billy would be his club's president. Billy agreed. Mara wrote a check.

Mara had never seen a football game. To help organize the club, he hired Dr. Harry March, an excellent doctor who loved football, and Bob Folwell, former coach at Annapolis. Mara also arranged with the Stoneham family to play in the Polo Grounds, home of the Giants, and named his team for the baseball club.

We all applauded Joe Carr's success. We knew Mara would tap a rich market and bring the game of professional football to the attention of sportswriters for the New York papers and for the burgeoning news agencies which distributed reports to newspapers throughout our country.

The tradition in those days was for the home team to keep gate receipts and pay visitors a guarantee that varied with its estimation of the visitors' drawing power. Soon a wide split developed among team incomes. Strong teams were becoming stronger and the weak ones weaker. I saw a deadly peril. Competition, I felt, was the lifeblood of all sport. Some of us thought we must try to equalize income. We talked long and hard and in the end agreed each visiting team would be given a choice: a guarantee sufficient to pay salaries plus travel expenses, or 40 percent of the gate after deducting 15 percent for park rental. It was an act of sharing unprecedented in sport. The principle of sharing became the foundation of professional football.

I was also giving more thought to the need to open up the game. I was bothered by low scores and the large number of ties. Fans liked to see a runner run. They liked the abrupt changes passing could bring. But other changes had to come first.

I was stunned when our first child arrived on January 5, 1923.

A girl!

I had assumed—and so had Min—that the new arrival would be George Stanley Halas, Jr. I already had visions of drawing my son into the thick of the Bears. We didn't even have a name for a girl. After some searching we decided on Mary Barbara, for her two grandmothers. But my brother Frank already had appropriated those names for his daughter.

I filled in the baby's certificate of birth, leaving the name blank. Many years later, upon getting a copy of her birth certificate for a passport application, my daughter discovered that the name we gave her—Virginia Marion—had been inserted in pencil.

She also learned that despite my wholehearted devotion to the Bears, I had not yet been sure the world would respect as father's occupation the designation of "football club owner, manager, coach and player." I had written in the more conservative career of "civil engineer."

The initial shock over, I was delighted with my daughter. I began plying her immediately with orange juice—the fad at the time for young babies—and stories of the Bears.

On September 4, 1925, Min was again in St. Anthony Hospital.

"It's a boy!" the nurse said.

She took me to Min and my son. Min was as happy as an angel. She cradled the boy in her arm. He was a wonderful sight to look upon. I bent over.

"Hiya, Mugs!" I said.

My chance remark was picked up. Mugs he became and Mugs he still is.

We had the baby christened George Stanley Halas, Jr. On his birth certificate under "father's occupation" I wrote "realtor." Ralph's fiancée, Florence, was godmother. Two months later Min and I attended their wedding. Both were Catholics. The service was at the Blessed Sacrament Church. Ralph had been my best man. Now I was his. Min and I had to hurry away from the wedding breakfast at the Oak Park Arms Hotel and missed seeing them off to Estes Park, Colorado, for their honeymoon. Min had to return to Mugs and I to football, which was about to undergo astounding developments.

Life was good those beautiful autumn days in 1925. Fortune had bestowed many blessings upon us. But a gift often carries a high price. That was to be true with the gift of our son. The birth had led to an aneurysm. The doctor told us it would be most unwise for Min to have more children.

CHAPTER SEVEN

The Golden Lad

THE MID-TWENTIES were the golden years of sport. Babe Ruth was hitting home runs. The smart, handsome Gene Tunney was stripping the formidable Jack Dempsey of his diamond-bright boxing belt. Suzanne Lenglen, Helen Wills and Big Bill Tilden raised tennis to a world sport. The gracious, meticulous Bobby Jones strolled the golf courses, astounding even the Scots at St. Andrews with his ability.

In football, great stadiums, the biggest since the Caesars erected the Coliseum, were rising all over America to accommodate the tens of thousands crowding into university towns every autumn Saturday. The country was booming. Pay was going up and working hours were coming down, leaving time, energy, and money for sport. Newspapers expanded their sports pages and sportswriters developed their flair with the written word. Radio brought into the home the excitement of hearing a game progress.

Across the land, movie palaces were rising and before Douglas Fairbanks swung on a chandelier to save Mary Pickford from a fate worse than death, the newsreel took the audience into the stadiums for last Saturday's best games. The players moved jerkily, the light on the screen flickered and the games were several days old—but there they were, the new national heroes, in action.

And week after week the figure who wriggled and squirmed and slid and darted across the screen was the handsome Red Grange.

In Wheaton, his hometown 30 miles west of the Chicago Loop, housewives spent next week's grocery allowance to buy a fancy dressing-gown in which to open the kitchen door to admit Red, with a 50-pound, 30-cent chunk of ice perched on a shoulder. Alas, sometimes instead of Red, the ice carrier was his younger brother Pinky.

Grange was a true rarity, a perfectly coordinated athlete. At Wheaton High, the skinny 140-pound youth won sixteen letters. Each year he was state champion in a different track event. In three years he made seventy-five touchdowns. Sometimes excited fans would move onto the field. Red would run behind them and, shielded by them, take a pass and score. The manual training teacher was the coach. If a player's ego became inflated, the others gave him the ball, stood back and let all eleven opponents hit him. That, Red says, taught everyone the importance of team play. "If blockers knock everybody down, your grandmother can score," Red says. In Red's senior year, Wheaton High beat the all-Chicago champions, Austin High.

Red's father, the police chief, demanded Red go to college. A neighbor attending the University of Illinois

99

persuaded him to go there. Red arrived with a $4 trunk and some photographs of admiring girls. Red planned to go out for track and basketball but fraternity brothers persuaded him, with a paddle, to add football.

The freshman team, with three future All-Americans—Frank Wickhorst, Moon Baker, and Red—regularly beat the Varsity. When the freshmen moved up, Illinois went from being a losing team to being unbeaten and tying Michigan for the Big Ten championship. As a sophomore, Red made 1,200 yards and twelve touchdowns in seven games. Walter Camp chose him as an All-American. Grantland Rice wrote a poem about the "Galloping Ghost."

In 1924, the Illinois team had even more scoring ability. The university completed a stadium that could accommodate 67,000 fans and every seat was taken for its dedication. Some came for the event; more came to see Illinois meet its strongest rival, Michigan; most came to see Grange.

The day was hot. Zuppke sent his men on the field without stockings. Fielding Yost, the Michigan coach, protested. He thought Zuppke had greased the boys' legs to make tackling a slippery task.

Yost centered his strategy on stopping Grange.

"Nail him now," he ordered. He instructed the kickoff be directed at Grange. Michigan tacklers would bring him down hard and—poof! There would go the image of the "Galloping Ghost."

Grange was off and running before the kickoff dropped into his hands on the 5-yard line. He spun and twisted and slid, darting this way and that, moving ahead like a stick in a rapids, swirling around every obstacle and racing through the swift clear narrows.

A touchdown!

So much for commands from the coach.

In the next twelve minutes Grange made three more touchdowns. Then Zuppke took him out. Grange returned in the third quarter to throw a touchdown pass and make a final touchdown himself. The score: 39–14.

For the next game with the University of Chicago, Amos Alonzo Stagg devised a strategy to keep the ball away from Red. Chicago won the toss. Concentrating on plunges, content with picking up 2, 3, 4 yards, Chicago scored twice before Grange touched the ball. Stagg also strengthened the ends, closing Red's favorite route to the goal, so he had to go through the line. It was painful. Each Chicago tackle was aimed at sending him to the sidelines. But each time Red jumped up and trotted back into position. The drive produced a touchdown. Chicago added a third. Grange countered with a second for Illinois. In the third quarter Grange wriggled through the line, befuddled and dodged the secondary and the safety, and covered 80 yards to tie the game.

As the end neared, Grange got free for another 51-yard scoring run but the referees called back the ball. A teammate had been caught holding. The game finished. A 21–21 tie.

As a junior, Red made thirteen touchdowns and 1,164 yards. He was again All-American.

Graduation took away most of that memorable Illinois team. As a senior, Grange made six touchdowns. He went East for the first time for a game with Pennsylvania at Franklin Field in Philadelphia. Easterners could not believe Red was so great as sportswriters said. The know-it-alls among the 65,000 studied the thick, slippery mud produced by a steady rain and predicted Grange would not gain 10 yards all day. He made 363 yards, three touchdowns, and brought a 24–2 victory. Now no one could doubt the superb running ability of Grange.

One Saturday in November of 1924 Ralph Brizzolara and I decided to drive down to the University of Illinois to see Red run. I didn't have to coax Min to come.

Ralph borrowed his father's open touring Hudson and picked up Florence—they were becoming serious. She wore a new fur coat. Min thought it would be a shame to get the coat wet but Florence said animals stay out in the rain so a little water wouldn't hurt her coat!

Min had made egg sandwiches. Mrs. Bushing had agreed to look after baby Gin until we returned the next day. During the drive I was in the pink. I belted out my favorite song, "Alice Blue Gown," alternating now and then with the old Illinois college song, "Hail to the Orange, Hail to the Blue."

When we arrived, the park was already full. Rain was falling. We soon were soaked. We brushed the rain off our faces and shouted all the louder for Red.

It is strange I don't remember the game. Perhaps I was living in my own dreams. I assume Illinois won. I do know that all evening Florence and Min talked about the exciting, handsome Red. We had seen the "Galloping Ghost" in the flesh. As an owner, manager, coach and player, I was determined to have Red on the Bears.

But how? For a year I pondered. I wrote Grange a couple of letters but received no reply. I spoke to him on the phone to no avail.

The pressures on Red were terrible. He did not know what to do. His father said he hoped Red would do something other than professional football. Fielding Yost said the same thing but Westbrook Pegler advised: "Grange may bring into a butcher shop many books of clippings but after he has exhibited them all, the butcher will say, 'The chops are still 68 cents.'" Zuppke told Red he should do what he thought best. Meanwhile, Major J.L. Griffith, commissioner of the Western Collegiate Conference, said baseball had been a big college sport until professional baseball came along. Fans moved over and college baseball died. He predicted that professional football would similarly rob college football of its crowds. Suddenly I had the answer to the question of why collegiate coaches opposed professional football.

One day late in October of 1925 a Chicago man named Frank Zambrino approached me. He was manager of a movie house and distributed films. He told me about a friend in Champaign named C.C. Pyle, who had been in vaudeville and now ran a movie theater in the college town. Pyle was thinking of trying to become Red's manager. Zambrino said Pyle wanted to know if, were he successful, I would be interested in having Red play with the Bears and, perhaps, make a big tour after our season.

I told him I liked the idea. Zambrino carried messages back and forth.

Early in November, Pyle saw Grange enter his theater and take an aisle seat halfway down. Now was the time! During the movie, Pyle sent an usher to Red. "Mr. Pyle would like to speak to you in his office," the usher said. Red asked, "Who is Mr. Pyle?"

"He owns the theater," the usher said. "He's waiting in his office."

After the movie Red went to the office. The door was open. Pyle sat behind his desk. Without even a hello, he said, "Grange, how would you like to make a hundred thousand dollars?"

Red was astounded. He thought Pyle must have

103

something crooked in mind. "I don't do those things," Red said. "You'll have to get someone else."

Pyle said, "I mean, how would you like to make a hundred thousand dollars playing football this winter?"

That caught Red's attention.

"Playing football where?"

"With the Bears, in Chicago and on tour."

Red said he couldn't sign any contract until after the last Illinois game. Pyle said nothing need be written now. He and Red would merely have an understanding between them that after the season Red would make Pyle his manager for two years. There would be a lot of money. Pyle would give 60 percent to Red and keep 40. "I'll guarantee that you will get at least one hundred thousand dollars this winter," he said.

Red said it sounded promising.

"All right," Pyle said, "I'll go to Chicago and get back to you on my return."

Pyle sent word through Zambrino that he'd come to an understanding with Red and was ready to talk with me. We knew we couldn't be seen together so I took a room at the Morrison Hotel. Pyle joined Sternaman and me there.

Pyle was an interesting man. I noted how carefully he dressed and how well tended was his mustache. His shoes were brilliant. He spoke well. He was suave. I felt I was in the presence of a born promoter.

I told him at once I hoped Red would join the Bears immediately after the last Illinois game the Saturday before Thanksgiving and play with the Bears in our final two games. Pyle agreed. He said we should then go East, to New York and Washington and other cities where people were eager to see Red. Then, after Christmas, we should go South to Florida and work our way across to California and up the West Coast.

It was a powerful idea. I would never have dared think of such a sweeping enterprise. But Pyle had unlimited vision. I asked who would make the arrangements.

Pyle said he would.

I liked the proposal. I would not have known where to begin. Pyle had been around. I was just a country boy.

It was obvious all of us had to share earnings. I could not possibly make a cash offer. I had no idea how much the tour would bring in. I had no spare cash for an advance. I said I thought a two to one split would be about right.

Pyle agreed, much to my surprise. Without a word, a single word. I anticipated at least some discussion. My astonishment may have stirred my generosity, because I then volunteered that the Bears would pay costs. "Of course," Pyle said. I said I hoped Grange would find the arrangements acceptable.

"He will," Pyle said.

A sense of uneasiness came over me. The negotiations had moved too easily. I thought I should begin again. "All right," I said, "it is agreed the Bears will get two-thirds and . . ."

Pyle cut me short. He said, "Oh no, George, Grange and I will get two-thirds. The Bears will get one-third."

I said that was impossible. After I paid the players and the tour costs, I'd be lucky to break even.

The sweetness went out of the discussions. We talked through the afternoon and the evening and the night and the next morning and on into the afternoon. After twenty-six hours, we did come to an agreement. We would split the earnings fifty-fifty, I would provide the

105

Bears and pay the tour costs. Pyle would provide Red. Red would provide the crowds. It was a fair arrangement.

We put it in writing. The last clause stated if any of us were asked about a contract we would declare none existed. The date was November 10, 1925.

We tried to keep our arrangement secret, but when Pyle went East to arrange games, he had to tell people managing other teams that Red was sewed up with the Bears. They blabbed. The press phoned me to ask if we had signed Red. I said no. I was speaking the truth. No one asked me if Pyle had signed Red.

A lot of people also asked Red if he had signed. Red truthfully told them he had signed nothing. Even so, many people demanded he be put off the Illinois team before the final game with Ohio State at Columbus. The athletic director there was very helpful. He said, "Red Grange says he has not signed a contract and that is good enough for me. He will play."

What a crowd! Eighty-five thousand. The biggest sports turnout up to that day. And what a game! Illinois won.

After the game Red went with the team to a hotel. The press gathered in the lobby. A friend brought Red a black wig to cover his red hair and gave him a big cigar. Red had never smoked. He put the cigar in his mouth, went along the hall to the freight elevator and rode it to the back door. He walked to the station and caught the midnight train to Chicago, where he checked into a hotel under another name.

In the morning, he met with Pyle, Dutch and me in my room at the Morrison Hotel. Red signed a contract making Pyle his manager.

We called in the press and announced Red would play the last two games with the Bears and then we would go on tour.

The reporters wanted to know how much Red would receive. Red correctly declined to say. Pay should be private. No one ever did say.

The press asked why Red was turning pro. I have always admired his answer: "I am going into professional football to make money. I see nothing wrong in playing pro football. It seems to me to be the same thing as playing professional baseball. I have to get money now because people will forget all about me in a few years. I am still loyal to Illinois but I don't think I owe my college anything more. I had to pay a price to play college football. It was hard work and I had little fun out of season."

Zuppke again came to Red's aid. He said whatever Red did was his business and if Red could live up to the Ten Commandments, he would get through life all right.

I was lucky to get Red. I suspected many other owners had tried. Tim Mara had come to Chicago to sign him, and Tim telegraphed home he had been partially successful: Red and the Bears would play the Giants in New York. Leo Lyons, who had the Rochester team, wrote me twenty-four years after the event that he too was in the Morrison Hotel that day. Leo was so certain he would sign Red for $5,000 a game that his partner had come out with a certified check. While waiting in their hotel room, they heard a lot of noise, looked out and saw Red telling the press he had signed with the Bears.

Red sat on our bench that afternoon. The next morning a line, four wide, reached from our ticket office in the Spaulding store, down State Street, along Monroe, and up Wabash, almost around the block. We sold all 36,000 tickets and could have sold 30,000 more. We could have doubled the price, or tripled it, but I did not want people to think the Bears were greedy nor did I want to price the game out of the average pocket. I did raise the tickets by a quarter, to $1.75, to pay the cost of reserving seats, something new for us.

Red didn't do much on Thanksgiving Day. Paddy Driscoll kept punting the ball away from him. The game was scoreless. At the end people booed. When Paddy came home, he told Mary, his wife, "Isn't it terrible the way people booed Red?" Mary said, "Paddy, they were not booing Red. They were booing you for not giving Red a chance."

Snow fell heavily but three days later 28,000 came to Wrigley Field again just to see Red. He ran 140 yards. We beat the Columbus Tigers.

I had no difficulty getting all sixteen players to agree to the tour. What a tour! There never has been one to match it. There probably never will.

After a two-day rest, we played in St. Louis, beating a mediocre pick-up team 39–6. The gate was a disappointing 8,000. On Saturday 35,000 Philadelphians came to Shibe Park in a drizzle to see Red make two touchdowns. We won 14–7. The next day, 73,000 New Yorkers packed the Polo grounds. We didn't have time to wash our muddy uniforms. Red grabbed a Giant pass and ran 30 yards for a touchdown. We won 19–7. The game was rough. Westbrook Pegler reported: "Red was slugged by a Giant who wound up like a barroom fighter throwing a cuspidor. Red stumbled but officials saw nothing. They

108

were as hostile to fighting as Tex Rickard. Soon Red was kicked in the arm. Then Joe Alexander tried to twist off the red head. The officials still saw nothing." The game wiped out Tim Mara's losses for the entire season and encouraged him to stay in football.

The team rode the evening train to Washington but Pyle stayed behind in New York holding open house in his hotel room for anyone wishing to use the Grange name. He picked up $13,000 from a sweater maker, $10,000 from a doll maker, $5,000 from a shoemaker, $5,000 from a ginger ale maker and $2,500 from a cap maker. He turned down a cigarette maker's $10,000 until the maker agreed to the wording: "I don't smoke but my best friend smokes . . ." He signed Red to make a picture for Joe Kennedy's FBO—later RKO—studios in Hollywood during the summer. The press said Red would be paid $300,000. In fact, he got $50,000. The picture was well received and led to a sequel and then a serial. C.C. Pyle established himself as Cash and Carry Pyle, alias Cold Cash Pyle.

The team had Monday off. We washed the uniforms. Senator McKinley of Illinois sent his limousine to take Red and me to the White House to meet President Coolidge. The senator introduced us, "Mr. President, this is George Halas and Red Grange of the Chicago Bears." President Coolidge replied, "How are you, young gentlemen. I have always admired animal acts." It snowed that night. Only 8,000 came to our game. Red made just 6 yards but we won 19–0. We went on to Boston.

The press was saying unpleasant things about Red. Babe Ruth came to the hotel and told him: "Kid, don't believe anything they write about you. You've got to take a lot of insults in this game. You've got to develop a thick skin. Get the dough while the getting is good and don't pick up too many meal checks."

Late in the morning Red went, on Pyle's request, to Joe Kennedy's office. "I suppose it was just a courtesy call," Grange remembers.

> Mr. Kennedy hardly mentioned the film. He spoke almost entirely about what wonderful athletes his sons were. He said they were best at touch football. He was specially proud of young Jack, then five or six. He said he thought they would all do well in athletics. I decided to keep the family in mind and maybe someday George Halas could sign young Jack for the Bears. Things didn't work out quite that way.

In the afternoon 25,000 fans saw us lose to the Providence Steamrollers 9–6. The New York kick on the arm had produced a painful purple welt. Red made only 18 yards.

We were in Pittsburgh the following day. Only ten men were fit. I filled in for a while with our trainer. Red's arm grew to twice its normal size and he had to leave the field. We lost 24–0, in snow.

We were due in Detroit two days later. I telegraphed ahead that Red would not be able to play and the club should refund money to people who bought tickets to see Red. Six thousand asked for their money. Another 6,000 didn't. We lost 21–0. The very next day we had to take on the Giants again, in Chicago. We lost 9–0.

That was it. Eight games in twelve days, 10 in 19. The date was December 13. We had nothing to do until Christmas.

Red summed up his initiation into professional football:

The game is cleaner than the college game because they have no vendettas and no personal spites. It is faster. I look for professional football to be the football of the future. The public wants it because the public interest primarily is in the game, not in the college. But, professional or amateur, I have had all the football I want. I'd sooner be back on my ice wagon. I took on too much. The human frame can't stand thirty games in twelve weeks but I've got to go through with it because it will mean my financial independence. Being famous is bunk. I've never felt worse. The newspapers have had me engaged to eighteen girls I've never met. When you're under the spotlight, you can't tell a strange woman the way to the station without being mentioned in a divorce case. I'll never coach. I'll never marry unless I find someone far more sensible than the flappers who flock around. I'll never be a millionaire. I'm glad I turned pro, but I'll be glad to quit.

The Eastern tour taught me we could not go South with only sixteen men. With Jim Carr's permission I picked up another half a dozen and off we went. The railroad supplied a Pullman car named Bethulla to be our home for five weeks.

Min, with new baby Mugs and little Virginia, came along as far as Florida. Min's sister Lil came to help with the children. Lil had made Virginia a red coat and hat. Red called her his Little Red Riding Hood.

When we arrived in Florida, the press and a lot of autograph seekers were waiting. Red borrowed Virginia and, with her on his shoulder, walked through the crowd unnoticed.

First stop, Coral Gables: The sponsors had guaranteed $25,000. Florida's land boom was shrinking and they were anxious to get some publicity. I took a taxi to the stadium. What did I find? A field. An open field! I thought surely the game would be cancelled. But no, two days before Christmas hundreds of carpenters arrived by the truckload. I didn't know there were so many hammer wielders in the world. Lumber arrived by the trainload. The men worked day and night and, lo and behold, on Christmas Day there it stood, a beautiful stadium, a bit splintery, perhaps, being made entirely of wood, but big enough to hold 30,000 spectators. The sponsors put a top price of $18 on the tickets. I couldn't believe it. In Chicago our top ticket price was $3. Only 5,000 people came. The sponsors asked that we settle for a split of the gate. We said no, the guarantee, please. Citizens came up with the money. Red carried the ball nine times, made 98 yards and our only touchdown and sat out the third quarter. We won 7–3.

Second stop, Tampa: New Year's Day. We won 17–3 against a team called the Tampa Cardinals, but really the Rock Island Independents. Red ran 60 yards for a touchdown. Jim Thorpe was still hanging in there. He said, "I won't stop playing football until I'm pushing up daisies." The crowd was 8,000. Tickets a modest $2.20 to $8.80.

Third stop, Jacksonville: We won 19–6. The game introduced Ernie Nevers to professional football—the great Ernie Nevers, rough, ready and capable, the West Coast's answer to Red Grange. It was a dirty game. We chased one player into the stands.

Fourth stop, New Orleans: I put Healey in charge of the boys on Bethulla and parked it in a remote part of the yard. Dutch, Pyle, Red and I moved into the Roosevelt Hotel. Healey took the boys to fights and the races. They did not do well on the track until Healey met an old friend who produced a tout who produced three horses, Princess Dorene, Redder and Ailing-P. The boys came home restored in pocket and spirit. In the game, Red played 53 minutes and ran 136 yards in 16 carries. Police broke up a crowd-supported protest to a penalty. We won 14–0.

Fifth stop, Los Angeles: The Big Money game. William Wrigley invited us all to his island, Catalina. Mary Pickford and Doug Fairbanks entertained us all at Pickfair. On Saturday, January 16, 75,000 people came to the Coliseum. No West Coast game ever had drawn so many people.

The boys had been shopping. They bought belted camel-hair coats and snapbrim hats. They became a classy lot. Not surprisingly they felt a need for money. They looked out at the huge crowd and decided the time had come to collect a half game's pay I had owed from the start of the tour. They said they wouldn't go until they got the money. I said "Okay, but don't go out until I tell you."

Pyle had not given me the Bears' share of receipts for the past two games. I went to the box office, confronted Pyle and told him that the Bears wouldn't play unless he gave me the overdue money, right now. He did so. I went back to the dressing room and told the boys to play.

George Wilson, an All-American halfback from Washington, was the Los Angeles captain. He had been promoted as a rival to Grange. We won 17–7.

Sixth stop, San Diego: We won 14–0. Another Grange touchdown.

Seventh stop, San Francisco: Gate 23,278. Tempers were rising. In the dressing room before the game, an old feud broke out between George Trafton and Dutch Sternaman. Dutch knocked George through the door into the runway filled with people. As Healey said, "It was a tiring season, long and arduous and rugged on manhood. There were a lot of things to laugh at. Propinquity lends enchantment into anybody's life, you might say."

We lost 12–7 to the California Tigers. Red carried the ball only six times. A sportswriter commented: "He must have been a real star back in his college days when he was playing for rah, rah, rah instead of quail on toast."

Eighth stop, Portland, Oregon: We won 60–3. Two Grange touchdowns.

Ninth stop, Seattle: The last day in January. Poor crowd, 5,000, despite very heavy press buildup. Four local radio stations broadcast the game. We won 34–0.

Throughout the tour, Grange proved himself excellent with the public. Of course, the money he made was turning some supporters of sports for sports' sake against him. But he remained helpful to the press and, generally, the press responded in kind. Read this Seattle report:

> Grange is still a boy, collegiate to the soles of his gold-bringing feet. He arrived in a light suit, gaudy shirt, wide necktie, wide wide trousers, socks all colors of the rainbow, no garters.
>
> He is about five feet ten, well proportioned with clean strong body lines. His unruly curly hair is a dull rusty bronze, parted in the middle. "It was once fiery red," laughed the goal and gold man.
>
> His face is full and strong. He has a powerful jaw.

Lines from his eyes are heavily creased and show the strain of twenty-three games this season. It is a tired face but one that smiles magnetically.

His day is mapped out as though he were the Prince of Wales. The mayor's man meets his train and escorts him to the hotel. There a thousand calls await. A barber comes. Red goes to the high school. His talk brings rapt attention and thundering roars. How the girls flock around him. He goes to the mayor's office, then to the Chamber of Commerce, then to the YMCA for a dinner, then to the College club where he is the guest star. Then to the radio station for a wedding. He is, of course, the best man.

The Bears had played thirty games since the season began in early autumn. That is more than a collegian plays in his entire three years of varsity football. Four hundred thousand fans had paid to see Red run with the Bears.

On the way home, I ran off on the back of an envelope a balance for the season. Red Grange had drawn people. Gate receipts almost trebled, from $116,534.34 the previous year to $296,900.68. The extra games had about doubled players' pay, to $41,335. Other salaries went through the ceiling, rising from $16,329.60 to $75,322.38. Opposing teams received $42,313.53. The travel cost $8,293.84.

There are two very modest figures, when compared to today's budgets. Advertising cost only $3,193.65. Had we paid for publicity, the bill would have been in the hundreds of thousands. Tax payments to the United States government were a comfortable $1,685.45.

Altogether, our costs were $282,226.67. Sternaman and I paid ourselves $2,600 in 1922 and 1923 and $5,800 in 1924. We raised our pay to $12,000 and gave each of us a $23,000 bonus. The Bears ended with our first worthwhile profit—$14,675.01. We declared our first dividend—$15,000.

Joe Carr chose his first All-Professional team. He included Ed Healey, Joe Sternaman and, of course, Red Grange.

Twice during the tour Pyle gave Red a check for $50,000. When the final accounting was made of receipts and royalties, Red received another $100,000. Red came to the Bears famous. Ten weeks later he was rich.

Frank J. Halas

Barbara Poludna Halas

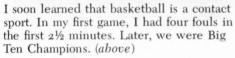

I soon learned that basketball is a contact sport. In my first game, I had four fouls in the first 2½ minutes. Later, we were Big Ten Champions. (*above*)

Bob Zuppke, our football coach at the University of Illinois, was a careful teacher who knew how to get the best out of young men. (*right*) (*Courtesy of the University of Illinois*)

Potsy Clark, on the left, was our star quarterback. We both were injured and an enterprising young photographer took our picture. He used it for a postcard with the caption: The Order of the Broken Jaw. The recognition brought me by the postcard was my first lesson in public relations.

Playing for the Great Lakes Navy Football team we went to the Rose Bowl and won 17–0. Left to right are Paddy Driscoll, Charlie Bachman, and myself. I intercepted a pass and returned it 70 yards. I should have scored but I was tackled on the 3-yard line. Anyone who can't dive 3 yards should play parcheesi. (*below*)

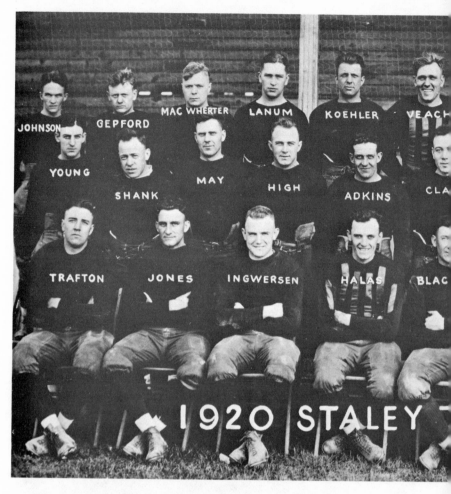

The 1920 Staley football team before our first game. The field had been built for baseball, so we leveled the mounds but didn't consider sodding the infield. After playing on cinders, I considered this surface to be as soft as a mattress. (*above*)

I played right field for the New York Yankees for a brief time. The man who replaced me was Babe Ruth, so after the season ended I took a job with the railroad. Mother was delighted. "A railroad job," she told me, "is secure." (*opposite page, top*)

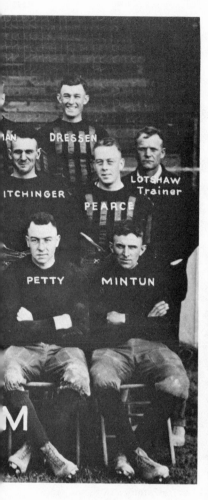

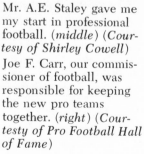

Mr. A.E. Staley gave me my start in professional football. (*middle*) (*Courtesy of Shirley Cowell*)

Joe F. Carr, our commissioner of football, was responsible for keeping the new pro teams together. (*right*) (*Courtesy of Pro Football Hall of Fame*)

The colors of our Staley uniforms were the same as those of the University of Illinois. We sewed the stripes on vertically to help us hold on to the ball, which, in those days, was fat and hard to pass. I only weighed 182 pounds and I played end. Blocking was my primary task. I was eager, but too light, so I tended to hold a bigger opponent whenever the umpire wasn't looking. (*left*)

The great Red Grange (with the ball) lead our Chicago Bears to a 17–7 victory over the Los Angeles Tigers in the Coliseum in January, 1926, before 75,000 fans. This coast-to-coast winter tour established the popularity of professional football. The Chicago Bears played a record-breaking 19 games in 47 days on this tour and we won almost every game. (*above*) (*Courtesy of World Wide photos*)

The whole family loved sports and we rooted for the Chicago Cubs. During our football games, Min would bring Virginia and Mugs and they always sat next to our team bench. I urged Min to move to the upper deck where she could see better. She said that Mugs might fall through the railings, but it was really too far away from the team. Here we're watching the Cubs. Front row, left to right: Myself, Mugs, Paddy Driscoll. Back row, left to right: Min Halas (standing) and Mary Driscoll (between Mugs and Paddy).

CHAPTER EIGHT

Hands Off Collegians

I ARRIVED BACK IN CHICAGO in early February of 1926 certain the golden era of football had arrived. The whole nation was talking of Red Grange and football, professional and collegiate.

I rejoiced that the days of small attendance, of continually having to squeeze every penny, were over. Prosperity had encased football—and the Bears—in a golden blanket.

I had long enjoyed the benefits of adversity. Now I was to learn of the perils of prosperity. I had barely walked to the bank with the final deposit when my old mentors from Illinois, Athletic Director G. Huff and Coach Zuppke, came to call. Their stern faces made me aware they had not come to congratulate me. No, they had come to talk about a very serious matter, Red Grange.

They said I had not offended League rules when I
signed Red Grange the day after his last college game.
But behind the rules was the desirability of collegiate
athletes not to leave college before graduation. My Illinois mentors said the debate over Red Grange's dropping out without his degree had intensified collegiate
ill-will toward professional football.

I saw the good sense in what they said and asked
what should be done.

They said the solution was simple. The National
Football League should declare flatly no collegian could
be signed until the class in which he enrolled graduates.
The change would deprive professional teams of collegians only for the final game or two of the regular season
and for post-season games, a small sacrifice. The probability of more tours such as the one C.C. Pyle arranged
for Red Grange was very small.

I accepted their proposal wholeheartedly and promised to see that the League would take action. I communicated the proposal to Joe Carr. He told me Mr.
Dooley, a lawyer in Providence, Rhode Island, and one
of the owners of the club there, had come up with the
same proposal. Carr said he was considering bringing the
matter before the annual meeting of the League scheduled for the following weekend at the Statler Hotel in
Detroit. I promised my support.

Mr. Carr told the League:

> The past season has been the most remarkable in
> many ways of any year in the history of the organiza-
> tion. Attendance at most cities increased many times
> and the feeling of the press and public was better
> than ever before. The addition of New York added
> much to both the class and prestige of the League,

118

but the outstanding development of the past season was the increased publicity.

The General Manager of the Associated Press has informed me the Associated Press will carry game results and League standing on its trunk wire, throughout the United States, Canada and Mexico.

Attendance and publicity were augmented when Mr. Grange elected to become a professional. Much discussion followed the entry of this most talked of athlete of modern times into our League. I am firmly convinced the net result has been all in favor of our organization. Thousands upon thousands of people were attracted to their first game of professional football through a curiosity to see Grange in action, and many became profound advocates.

Mr. Dooley brought in his resolution:

That the National Football League . . . hereby places itself on record as unalterably opposed to any encroachment upon college football and hereby pledges its hearty support to college authorities in maintaining and advancing the interest in college football and in preserving the amateur standing of all college athletes . . . It is the unanimous decision of this meeting that every member of the National Football League be positively prohibited from inducing or attempting to induce any college player to engage in professional football until his class at college shall have graduated, and any member violating this rule shall be fined not less than One Thousand Dollars, or loss of its franchise, or both.

Mr. Carr asserted that he would enforce the new rule decisively, and would expect the League to support him totally in any firm action he took against any offenders. The League pledged itself to do so. More than that, it approved without question action he had taken during the winter against two clubs, Milwaukee and Pottsville, for offending other League rules. The Milwaukee club had used four high school players in a game against the Chicago Cardinals. Pottsville had played a non-League team in Philadelphia, although Mr. Carr had warned them three times against so doing. Carr had fined the Milwaukee management $500 and given it ninety days to dispose of its assets and leave the League. He had fined Pottsville $500 and declared its franchise forfeited. He said he did not know for certain if the Cardinal club knew of the presence of the high school students so he did not withdraw their franchise but he did fine the club $500.

No one left that meeting doubting that professional football had a man to whom rules were sacrosanct. We reelected him unanimously, extended his term from one year to three, raised his pay to $6,500, raised the franchise fee to $2,500 and agreed each team would give the League 1 percent of its net gate receipts.

Our collegiate critics were not won over by our actions to protect collegians. Pop Warner maintained professional football might gain in popularity but would never equal college football in interest or in caliber of play. Stagg continued to take sweater letters from Chicago graduates who turned professional. And dear Mr. Yost said the good pay professionals were getting was only a deception. "Where will they be when they are thirty-five or forty?" he asked. I often asked myself and my players that question. Football is only a chapter in players' lives. They should use it to open doors and provide funds for their real life's work.

The Bears' contract with Mr. Pyle for Red's services ended with the Seattle game. I had hoped, and perhaps even somewhat expected, that Mr. Pyle would continue the very profitable cooperation with the Bears.

I broached the subject to Mr. Pyle. He said yes, he would continue to provide the services of Mr. Grange to the Bears in return for one-third ownership of the Bears.

One-third ownership? An equal partner with Dutch and me? No, no, no! In no way. No, first, last and always! The matter was not negotiable. A percentage of earnings, yes, that was negotiable, but a share of ownership, no!

Feeling thwarted by me, Mr. C.C. Pyle decided to establish his own football team in New York City. He would call it the Yankees and play in the Yankee Stadium. It would be a rival to Mr. Mara's year-old Giants.

Mr. Mara was highly alarmed. He was certain New York City could not accommodate two football teams. Someday, maybe, but not in 1926. Yes, 73,000 did come to see Red Grange play, but no other Giant game that season had paid expenses. Mr. Mara was certain a second team in the city, especially one with Grange on it, would bring disaster to the Giants.

Mr. Mara informed League members he would oppose with all his strength the League's giving a New York franchise to Pyle. Under League rules, Mr. Mara's veto was sufficient to deny Mr. Pyle his New York wishes.

Mr. C.C. Pyle was not defeated. He was merely deflected. He decided to have his own league as well as his own team. He would call the organization the American Football League. Pyle told Grange: "No blasted Irishman is going to keep me out of New York!"

Pyle set about luring players to the Yankees and selling players and promoters the idea of forming teams. He

121

offered Ed Healey $10,000 to obtain players and to coach. I offered a compromise that Healey accepted. He explained: "If Pyle was clever enough to have been married and divorced three or four times, he was the kind of guy I didn't want any part of."

Pyle took Ralph Scott from the Bears to play and to coach. He signed Pooley Hubert from Alabama, Eddie Tryon from Colgate and George Pease from Columbia. He used our offensive and defensive strategy. Grange had one-third ownership.

In Chicago, Joey Sternaman announced he was forming a Chicago club, the Bulls. I was most sorry to see him go. He had been our biggest scorer and our most popular player, apart from Grange.

Worse, I suspected his brother, Dutch, my partner, would be tempted to find blood is thicker than ink on a contract. Indeed, the Disabled War Veterans soon claimed that Pyle had spoken to them about organizing with help from the Sternamans a Chicago club to be called the Marines. The Veterans claimed the brothers had agreed but after the Veterans had spent $10,000, Pyle and the Sternamans backed off. The Veterans asked a court to order Pyle, the Sternamans and Red Grange to reimburse them. Dutch told me he had never talked to the Veterans. Joey told me he had talked to them and had become convinced the Veterans would not be able to form a team so he was going ahead on his own.

The situation created considerable ill-will between Dutch and me. Dutch offered to sell me his half of the club. How I wish I had bought him out at once!

When the League met in July in Philadelphia to confirm the schedules for the 1926 season, Dutch and I were working at cross purposes. Each was scheduling teams.

122

The crucial date was October 17. On my schedule I had penciled in for that day a game with our old rivals, the Cardinals, a match that usually produced the biggest gate of the season. Dutch wanted to play the Cardinals on the traditional date, Thanksgiving Day. When other League members learned that October 17 was the day Joey Sternaman had scheduled a game in Chicago between his new club and Mr. Pyle's New York Yankees starring the great Red Grange, the reason for differences between Dutch and me became obvious. A double bill in Chicago on the day I proposed would hurt the Bulls; keeping the Cardinal game on Thanksgiving Day would help them.

The situation caused me heartache. Dutch, Joey and I had gone through hard times together. Now, when prosperity was here, we were divided. I was finding adversity more pleasant than prosperity.

My will prevailed at the League meeting. The Bears and the Cardinals would play on October 17.

It was not a happy League meeting. The spirit of comrades-at-arms had gone. The small group who first gathered in Ralph Hay's Hupmobile showroom was swallowed in a sea of newcomers. So many people came—forty-two in all—that we had to hire a hall. The sessions went on for two days until midnight. They were filled with bickering. Much of the discussion was not over football or how it should be played or organized but over money and the acquisition thereof. There was an air of greed.

Soon a new peril arose. For years, the Cardinals had played in the White Sox baseball park. The Cardinals paid a percentage of the gate. Joey offered a fixed rent which Chris O'Brien, the Cardinals' owner, could not meet. Chris moved to the much smaller Normal Park. His financial outlook was dismal. He had to cut expenses. The most expensive player was Paddy Driscoll, and common sense told Chris that Paddy deserved a raise, not a cut.

Joey Sternaman offered Paddy a raise, and a big one, to join the Bulls.

Alarm bells rang in my head. If they got Paddy, the Bulls might be a better club than the Bears. I could never let the Bears be second best in Chicago.

I offered Chris O'Brien $3,500 if he would sell Paddy's contract to me. He accepted. National League rules made it impossible for Paddy to play for any National League team other than the Bears, but Paddy was under no prohibition to join Joey or any other club in the new American League.

Paddy wavered. He had long wanted to play with the Bears. He and I had played together most happily on the Great Lakes team. He admired the Bears. In the end, he decided to play with the Bears for $10,000. Once again, adversity brought a great benefit to me. Paddy could have earned more money that year playing with Joey Sternaman but how long would the Bulls survive? Indeed, how long would the new league survive?

By mid-August we had a good team. We had picked up a great Nebraska tackle, Link Lyman; another tackle, Earl Evans from Harvard; a guard, Bill Buckler from Alabama; tackle Clifford Lemon. All good players. But could they draw? Could Paddy draw as well as the lost Joey Sternaman? Could any team bring in people who had come to see Red? Could Grange himself still draw?

We hoped the common answer was yes. We hoped that the magic of Grange and the power of the press, radio and newsreel which had aroused so much curiosity about professional football would convert the curious to loyal supporters of the game.

We opened the season full of hope. Wrigley Field would not be available until the baseball season ended so we had to go abroad for our first three games. We went to Milwaukee and beat a team reconstituted without high school players 10–7. We tied Green Bay 6–6. We beat Detroit 10–7.

In scoring points, Paddy at age thirty-one was proving greater than ever. He ran for a touchdown. He threw a 50-yard pass for a touchdown. His toe was faultless kicking field goals and conversions. After the three games we were top of the League.

Attendance was larger than in the previous year, but only by a bit. We told ourselves Green Bay and Detroit and Milwaukee had not really been touched by the football hysteria. Wait until we come into Chicago. Then the crowds would come.

We came into Chicago. Our first guests were the Giants. We rolled out tickets by the reams, our eyes still filled with the glorious vision of all 73,000 seats at the Polo Grounds filled with screaming fans last season.

The Giants brought five All-Americans.

We had picked up from tiny Knox College an agile runner named Bill Senn. Optimists said he was about as good at getting through an open field as the great Grange. It was an exciting game. Senn got loose and ran 70 yards. Later we got to the Giants' 4. Three times they held us cold. On the fourth, Paddy went over for the only touchdown of the day. We won, 7–0.

125

Four games. Three victories. One tie. What a season!

What a season, yes, for the score books, but not for the cash box. Fewer than 8,000 people saw the game with the Giants.

We did not allow hope to die. It had rained that day, we told ourselves to keep our spirits high. Next Sunday would be better.

Next Sunday was the 17th, the day Chicago would have a double treat, Paddy playing with the Bears against his old teammates on the Cardinals at Wrigley Field; Red Grange and the Yankees taking on Joey Sternaman's Bulls at White Sox Park.

As an extra attraction, we brought Jack Bramhall's band to play during the halftime. An innovation.

In White Sox Park, Joey also introduced a bit of show business. He had a man with a megaphone run up and down the sidelines identifying the players, pointing out the fine points and leading cheers.

Paddy was magnificent. He kicked one field goal from 38 yards, a second from 40 yards, a third from within the posts' shadow. He made our only touchdown and he kicked the conversion. He pulled an old trick: on a first down when the Cardinals were expecting a run, he punted almost straight up so the Bears could recover the ball and make a gain.

I added a bit of drama, unwittingly. I took a blow on the head that knocked me out. I was carried from the field. I came to in the dressing room.

"Who are we playing?" I asked.

"The Cardinals," Andy said.

"Well," I said, "I hope Min has the turkey on."

We won 16–0. It was a great game. Paddy and the Bears proved themselves to be in a class above Paddy and the Cardinals. As Healey said: "It was a pleasure to

126

have such a charming model gentleman and great athlete with us. John L. Driscoll was a terrific ball player, a real competitor."

At both of the games, everyone, I am sure, had a good time.

But I wasn't happy. Nor, I think, was Joey nor even Cold Cash Pyle. Without Red, we drew 12,000. With Red, Joey drew 20,000. Put the two together and what do you have: 32,000. A year earlier, before Grange, we would have been astounded at such a turnout. But coming after the winter tour, 32,000 was dismal for the biggest professional football day Chicago ever had, and perhaps ever would have.

It was the same everywhere. We were back to the small gates, the hard grind, the search for fans, the pinching of the penny. The Maras learned the Red Grange euphoria had vanished. The Giants drew only 3,000 or 4,000. Mara would look through binoculars at Yankee Stadium and say, "There's no one over there, either." A third team had been formed in Brooklyn and a fourth in Newark. Mara bought the Newark team and folded it. When the Brooklyn players went two weeks without pay, he paid them off to go home.

On Armistice Day, we met the Cardinals again, for charity, in Soldier Field. It was a holiday. Nobody had to work. There was no rain. In vast Soldier Field, the 10,000 fans were lost.

Three of the new American League teams had folded. Two more quit the following week. Only Pyle's Yankees with Grange were making money—in pennies and nickels instead of dollars. Joey may have been breaking even.

Pyle came to Columbus but denied he had come to talk with Carr about the possibility of merging the two

127

leagues. He said he didn't even meet Carr. He said he came to Columbus to see Suzanne Lenglen play indoor tennis. The gorgeous French lady was Pyle's newest discovery and indoor tennis was his newest promotion. She and the game proved to be ahead of the times, and costly to Cold Cash.

Still, it was a great season on the football field. Ernie Nevers came North to play with a traveling team, the Duluth Eskimos. We beat them 24–6. We beat the Canton Bulldogs 35–0. Altogether we amassed 216 points to 63 for our opponents. We won twelve games, lost one and tied three. Our loss was to the Frankford Yellow Jackets. Guy Chamberlin, our own Staley days' Guy Chamberlin, was coaching the Frankford team and decided to get into the game. He blocked a kick for conversion after our only touchdown. He blocked a field goal. With two minutes left, the Yellow Jackets scored and converted. We lost 7–6. Despite the defeat, we could have won the championship except in the final game we tied Green Bay 3–3. The Frankford Yellow Jackets won the championship. I determined the time had come for the League to take over scheduling and put the title race on a more even basis.

I sat down with a pencil to work out the financial accounts. Receipts came to $151,631.80. That was a good gain over the $116,000 for 1924, but a big drop from the 1925 total of $296,900. Of course I didn't have to hand over $66,031.25 of our home gates to Pyle and Grange as I did the previous season, but player salaries had jumped from $21,422 in the last normal year to $60,490. Altogether costs were $150,641.84. We had a profit: exactly $989.96!

We did not declare a dividend.

CHAPTER NINE

Ralph Jones—
A Call for Brains

MY FAITH IN THE BEARS and professional football continued, but I could not just sit and wait for the public to catch fire.

In Washington, George Preston Marshall had formed a basketball team, the Washington Palace Five. He and Joe Carr persuaded me to start a team in Chicago. I did so, but only after Joe promised to serve as president of the American Basketball League. I called my team the Chicago Bruins. Max Rosenblum, a department store owner in Cleveland, formed a club there under an excellent coach, Marty Friedman. Harry Heilmann, of baseball fame, financed a club in Brooklyn, the Arcadians, with Garry Schmeelk as coach. Other clubs were the Buffalo Germans, the Rochester Centrals, the Fort Wayne Caseys sponsored by the Chamber of Commerce, the Detroit Pulaski Post Five and Boston Whirlwinds. The New York Celtics, who won twenty games for every game lost, refused to join the league, preferring to barn-storm. I didn't have to look far for a coach I could afford. I chose myself. We played in an armory, and we did not do well. In the first half, we tied for sixth place with Boston and Detroit—six games won, ten lost. Boston then dropped out. In the second half we were next to bottom, three wins and eleven losses. Financially I broke about even. I considered that acceptable for the first year of a venture. Marshall lost $65,000 and gave up.

I hired John "Honey" Russell of New York to coach and signed a great player, Nat Holman, for $6,000, for half a season, more than I could afford. Hope, hope, what can be accomplished without hope! Hope carried me through the next two years. Hope led me into taking the team into the vast Chicago Stadium, giving up half of the gate as rental. It was a sporting success but a financial disaster. After three years I gave up basketball.

Real estate looked like a good thing. Chicago was growing fast. I had joined a friend, Howard Kraft, in buying land in Cicero, from 35th Street to 39th Street and from Austin Boulevard on the west to Central Avenue on the east, dividing it into lots and building houses. We did well. In Racine, Wisconsin, John Deering, founder of a large and very profitable farm equipment manufacturing firm, had died. His large estate on Lake Petite fell into the hands of the First National Bank of Antioch, of which Mr. C.K. Anderson was president. We helped subdivide it. We put in a golf course.

During the summer of 1927, Mayor Cermak arranged for Gene Tunney to train at Lake Petite for his second fight with Jack Dempsey. He and his entourage lived in the mansion. A lot of newspaper people came. We put in pay phones. Every night Tunney would spend hours at a phone dropping in quarters and talking to a girl. I presume it was the rich young lady he married the next year, after the fight in Soldier Field, when he took the long count and held the title he had won from Dempsey two years earlier. It was a tremendous sporting event, the first time, I think, any event drew a million-dollar gate.

Mr. C.K. Anderson was very happy working with us and we were very happy working with him.

"Anytime I or the bank can be of service," he said, "let me know." What a life-saving promise that turned out to be!

Pyle surrendered early in 1927 but, with twenty-eight teams in some stage of operation, League affairs were in disarray. League meetings in New York and Cleveland failed to produce a schedule. We had to sort the men from the boys. In July at Green Bay, President Carr said teams must, right now, put up a $2,500 guarantee. Eleven teams did so: Buffalo, Cleveland, the Bears, the Cardinals, Dayton, Duluth, Frankford, Green Bay, the Giants, Pottsville and Providence. For the first time we drew up a League schedule. Order had come at last into professional football. Green Bay served us an excellent banquet.

Pyle's contract with Red Grange had another year to run. Pyle also had Yankee Stadium. But where could he find worthwhile competitors? He approached Carr and Mara. The three agreed that Pyle could acquire a dormant Brooklyn franchise, play in New York on Sundays the Giants were away and, on Giants' home days, play in other League cities. We all welcomed the arrangement. We all were eager to have Grange, still the magnetic Grange, play in our stadiums.

I would have welcomed Joey Sternaman back on the

Bears but he became a playing partner with Chris O'Brien on the Cardinals. Chicago's two most popular players, Paddy Driscoll and Joey, would again be matched against each other although on exchanged teams.

Rock Island, which had jumped to Pyle's league, wanted to come back into our League. We said no. The team had not been able to keep up. With the remarkable exception of Green Bay, professional football was becoming a big-city enterprise.

My biggest problem was personal. My relationship with Dutch Sternaman was worsening. Mutual trust had almost vanished. The split hurt the team. I developed plays. Dutch would drill them into the backfield, I into the line. I was steadily moving toward an open game, with a sixty-forty division between running and passing. Sternaman wanted a tight game. The consequence was that I would tell the team to do this and Sternaman would tell them to do that.

The results soon began to show. In the 1927 season, we won only nine and placed third; in 1928, we won seven and in 1929 only four. Receipts, too, were off. We lost $3, 486.35 in 1927, $563.71 in 1928 and $1,082.92 in 1929. The last 1929 game drew only 2,123 customers. We couldn't pay our guarantee to the visitors from Frankford. The Bears were kept solvent thanks to program sales. These little sheets steadily earned about $2,000 a year. We were not alone. Wellington Mara recalls the period as very discouraging: "Many times my father had second thoughts about football, advancing money and writing off losses. His friends told him he was foolish to keep the Giants but he stayed firm, I am sure, because my brother Jack and I were so interested in the sport."

I eagerly awaited the coming of Red Grange to Chicago to play the Bears. Little did I suspect disaster was near.

As Red recalls the game:

> I went over center to get a pass. Trafton, the Bear center, followed me out. We both went up in the air. Coming down I caught my cleat in the sod. Trafton fell over my leg and it twisted. The twist tore the cartilage. It wasn't anybody's fault. I thought I would never play football again. For months I walked on crutches. A doctor told me to play golf. In time I dropped one crutch and then the other. I resumed running.

Ed Healey retired after the 1927 season. His story of his last game with the Giants in New York is memorable. As he told it:

> On defense, I came in contact with the great Cal Hubbard, who was no small toy to try to move around. On offense, I came in contact with Whitey Nesser, a tough hombre who could do just about everything with his hands and his elbows and had a terrific capability of breaking through to catch the runner or the kicker. All the time there was Joe Guyon, all elbows, knees, feet, cleats, everything. If he didn't scratch you up, he'd break a bone. It was a pretty tough day for me. That evening, my new wife's sister and her husband gave a party on Long Island. You can imagine what a mess I was to be presented as the husband of a darling wife I had just taken unto myself!

Red was out the entire 1928 season but I heard that his knee was improving. I called him and asked if he would join the Bears for the 1929 season. Red told me that although he could run again, he had lost his old ability to change pace and direction. "I can't cut," he said. I told him that did not matter. "I want you back," I said. I realized he would no longer gallop for touchdowns but I liked his intelligence, his determination and his desire. I thought he still had a great contribution to make to football. Too, there was still magic in the Grange name. He agreed to join us.

Red's kid brother Garland also joined the Bears for the 1929 season. So did Harold Cunningham, an end from Ohio State; Ralph Maillard, a tackle from Creighton; Everett Nelson, a tackle from Illinois; Madison Pearson, a center from Kansas; John Polisky, a guard from Notre Dame; John Ryan, a tackle from Detroit. And, more or less by default, we picked up Luke Johnsos. I went to Northwestern to offer a fullback, Walt Holmer, $5,000 a year. He stalled until I signed his roommate, Luke, for $100 a game.

"I was only bait for Holmer," Luke reminisces. "I thought it was kind of funny but when we began playing, the humor departed. Holmer didn't make the team. I was out there sixty minutes getting the devil knocked out of me for a hundred bucks and Holmer was getting his $5,000 sitting on the bench."

I traded Holmer after two years. Luke became a powerfully important Bear.

Before the football season began, Paddy and his wife Mary, Min and I, and a stockbroker, Howard Hanson, gave ourselves a vacation motoring in Canada. While we were having a most enjoyable time, Wall Street collapsed. I had bought stocks on margin with my Grange earnings. Everybody was doing that, expecting to get rich. Stock values fell so fast that J.J. O'Brien, of Paine, Webber and Co., sold me out. He didn't even ask. Of course, it was their privilege. My partner, Dutch, had played safe, buying an apartment house and a super gas station. Life does have its ups and downs and a man must accept them and try to make the best of it all.

The stock market collapse stopped real estate business cold. Kraft and Halas, Realtors, folded—honorably.

Misery extended to the football field. The Packers ran over us 23–0, the Giants 34–0. And then we again met Ernie Nevers. Since our first coming together at Jacksonville on the Red Grange tour, he played with the Duluth Eskimos. In three seasons he had missed only 27 minutes of play. Not even appendicitis could bench him. Then the Eskimos folded and Nevers came to the Cardinals. By then, that team had changed hands. It was losing money and Chris O'Brien could not subsidize it. I was concerned the buyer might be undesirable. I induced a great Bear fan, Dr. David J. Jones, to buy the club. He had served as city physician under four mayors. I promised him that if the losses continued, I would absorb 40 percent; if there were a profit, I would take none of it. That was some partnership! Heads you win; tails I lose.

In our game with the Cardinals at Comiskey Park Nevers ran 20 yards for one touchdown. He plunged 5 yards for a second touchdown. He plunged 6 yards for a third touchdown. He dived 1 yard for a fourth touchdown, and another yard for a fifth touchdown. He ran 10 yards for a sixth. Four times he kicked the extra point. The final score: Bears 6, Nevers 40! Nevers was properly cheered by 8,000 people, including the entire Notre Dame team brought there by Rockne for a post-season course.

135

As the 1929 season deteriorated, on its way to a miserable 4–8–2 ending, loss after loss drove home two lessons:

First, the time had come for me to stop playing. I was thirty-four. I no longer had speed. My muscles were no longer strong enough for me to shift supersized linesmen. Dutch had ceased playing regularly.

Secondly, the time had come for Dutch and me to stop coaching, or, more accurately, miscoaching. We had to put coaching under one mind. We decided to bring in someone who would pull the team together.

I wanted, first and foremost, an experienced coach who was a good teacher. I could think of no one who better met those qualifications than Ralph Jones, my freshman football coach and Varsity basketball coach at Illinois.

"Don't give out too much at one time," Jones used to say. "Give a little and let the student absorb that before giving more. If you give too much at once, you'll only confuse him."

Ralph Jones had left Illinois in the mid-twenties to become athletic director at Lake Forest Academy, a small but excellent secondary school in the north Chicago suburb. He was happy there but I persuaded him to come to the Bears.

It astonished everyone that the Bears should go to an academy for a coach. The announcement said we would pay Jones $10,000. Actually, the contract was for $7,500, but overstating salaries has rarely been disagreeable to employee or employers in many professions.

Ralph Jones was a sound strategist. He believed muscle, guts and spirit were not enough. He believed it

136

also took brains to win games. Brainwork reduced the amount of profitless and painful crashing and thrashing about. Brainwork properly applied could add excitement and make the game more attractive.

"I'll give you a championship in three years," Jones said. I believed him.

In 1930, the line, on offense, formed up with guards 1 foot from the center, tackles 1 foot from the guards and the ends 2 feet from the tackles. On defense, the center moved back to become a linebacker and the other six bunched together closely. The tight formation led to pileup after pileup after pileup.

From time immemorial, the backfield had lined up in a T, the quarterback directly behind the center, the fullback directly behind him 4 or 5 yards with a halfback on each side. The ball went to the quarterback who pivoted and handed or lateraled to one of the backs. The other backs became blockers or receivers. The formation made sense for driving straight ahead. The objective then was power, power, power. Power in a tight backfield. Power in a tight line. Met by power on the defense. The result was crash, crash, crash—and boredom.

College coaches had tried to add opportunities for nimble runners and expert passers. At Notre Dame, Knute Rockne, the great Knute Rockne, had created the Notre Dame box. The backfield lined up in a T and shifted to a box, either left or right, like this:

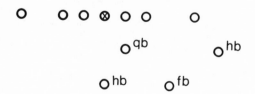

The center passed the ball to the back designated to run, pass or kick. The quarterback directed the team and called the signals. After the snap he became basically a blocker.

Pop Warner, the great Pop Warner, created the single wing and the double wing. Warner pulled the two guards back. The backs lined up in the T. On the shift, the two guards went together into the line on one side of the center, making four men on one side, two on the other. For running plays, the backs shifted into a lopsided version of Rockne's box. He called it a single wing. The backs and guards shifted to the same side, adding a lot of power to that side.

After the shift the single wing looked like this:

O O ⊗ O^{lg} O^{rg} O O

O^{qb}   O^{hb}

O^h   O^{fb}

The double-wing shift ended like this:

O O ⊗ O O O O

O^{hb}   O^{qb}

O^{hb}

O^{fb}

The halfbacks were in good position to go for passes.

The box and the wings did add dimension to the game but I felt they were not much of an improvement over the T. I had grown up with the T. I had played it at Illinois, with the navy, with Hammond. I had used it with the Staleys. I kept it all through the twenties with the Bears, although I cannot recall how often critics denounced the Bears as an old-fashioned team.

Rules required that while signals were being called, a team could shift but the players had to hold the new position for a full second before the ball was snapped. That supposedly gave the defense time to adjust its positions. The shorter the pause, the more likely the defense would be caught unprepared. At Notre Dame, the one-second pause frequently was not much longer than the blink of an eye. The officials had a problem trying to determine when a second was a second.

Jones began by readjusting the offensive line. He increased the distance between center, guard and tackle from 1 foot to 1 yard and the distance between guard and end from 2 feet to 2 yards. The change gave the defense new opportunities to enter our backfield. To remove this gift, Jones needed to speed action in the backfield, to improve the blocking and to open holes in the line quickly. For plays coming through the line, the blockers should try not to bring down the assigned defense men but merely deflect them. For example: On a quick opening play between our right guard and tackle, our guard would hit their guard on the outside, moving him to the left, and our tackle would hit their tackle on the inside, moving him to the right. The two defense men would be out of action for only a few seconds but long enough for our back to get through with the ball.

To speed up action in the backfield and add diversity, Jones began applying a little-used rule which allows one man to move as soon as the signals begin and continue moving. The one-second halt after the shift does not apply to him. Jones saw tremendous opportunities in the rule. In Carl Brumbaugh and Red Grange he had ideal experimenters. They were smart. Brummy was a good passer, Grange a good receiver. Both could run and block.

Jones began by having Grange, playing left halfback, run to the right behind the line. By the time the ball was snapped he was outside our right end. He could take a lateral and run straight ahead, or he could run downfield to take a long pass, or he could come in behind the defense line to take a short pass, or he could join the end in blocking for another back coming around with the ball.

For variety, Jones would send the right halfback to the left.

One day, in a game against Green Bay, Brummy noted the defensive halfback followed Red, creating a gap in their secondary. Brummy told Red to go in motion but only as a lure. Brummy gave the ball to the fullback who went through an opening in the line, on through the gap and 54 yards for a touchdown.

In time Jones had so many plays the defense was totally confused.

"Playing football," said Red, "became a lot more fun."

Thus was born the modern T-Formation with man-in-motion. It broke the game wide open. Football became a game of brains. Instead of knocking men down, Jones tried to entice the defense into doing something helpful for us. Best of all, the public found our new brand of football exciting.

Jones worked out meticulous positioning. The quarterback was directly behind and tight up against the center. He placed his left hand, palm down, against the center's crotch, so the center could feel it and know the back was there. The right hand was about four inches below the left, palm up. On the count, the center would snap the ball into the quarterback's hands.

The quarterback would clamp both hands on the ball, pivot and move back to do whatever the play called for. He could hand the ball to one of the backs already charging forward for a quick opening play. He could pretend to hand it to a back, hide it, fade back and pass or hand it to another back. He could lateral it to one of the backs. If we needed a yard, he could do a quarterback sneak.

With the wing formation or the box, the center had to look back between his legs and pass the ball to the back. He would usually watch to make sure he had made a good pass. Only then would he be ready to block. By then, everybody else was in action. He had missed the explosive moment. Sometimes his pass to the back was faulty. That was costly.

With our T, the center could pass with his head up. On the count he became the first man to explode because he was the only one who knew the instant the play started. One of our great centers, George Trafton, began using only one hand to give the ball to the quarterback, increasing his readiness and ability to block. This is common procedure now.

For passes, Trafton would hand the ball with the laces in exactly the position Brummy wanted them. When throwing to a back for punts, field goals, or conversions, he could spiral the ball just enough to make it end up in the kicker's or holder's hands with the laces in the right position. It saved perhaps a half-second, but that was long enough to reduce the danger of a blocked kick.

141

We developed a simple system of signals. It was based on two two-digit numerals. The holes to the right were numbered 1-3-5-7-9; the holes to the left were 0-2-4-6-8. We numbered our backs in this manner: The left halfback was 2, the fullback 3, the right halfback 4. The first of the first two-digit numeral specified which back got the ball. The second number told where the hole should be opened. The second two-digit numerals told which back was going in motion and on what count the ball would be snapped.

If the quarterback called 31–26, plus some dead numbers added to disguise our real numbers, the fullback, 3, would get the ball from the quarterback and go through the 1 hole opened between center and right guard; the left half, 2, would go in motion to the right and the ball would be snapped on the count of 6.

The success of any play depends upon the ability of each man to carry out the assignment given him. That means hours and hours of practice.

Jones marked everything from the ball. He placed the fullback exactly 4 yards directly behind the ball. The right halfback lined up straddling the outside leg of the right tackle; the left halfback straddled the outside leg of the left tackle. Each halfback placed himself so his heels were on a line with the fullback's toes.

Because everyone began from a precise position, we could work out exact timing. Each back knew exactly how many steps he would take, what route he should follow. Every Monday the coaches would review the defense of next Sunday's opponents and then prepare a "short list" of plays against them, consisting of a dozen runs and a dozen passes.

We would give the plays to the players on Tuesday

142

morning. Twice a day until Saturday, the team would go through the plays, over and over and over until each play became almost automatic. At night, each man would draw diagrams of the plays so each knew all assignments.

During the game, the quarterback would intersperse the new plays with others worked out for earlier games. If a play worked, we'd repeat it several times. In a usual game a team has the ball about seventy times. In the old days, the routine was pretty well frozen: run on first and second, pass on third if more than a yard or two was needed, punt on fourth. Using our modern T-Formation with man-in-motion, we would pass on any down.

Blocking took on new dimensions. Hunk Anderson's reverse body block gained new importance. We developed many ramifications of it. The blocker had to shoot off on the proper foot and pivot at exactly the right time to give thrust to the body. If done correctly, this block would remove from play a man 50 pounds heavier. If a defensive linebacker came in low, the blocker would shove him down with a hip and then step over him. If he came in high, planning to wrestle, the blocker would throw a body block at his knees, or lower, and flatten him.

Jones impressed on each player the need to watch his opposite number closely and seek a clue which might give away the opponent's intentions. A linebacker about to blitz the quarterback might place his feet in a different position. A receiver might wipe his hands on his trousers. A back might look at the intended receiver as the team lined up.

Sometimes we found clues. Sometimes they proved useful. Sometimes we guessed wrong. It always added interest and, now and then, a score.

143

I told my boyhood friend, Charlie Pechous: "Charlie, we're five years ahead of everybody."

To make our T really work, we needed a powerful running back. For some time I had been hearing about a big strong man from the north woods who was good for 10 yards or so every time he carried the ball for Minnesota. The coach there, Doc Spears, said he had found his Hercules one day when driving through the woods along the Rainy River which separates Minnesota from Canada. He was seeking a boy he had heard about and saw a young man pushing a plow without aid of a horse. Doc said he stopped and asked the plowman the way to the house he was seeking.

"Right over there," the plowman said, picking up the plow and using it for a pointer. Doc said he forgot about the other boy and went for the plowman. His name was Bronko Nagurski. Bronk does not tell the story himself but he does not deny it. Doc finished with Bronk in 1929. I made sure the Bears got him.

Halfway through the 1930 season, Notre Dame expelled one of its more colorful players, Jumping Joe Savoldi, for offending a Notre Dame rule against marriage. The expulsion became a popular subject of discussion for press, radio and the public. I offered him a place on the Bears. He accepted quickly. I was well aware of the very solid rule the League had made, with my help, against teams signing players before their class was graduated but I told myself, and anyone who asked, that Jumping Joe was a special case. I was not taking him out of school. Notre Dame had put him out. He was no longer a collegian, by action of the college officials.

Before long Mr. Carr told me I was guilty of offending the League rule. I put my case. He said the expulsion did not change the rules. The rule said a player could not be signed until his class was graduated. He agreed the rule did not allow for the possibility of expulsion and, because of that, he would not impose a fine although he would declare me guilty. I said in that case, he must fine me. He did. I had to pay $1,000. Perhaps Savoldi was worth it.

Coach Jones, the T, Bronk and Red put us back onto the winning side. We ended the 1930 season with nine wins, four losses, one tie. We were on our way to becoming the Monsters of the Midway.

CHAPTER TEN

Adversity Returns, with New Benefits

MONEY WAS SHORT EVERYWHERE, including the Halas household. Mother had given the children money every Christmas and birthday. Almost all had gone into savings. I raided their accounts. I fell behind with the apartment rent. The real estate office lay between our place and the grocery store. Min always made a detour. One dark day stands out in my mind. Virginia needed gym shoes. Girls wore white shoes, boys black. The black were cheaper and Min bought those. Virginia was unhappy until at school the next day she saw more than half of the girls had black shoes.

I'd leave home about 8:00 A.M. and not come back until 8:30 P.M. or so. Min and the children always ate at six. "Except one day," Virginia recalls. "Five-thirty and no Mother. I was very worried. At last, Mother came in, totally distraught. She had gone to the hospital with Edith Walquist, the wife of one of our quarterbacks,

146

Laurie, for the birth of a Walquist child. The baby was delivered. Edith hemorrhaged. Doctors could not stop the flow of blood. Edith died."

When I would come home Min would fix something and we would sit in the kitchen talking over events of the day. During the season when the weather forecast was good, the phone would ring with people asking for passes. "Not again!" Min would say. I would assure her passes built fans.

To keep the Bears going, I gave IOU's. Jones accepted one for $1,000 and another for $500. Bronko, McMillen, Holmer and Savoldi each took one for $500, Red Grange for $1,000. I could not pay Frankford their $2,000 guarantee. We had a drawerful of bills and we were overdrawn at the bank by $1,147.44. Altogether, the Bears owed $11,791.88, and no change was in sight.

The Depression was deadly for many League teams. Of the twenty-two clubs in the League in 1926 and eleven which had formed subsequently, only ten were operating in 1931, and four of these disappeared during or after that season.

In the summer of 1931, my partner, Dutch Sternaman, couldn't meet mortgage payments on his apartment house and his super gas station. His only other asset was his partnership in the Bears. He asked if I would buy him out for $38,000, enough to meet his financial needs.

I did want control of the Bears. My faith in the Bears was boundless. I scurried around to find the money. Ralph Brizzolara sold some Swedish match stock he had inherited from his father to raise $5,000. Jim McMillen was having a rich year wrestling and he put up $5,000. Charlie Bidwill, by some magic, raised $5,000 from a bank that was already closed. George Trafton's mother

147

supplied $20,000 and my mother $5,000. On July 3, 1931, I did buy out Dutch. I paid him $25,000 in cash and promised to pay $6,000 on January 25, 1932, and the final $7,000 on July 31, 1932. I placed my Bears' stock in the bank as collateral. I paid off pressing bills and had $6,000 left for the January payment. I always went to the bank to borrow money for the new season and I assumed that if worse came to worst, I could borrow the final $7,000. The fine print said if I failed to make the payments, the stock would go to Sternaman. I considered the clause merely legal hocus-pocus, something I was soon to learn a person must never do.

By the next July, the worst was worse than any worst I could conceive. Many banks were closed and those open would make no loan. On July 31, I had just $2,000. I was $5,000 short and, as the fine print stated, the stock passed into the control of Sternaman. On August 3, his lawyer wrote a letter informing me that the stock would be put up for public auction in his office at 12 o'clock sharp on August 9, six days away.

I tried everywhere to raise the $5,000. I called everyone I knew. No one could help me. August 9 came. I was desperate. At noon I would lose my Bears. Years of effort would be negated.

About 11 o'clock Mr. C.K. Anderson, the president of the First National Bank in Antioch, phoned. He is the banker who had worked so happily with me on the Lake Petite development and in being host to Gene Tunney. He said he understood I needed $5,000 urgently.

"How true!" I replied. "I must have the money by noon or I will lose my Bears!"

He said he would lend me the money. I raced from my office at 111 W. Washington to his Chicago office at Randolph and LaSalle Streets and collected his check with grateful but quick thanks, and then ran to the lawyer's office and handed in a check. It was 10 minutes to noon.

All had come right. The Depression and hard times had forced by fifty-fifty partner to sell. I did have new stockholders but together they held only minority interest. I had firm control of the Bears. Again, adversity had bestowed its benefits upon me.

Some years later another problem arose. Mrs. Trafton thought I should make her son George coach. We held a stockholders' meeting. She was outvoted. My brother Frank voted my mother's stock, and McMillen sided with me. As a result, Mrs. Trafton said she would like to sell her stock. I bought it from her for $40,000, doubling her investment of $20,000. McMillen kept his stock until 1954. He then had two children in college and needed money. I offered him $25,000 for his stock, five times its cost. We settled for $40,000. A quarter of a century later McMillen regarded the price as more than fair. "Of course," he says, "if I had held it, the stock would have increased many, many times. But no one in 1954 saw the large audiences and the tremendous amount of money television would bring."

I kept one eye open for business opportunities which might provide extra funds for the Bears. A mail-order house selling sporting goods and jewelry folded. I bought some of the assets and revived the business as May and Halas. One of the employees, Max Swiatek, became my right-hand man and the Bears' archivist. His loyalty and his honesty have been of paramount importance to me.

One day "Colonel" William C. Hauk, who managed

the Flat Iron Laundry and sold advertising space in our programs, told me he knew of a wholesale laundry that could be purchased cheaply. We bought the defunct Chicago laundry and named it The White Bear Laundry. The "Colonel" ran it. Later his son and daughter-in-law, Rita, joined. Much later Rita was to become very dear to me. The laundry did well over the years.

Dr. David Jones was losing interest in football. He saw a dark financial future for football and his Cardinals. Undesirable characters again sniffed about. I looked around for another owner. I favored my old friend Charlie Bidwill. He loved the Bears. He was one of our most ardent fans. He was owner of a printing company and part owner of Sportman's Race Track. Both were profitable. Charlie had an associate named O'Hare, who was shot in a power struggle for control of the track. Early in World War II, O'Hare's son Butch was shot down while attacking a Japanese battleship. President Roosevelt gave the family the Medal of Honor, and Chicago named its airport for the hero flier. Bidwill offered me a third of the track to induce me to become the president. I lacked enthusiasm.

One night Dr. Jones and I were guests aboard Charlie's boat. Bidwill said he heard Dr. Jones might be willing to sell the Cardinals.

"If I get my price," Dr. Jones said.

Bidwill asked the price.

"Fifty thousand," Dr. Jones said. That was double the sum he had paid for the club.

The doctor thought Bidwill was only making polite conversation but a couple of nights later Bidwill called Dr. Jones and told him he'd take the club for $50,000. I rejoiced. The Cardinals remained in good hands.

Carr persistently watched for any attempt by gamblers to move in on football. He let all managers know that if he caught any owner or manager betting on the result of a League game he would ban the individual from the League forever. The warning sufficed. Joe hated gambling. He said it could lead only to dishonesty, and dishonesty would ruin professional football. All of us early members were deeply appreciative of his firm stand.

Carr and I worried about the shrinking League. We needed new clubs. We proposed that George Preston Marshall start a club in Boston, a good baseball town. George Preston Marshall knew little about football but he was a promoter. He had good connections and a source of money. His father had died when George was in the army during World War I and left the son the Palace Laundry, a small but growing enterprise in Washington. George took it over on returning from the war. He made it grow and grow. In time he had forty or forty-five branches in the Capital.

George Preston Marshall enticed four monied men into his football club, each putting up $7,500, I think. He put in an equal amount and they started the club in Boston. They arranged to play in the Boston Braves' baseball park so they called their team the Braves. It did not do well. After it lost $40,000, the partners dropped out. Marshall carried on. He had problems with coaches who thought an owner should sit quietly in the owner's box. Silence did not come easy to George Preston Marshall.

Boston ignored the team, even when it began winning and after Marshall changed the name from Braves to the more colorful Redskins. When in 1936 the club topped the division and the achievement went unnoticed

151

in the Boston press, Marshall moved the team out of Boston. Homeless, it played the title game with Green Bay as guest of the Giants in New York. The next year Marshall found a new home in Washington. There the Redskins became formidable. They deserved the magnificent 110-piece band Marshall marched up and down, their Indian headdresses swinging.

The Giants were always a threat. One reason was Benny Friedman, a Cleveland boy who had developed greatness as a quarterback at the University of Michigan. Benny was an innovator. He did much to develop passing as an art. One afternoon he threw four touchdown passes against us. Curly Lambeau at Green Bay created a strategy to deal with Benny. He pulled his best defense man, Cal Hubbard, out of the line and told him his sole job was to take out any potential receivers who came through the line. That left the other linemen with the task of sacking Benny. It was a rough afternoon for Benny.

Benny was specially dangerous because you never knew when he was going to pass.

"One day in Chicago," Friedman recalls, "we had the ball on our seven-yard line. It was third and seven. In those days it was automatic that if you had long yardage, you kicked on the third down. We went into punt formation. Then I saw that the Bear halfback had gone back for the kick. That created a hole. I called a pass play. The ball went to our fullback, Tiny Feather. He handed it to me as I faded back to pass. The kicker, a fellow named Wilberg, came up to block for me. The play went exactly as planned except that I couldn't see the intended receiver, Sedbrook, anywhere. However, I saw that our right end, Lyle Munn, was clear. I hit him with the ball.

152

Coming back into the huddle, I sought out Sedbrook and asked him where he had been. He said, with some pride, he had taken out the Bears' tackle, his job when it was third and seven and we were going to kick. I said, 'You dummy. You should play with the Bears.' It was the worst insult I could think of. We won, 7–6, but what made the game for me was the knowledge we had outsmarted Halas and his Bears."

Pittsburgh had been a great football town since the early days but professional football was blocked by a state law against Sunday sport. The ban was erased in 1933 and a delightful Irishman, Art Rooney, bought a franchise for $2,500 and started a team first called the Pirates and then the Steelers.

The team was not an immediate success on the field, nor with the bank, but it brought a wise, gentle sportsman into the League. Rooney was to make a fortune in racing and raising horses. The earnings supported the club.

For years, the Yellow Jackets, operating in the Frankford section of Philadelphia, had been a power in professional football. They beat us for the championship in 1926 and were second in 1928. By 1931 they were bottom and dropped out. How fortunate that was for the League and for professional football because into the opening stepped Bert Bell.

Bert was different from most of us. He was High Society. His mother was named Fleurette. His father had Cromwell for a middle name. Bert was christened de Benneville. A brother was governor of the state, his father attorney general for the state and his grandfather a congressman. Of course the family was rich. Bert had, in turn, a nanny, a pony, a Marmon sportster. His mother

153

died when he was seventeen. His father spoiled him expertly. Bert was thrown out of three prep schools. At the University of Pennsylvania he found joy in quarterbacking the Varsity. He collected a broken nose and broken shoulder and began losing his front teeth. He left college after his third year to drive an ambulance in France. After the war and a final year in college, he helped coach at Pennsylvania and at Temple. Off campus he was a heller. The stock market crash eliminated his fortune. He continued to be a heller, but on a reduced scale. In 1932 he fell for a Ziegfeld Follies girl, Frances Upton. He wanted to marry her. "It's alcohol or me," she said. He finished his glass, turned it upside down and never again drank anything stronger than coffee.

The Yellow Jacket franchise could be bought for $2,500. Bert didn't have the money; Frances did. Four former college friends provided operating capital. The new law permitted Sunday games. President Roosevelt was raising the eagle of the National Recovery Act over the country so Bert changed the club's name to the Eagles. The new name didn't create spectators or victories. Philadelphia baseball fans, like those in Boston, seemed immune to football. One cloudy day Bell sent a hireling to the Athletics' field with a megaphone to shout that the baseball game was cancelled because of rain, but the Eagles were playing football at their park.

We gained a fourth new owner, George Richards. He bought the Portsmouth franchise and moved it to Detroit. Richards was a promoter. He said Joe Carr was a nice guy and good at paperwork but the League needed a real promoter, a man with new ideas, someone who could get things rolling. He proposed we dump Carr and take on an agile-minded gentleman who had been very successful selling Miami to Americans. To show our faith in Carr, we gave him a ten-year contract.

Although scheduling had become a League enterprise, teams were still selective in lining up opponents, seeking games with teams that would draw the largest crowds.

The Bears always brought the largest crowds [Art Rooney recalls.] We couldn't put up a tough fight but George Halas would come and play. He kept me alive. One year we were scheduled to play in New York and New York was scheduled to play in Chicago. We figured there would be a better gate all around if Halas went to New York and I went to Chicago. Halas promised to add $500 to our usual guarantee of $2,500. The New York turnout was great. In Chicago we didn't draw very well and George wanted to pay me only $2,500. We argued. Finally he said, "Do you want to fight me for the 500?" I said, "No, George, I don't want to fight you. I just want the $500." He gave me the money. At the door I said, "Hey, George, I'm not so sure you could have won the fight." He laughed. He knew that in my earlier days I had been U.S. lightweight champion.

Another year Halas and I were asked to take our teams to Lexington, Kentucky, for a charity game promoted by a minister. The gate barely paid costs. Halas said, "Art, we can't go home and leave this charity with no money. We'd better give them something." We kicked in something, $2,500 each, I think.

George Marshall thought the season would be more interesting if the teams were divided into two groups of five teams each. The top division teams would play for the championship. Baseball had long found that arrangement productive of interest. As World Series time neared, the excitement rose. The series itself was a national spectacle. We copied our older brethren. It was the forerunner of the Super Bowl.

We all believed professional football was earning public respect. Yet collegiate coaches, as a group, remained opposed. The Western Collegiate Conference took two fierce actions against us. It ruled that no person who officiated in a professional game could perform at a collegiate game, and no player who had signed with a professional team could be hired later by a conference university as a coach. As a group, and as individuals, we labored to have these restraints removed.

Among ourselves the arguments were ceaseless. "My father and Halas were so often on opposite sides," Wellington Mara remembers,

> that I grew up looking upon Halas as an enemy. They had bitter arguments. They had deep feelings. Neither was afraid to take positive positions and let his position be known. When they agreed with you, it wasn't out of deference. It was because you had convinced them. Now I see Halas in a different light. I realize he and my father were on the same side, working for the good of the League.
>
> At the League meeting in 1934, some members wanted to make a dropped lateral a live ball. George was bitterly opposed. He gave one of his most passionate speeches. He said the change would introduce a very big hazard into the use of the T-Formation with a man-in-motion, a strategy which called for a lot of such laterals, frequently dropped. "You gentlemen will destroy me and the modern T-Formation," he said. "You are taking away my bread and butter." He really cried. Real tears. He had his way.

156

One evening at a civic dinner, Clark Shaughnessy introduced himself to me. He was head coach at the University of Chicago. He said he was fascinated by our modern T-Formation with man-in-motion and would like to learn more about it. We rearranged place cards so we could sit together. We passed the evening talking about the formation. We merely touched basic principles. I invited him to come to my office to learn more. He came regularly for several years. I told him how Ralph Jones had created the formation. I explained the reasons behind it and kept him current with developments. Starting in 1935 he assisted me with terminology and analyzing game scout reports. I paid him $2,000 a year. He continued to improve his knowledge of the modern T-Formation with man-in-motion. In 1940 he became coach at Stanford and introduced the Bear formation there.

The League gradually increased the team player limit; from sixteen to twenty in 1930; twenty-four in 1935; twenty-five in 1936; thirty in 1938; thirty-three in 1940. We raised the franchise fee to $10,000. We settled money disputes between clubs. We awarded championship cups. We hired a publicity director—part time. We organized officiating to get rid of sloppy officials and homers—officials who favored the home team.

"At one meeting," Rooney remembers, "we had a big discussion about how much air should go into the football. If you put 13 pounds into it in a cold room, what happens when the ball is taken outdoors where the temperature is 100 degrees? Everyone was putting in his two bits worth. I said, 'Why are we wasting all of this time? Ask George! If anybody knows what can be done with footballs or baseballs he knows, because I am sure he has already tried everything.' He knew."

157

By the mid-thirties, Bidwill, Marshall, Rooney and Bell needed help. The League was out of balance. The Bears, the Giants and Green Bay were always close to the top. The others scrambled for lower places. We three drew the biggest crowds. We had the most money. We could pay more for players. Good college players wanted to join our winning clubs. The prospect was that each year the strong would become stronger, the weak weaker.

The situation might be good for the strong teams in the short term because it is always pleasant to win. But I had seen thousands of people walk out of games in which one team was running away. People stayed away from a game certain to be one-sided. It was a reappearance of the problem we had tackled more than ten years earlier by introducing the principle of sharing. Mara agreed. He argued:

> People come to see a competition. We could give them a competition only if the teams had some sort of equality, if the teams went up and down with the fortunes of life. Of course, that meant that no team would in the future win a championship every third year and people would start saying, "What's happened to the Giants? They aren't the team they used to be." That was a hazard we had to accept for the benefit of the League, of professional football and of everyone in it.

At the 1935 League meeting, Bell proposed League teams organize a draft of the best college players. Each team would produce a list of graduating players it thought attractive. The lists would be posted. Each team would select players, one at a time, in inverse order to the League standings the previous season. The team that finished last would get first choice, the winner the last choice. Each team would negotiate with the players it selected. If terms could not be agreed, the League president would arbitrate. If that failed, the team would try to arrange a trade with some other team. If that failed, the player would have to wait a year before he could negotiate freely. All unchosen or unlisted players could negotiate with any team, and any team could approach any nonselected player.

I thought the proposal sound. It made sense.

Mara also approved. He and I had more to lose than any other team. With our support, the proposal was adopted unanimously, to become effective with the 1936 season.

Of course some people saw in the draft an aspect of selfishness on the part of owners. They claimed we were trying to hold down salaries by reducing the negotiating rights of the best players. There is some truth in this argument. But time proved that by leveling the clubs, the draft system heightened the attractiveness of the sport. It created bigger audiences, which brought bigger revenues which brought higher salaries for all players.

In the thirties Los Angeles was growing fast. Collegiate sport was big there. The Rose Bowl was becoming a major national sports event. A Los Angeles gentleman, Harry Myers, came to our 1936 meeting saying he represented the Los Angeles American Legion and three Los Angeles newspapers. The group would like a franchise. They would pay the $10,000 fee. They were prepared to play twelve games, six in Los Angeles, six in the East. To the usual· guarantee for visiting clubs they would add the cost of transportation to and from Chicago, about $2,300, although when Los Angeles came East it would expect only the usual guarantee, providing six games could be arranged in consecutive weeks.

It was an interesting proposition but it meant radical departure. The League decided that, as a test, the Los Angeles club could negotiate games with any League team individually. Only Bell and Rooney made such agreements. To get other games, the Los Angeles team joined with five other independents and formed a league. It did not do well. The next year Myers again asked for a franchise. Bell and Rooney said their experience led them to advise the League not to expand to the West Coast. But our Detroit man, Richards, said a game could be arranged in Los Angeles between the winning League team and Pacific All-Star collegians for a gate of not less than $100,000. That was the kind of money we had not seen since the Red Grange days. We told him to see what he could do.

Another situation was arising in radio. Various clubs arranged with local stations to broadcast games under commercial sponsorship. The League favored interchanging broadcasts but left arrangements to teams.

Joe Carr suffered a heart attack. He was hospitalized for a month, and we pleaded with him to take a long vacation. He refused. On May 20, 1939, he died. Red Grange summed up Carr's contributions to our game:

Joe E. Carr was the single individual most responsible up to that time for the growth of pro football. He was a kindly, sympathetic honest gentleman. He had vision and common sense. From the start he insisted pro football would one day be one of America's outstanding sports. A lot of people talk about the Golden Rule. Carr put it into practice. He saw that everyone got a square deal. He left a League with a sound foundation. When Joe Carr died 90 percent of the players were earning more during the short football season than the economic situation would permit them to make in a year in other pursuits. The high earnings brought in top college players, improving the caliber of play. Nearly half used their earnings to further their education. Others used the money to get a running start into the business world. All this was due to the sane, honest administration provided by Joe Carr and supported by the owners. He has been justly enshrined in our Hall of Fame.

Shortly before he died, Carr spoke one hard truth: "No owner has made money from pro football but a lot have gone broke thinking they could." In 1930 the Bears made a profit of $1,695.93 on receipts of $155,294.69. After ups and downs, in 1939 we earned $14,535.19 on receipts of $226,426.63. Players' pay had gone from $53,469.83 to $89,370.02. As coach I received $5,000.

Football had also become a very complex game. Good rules were mandatory to reduce the danger of injury. The 1930 collegiate rule book contained eighty-six pages. Not surprisingly, a rule devised to meet a particular situation might conflict with other rules. Officials had to decide which rule to follow. The rules became a maze.

In 1932 the League set up our own rules committee. I was made chairman. Our first need was to make radical changes to open up the game: permitting passing anywhere behind the line of scrimmage, bringing in out-of-bound balls and restoring the goal posts to the goal line. Also we needed to pull the sprawling body of rules together. The task required a man with special talent and experience. It required Hugh Ray, known as Shorty. He was 5 feet 5, 135 pounds. He taught mechanical drawing at Carter Harrison High School in Chicago. One word sums up Shorty: precise. As a football fan, he was appalled at the sloppy application of rules in high school sport. He toured Chicago schools preaching the need for good officiating. He gained adherents and in 1925 brought into being the Chicago Public School Athletic Officials Association. Other cities soon copied the system.

Shorty rewrote the high school rule book, bringing together companion rules, eliminating conflicts, indexing. He produced a handy booklet small enough to be carried in a hip pocket. To help officials apply rules uniformly, he set forth a variety of situations and explained which rules apply and why. He conducted clinics and tests for officials. Above all he emphasized quickness. He said that every second, or part of a second, used by officials was stolen from the players and fans. Shorty carried a stopwatch and used it as a deadly weapon.

In 1935, the American Football Coaches Association hired Shorty to produce a new collegiate rule book. He stormed through college officialdom. He was neither polite nor politic in pointing out errors, slipshod ways and favoritism. In two years he irritated so many people the collegiate coaches dumped him.

Since 1932, our League had made much progress ridding itself of homers, but the quality of officiating still varied greatly. We needed a system to examine and supervise officials.

In 1937, I persuaded the League to hire Shorty as full-time technical consultant. It was one of my finest contributions. Shorty set about with enthusiasm. Within a year he codified our rules. He sent three observers to games. One watched the officials for errors; the second recorded the time officials needed to get a dead ball into play—Shorty fixed 8 seconds as maximum; the third checked on the time teams used between plays—rules allowed 30 seconds. By saving a second here, 2 seconds there, Shorty increased the number of plays in the average game from 145 in 1936 to 174 in 1950. The extra plays helped raise average scoring from 24 points to 46 points—the result of thousands upon thousands of stopwatch measurements by Shorty and his helpers.

Shorty was sixty when he came to the League in 1937. He continued until his death in 1956. I enthusiastically proposed for the Hall of Fame this small energetic man.

As years passed, I saw the benefits that might come from bringing the club together for training in late summer. Players could become a more closely knit team. There would be less temptation to break training, fewer distractions. We could devote more time and energy and thought to the game.

In 1935 I made arrangements with St. John's Military Academy at Delafield, Wisconsin, to use part of a dormitory and the field for three weeks.

"Training camp was hard," George Musso comments.

Because you played last season or made All-Star or something didn't mean you would play the next year. You never knew what new player would show up. Halas had his own measuring sticks. Interior linesmen had to be tough; they had to bang you. Receivers who thought they had only to run out and wait for a pass should pay to get into the ball park; the good receiver came back as a linebacker or halfback and blocked so the ball carrier could get past. The way a guy blocked showed how much determination he had. Halas rated determination very high. If you got a knee in the ribs while blocking, that hurt. But if you blocked properly you didn't get hurt. You came up to your target until you were close enough to shake hands with him. Then you threw your body against him. You didn't go at him with a shoulder because if the target moved 10 inches, you missed him.

I tried to generate a team spirit. Generally, the Bears did pull together. One season, however, the team split into two cliques. One was made up of players who lived in the Sheridan Plaza Hotel. The others made up the second. The split hurt our play, so one day in the dressing room, I said, "Put on your full equipment including shoulder pads and head gear." One by one I called the names of the men in one clique. "You line up over there." I told the others, "You line up on the opposite side of the room." The players wondered what was going on. When they were lined up, I said, "That's the way you have divided yourselves. You've got one group against another group. You are messing up the whole ball club. So let's fight it out right now. Go to it. Fight like hell. Do anything. Gouge. Kick. Anything!" They were stunned. They didn't know what to do. They didn't do anything. That ended the split.

I assigned roommates. I tried to put together men who liked each other, but sometimes I had other reasons. "Soon after Sid Luckman came to the Bears," Moose recalls,

I told him to call a certain play. Sid said, "Moose, you play your position and I'll play mine." I thought I had

164

a lot more experience and told him off. After the game Halas called me aside and said, "I noticed you and Sid had some words out there today. Moose, Sid is going to be a great quarterback. I want you to get along with him." Coach put me in a room with Sid. We became good friends, and he did become a great quarterback.

I encouraged players to control their tempers.

"We need you," I told them. "If somebody slugs you, hit him harder with a legal block. Push the rules as far as you can but stay within the rules." One day when we faced a rough team, I told the players: "Men, it's easier to fight than to walk away from a fight. Today I'll give a $100 bonus to anyone who walks away from a fight." If an official threw a Bear off the field for roughness and fined him, I added my own fine.

Perhaps the team discipline carried into my home. Virginia recalls:

Dad would say something and that would be that. In the evening, he and I would sit at his big desk in the dining room. I would do my homework problems and he would check them. In high school I had to be home by 10:30. I'd be the first to leave a party. When it was my turn to give the party, Dad would drive the girls home. He enjoyed that. He wanted me to tell him beforehand the girls' names. He would be as careful to get the names right as he is today about the most important business associates.

Some evenings the coaches came to our apartment. They'd work out, turning this way and that, handing off the ball, blocking. When someone bumped into a chair, Mother would come in, saying: "What in the world are you doing!"

Virginia began absorbing football. As she grew older she sat with Min in the box closest to the team bench. For years I urged Min to move to the upper deck where she could see better. She said Mugs might fall between the railings, but it really was too far from the team.

"Every time I see a goal kicked, I think of my Mother," Virginia says.

She would always say, "Don't watch the ball. Watch the official. When he raises his hands, you will know the kick is good." Mother and Mugs would yell at the officials. Once in a while Dad would gesture in Mother's direction as though to say, "Shush."

One day at school the boys were talking about Red Grange. I said, "I know Red Grange." "What do you mean, you!" they shouted. I told Red. He autographed a photograph: "Dear Virginia, sure I know you and I think you are swell, Love, Red Grange." That made up for lots of things.

CHAPTER ELEVEN

My Beloved Monsters

THE START OF THE 1932 SEASON was totally frustrating. We had devoted two years to developing the modern T-Formation with man-in-motion to open up the game and bring in new skills for scoring. We had so many good players Jones could not get down to the League limit of twenty. I called President Carr and proposed the limit be raised to twenty-two. He telegraphed the other owners. They agreed. We kept all twenty-two.

Yet, we went through our first four League games without scoring. Not one touchdown. Not one field goal. Not even one safety. Our opponents scored only in the fourth game—with a safety. Finally we took off and went through the rest of the season unbeaten. There were some memorable moments.

A 235-pound rookie fullback, John Doehring, proved to have an amazing passing ability. I had found him in Milwaukee. He was one of the few professionals who did not come out of college. We called him Bull. One day Bull took a lateral. He was supposed to pass the ball to Luke. Luke got clear but Bull was being smothered.

"He didn't even have room to raise his arm," Luke says. "I looked away. Another effort had failed. I happened to look up and there, coming straight into my hands, was the ball. I was so surprised I dropped it. As we were walking to the dressing room, I asked Bull how he got rid of that ball. He said, 'Well, they were rushing me so I threw it behind my back.' And that is what he had done. Honest to God, he had thrown the ball behind his back. Forty yards. Right into my mitts."

In a tight game with the Portsmouth Spartans, Luke lingered near the sidelines to tie his shoelaces. The Spartans forgot him. He took a pass and scored.

We ended the season with seven wins, one loss, and six ties. The ties did not count in the reckoning. We shared top place with the Portsmouth Spartans, who were riding high on the kicking, passing and running of Dutch Clark. Their coach was Potsy Clark, my old friend from Illinois and co-member of the Order of the Broken Jaw. Fortunately for us Dutch was basketball coach at Colorado College, his alma mater, and could not get leave for the playoff. That would never happen today.

The championship game was scheduled December 18 in Chicago. In a mild year Christmas Week is no time to frolic on a Chicago football field. In 1932 the winter had come early and hard, bringing deep snow. William Veeck, Sr., released me from my pledge to play all home games in Wrigley Field and we moved into Chicago Stadium. The Salvation Army had sponsored a circus there so the concrete floor had a thick covering of what the management described as a very swell brand of dirt.

168

Permanent seats limited the length of the playing field to 80 yards and the width to 45. That required special rules. We put the posts on the goal line. To avoid solid-plank four-foot-high walls, we moved out-of-bounds balls inward 10 yards.

The game was a financial success—a capacity house of 11,108.

The game was scoreless until we intercepted a pass on the Portsmouth 7. Nagurski drove 6 yards. Second and one. Nagurski plunged. No gain. Third and one. Nagurski plunged. No gain. Fourth and one. Would Nagurski make it on the fourth try?

"I lined up as usual, four yards back," Nagurski remembers. "Red went in motion. The ball came to me. I took a step or two forward as though to begin the plunge everyone expected. The defenders converged, doubling up on the line to stop me. There was no way through. I stopped. I moved back a couple of steps. Grange had gone around end and was in the end zone, all by himself. I threw him a short pass."

"Actually, I was on my back," Red says. "Someone had knocked me down. But I got the ball and hung on to it."

Potsy Clark protested that Nagurski was not 5 yards behind the line of scrimmage as rules demanded. Nagurski insisted he was. So did I. The referees agreed.

After eleven years the Bears were again champions!

Ralph Jones had delivered. Everybody acclaimed him. The modern T-Formation with man-in-motion had delivered, but few seemed to notice and I was not going to inform the world. Let other coaches stay with their wings and boxes.

The game did have immediate and important effects

169

on football. At the League meeting two months later, we made three fundamental rule changes:

1. Passing was permitted anywhere behind the line. Potsy Clark's attitude was common: "Nagurski will pass from anywhere so why not make it legal?"
2. An out-of-bounds ball was moved in 10 yards, eliminating the usual waste of a down to gain room to maneuver.
3. The goal posts, which had been moved 10 yards behind the goal line three years earlier following the colleges, were restored to the goal line.

The changes opened and speeded the game, led to higher scores and reduced the number of scoreless or tied games. In five years we had played ten tied games. In the next five years we had just four.

For passing, we needed a slimmer ball. It had been pared from 27 inches to 23 inches in 1912 and to 22½ in 1929. We had to wait until 1934 to trim it to 21¼ minimum, 21½ maximum.

The Bears were ablaze with glory. I rejoiced in the championship. I saw nothing but success ahead.

But at this supreme moment, financially I was in deep, deep trouble.

I had gone into the 1932 season surrounded with IOU's. I had hoped attendance would pick up so I could pay off those notes. The opposite happened. I ended the 1932 season with a loss of $18,000. I kept afloat by giving more notes. I couldn't pay Green Bay its guarantee of $2,500. I told Lee Joannes, the Packers' president, "Lee, I am out of chalk."

Lee recalls the day: "It had snowed heavily in Chicago. The result was a very slim attendance. Halas gave me $1,000 and a note for $1,500.

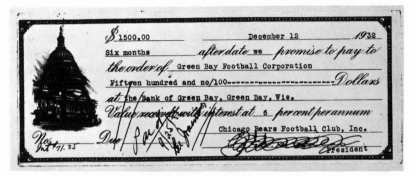

"The next year when the Bears played in Green Bay Halas said I should take the $1,500 out of the guarantee. I marked the note paid. But Halas will never get it back. I put it in our Hall of Fame. Halas did much more than pay me back. When Green Bay called a vote on a bond issue for a new stadium, Halas came up and did a wonderful selling job. We got the stadium."

I had to give other notes. Bronk and Red each took one for $1,000. Ralph Jones took one for $3,000, perhaps solidifying his poor opinion of the future of the game, and returned to college coaching, at Lake Forest College, at a reduced salary. I would not challenge any comment that the financial shortage contributed to my selection of Jones' successor. I studied the twenty-seven applications, and chose me. I came cheap. I would coach for nothing. I told everyone I was only filling in until I could find the right man.

All came right for the Bears in 1933.
Nagurski says:

Ralph Jones was a great strategist but Halas has a talent for handling people. He has immense enthusiasm. He is a fighter. He is always out to win. He treated everyone in a different manner. Sometimes he'd take a player into a corner and talk to him quietly. Sometimes he'd chew a fellow out in front of everybody. He seemed to know how each person would respond. He was around all the time. He was strict, but if the team was going well and the boys were behaving, he'd give us a lot of leeway.

"Mr. Halas had an advantage over the other coaches," Johnsos recalls. "He could run faster and holler louder. Once in a while, officials would penalize him when he shouted something like: 'You silly $%¢&*@$¢!'"

One day in Wrigley Field, [Wellington Mara remembers,] an official ran to retrieve a punt that had gone out of bounds. He dropped his cap to mark the spot. George Halas moved it a foot or so in favor of the Bears. The distance meant absolutely nothing, but the action was typical of Halas. He just couldn't resist getting every possible advantage for the Bears. Of course, the place was in an uproar. Another official moved the cap back. At the time, Halas' little act of enthusiasm didn't please me. I guess a person must become a little mature, a little mellow, to appreciate enthusiasm of someone who is always on the other side of the field.

I was always looking for new players to strengthen the team. Bronko told me about a tremendous goal kicker at Minnesota, Jack Manders. His goals were to win many games for us. He also became an excellent halfback. From Marquette I picked up a quarterback, Gene Ronzani. Bill Karr resisted my inducements but came out to Chicago from West Virginia to see the Chicago World's

Fair. He ran out of money and came to our training camp. He was half-starved. We fed him steaks. He picked up speed and stamina. When Luke broke an ankle, Karr moved in. From Green Bay I got Joe Zeller. I had noted that he seemed to have some success in stopping Nagurski. And from little Millikin College down in Decatur, where the Bears began, I found George Musso, the Moose. In high school in tiny Collinsville, in downstate Illinois, he weighed 240 pounds and played all sports. At Millikin he played tackle and guard. He planned to go into coaching. He was drafted for an All-Star game arranged in Soldier Field as special attraction for the Century of Progress, the World's Fair. I liked his performance. A few days later I sent him a telegram asking him if he would consider joining the Bears.

"He sent a money order for five dollars," Musso adds. "The roundtrip train ticket on the Wabash was three dollars. That left two dollars for me to really do the town. I came. Mr. Halas offered me ninety dollars a game. I accepted."

For the Bears that was a momentous event. Musso played with us twelve years.

Bronk, Brummy, Luke and Hewitt worked out one play of their own. Brummy faked into the line and gave the ball to Bronk who lateraled to Hewitt who passed to Luke. The play came in handy in a game with Green Bay. With two minutes to go, we were trailing 7–0. We had the ball on their 35. Luke asked Brummy to call their play.

Brummy said, "You'll get me fired."

"Try it," Luke said. "What have we to lose?" The play went perfectly. The ball traveled from center to Brummy to Nagurski to Hewitt and right into the arms of

Luke, waiting in the end zone. We converted. The game was even 7–7. We kicked off to Green Bay. We held them for three downs. With the clock running out, they punted. Hewitt got through, blocked the kick, picked up the ball and scored. We won 14–7.

When we won two more games in the last 2 minutes we became the story-book Bears.

Of our thirteen games in 1933 we won ten, lost two and tied one, giving us the Western title and taking us to New York for the championship.

There was a huge turnout. The teams were evenly matched. During the season we had beaten the Giants 14–10 and they had beaten us 3–0.

On the big day, Manders kicked two field goals, from 16 yards and 40 yards. Then, in four plays, the Giants made 75 yards and a touchdown. The conversion put them ahead 7–6. Later the Giants had the ball just inside the sidelines with room for one lineman between Mel Hein, the center, and the boundary. Both teams bunched up on the inside. Just before the ball was snapped, a back jumped onto the line at the far end and the lineman between Mel and the boundary jumped back. That technically made Mel an end and available as a ball carrier. The quarterback took the ball from Mel and with as much sleight of hand as he could manage gave it back to him. Mel hid it behind the seat of his pants. The quarterback pivoted, faded back and began grabbing at the air as though he had fumbled the ball. Everyone went for him. Mel slowly straightened and, holding the ball behind his back, walked forward. Nobody paid any attention. "Don't panic," the quarterback had told him when rehearsing the play. The strain of sauntering was too much.

He broke into a run. Our safety took note, ran over to investigate, saw the ball and brought Mel down. The play earned 15 yards. Had Mel taken a few more quiet steps he would have scored.

In the third quarter Manders kicked his third field goal, regaining the lead for us, 9–7. After our kickoff, the Giants reached our 1-yard line with only five passes. Max Krause scored and the conversion made it 14–9 Giants.

We tried an improved version of the 1932 indoor game quick pass, with Nagurski charging forward as though about to crack the line while one end veered out in one direction to draw the defense and the other circled back behind the line to take a short pass directly over the center. With Hewitt as lure and Karr as receiver, it worked for a touchdown. We led, 16–14.

Again four Giant passes plus a run brought the ball to our 8. Then came an unrehearsed play. Ken Strong took the ball and started around his left end. We trapped him but before we could bring him down, he lateraled to Newman, the quarterback. Newman ran this way and that and, in time, found himself trapped still behind the line of scrimmage. While all this was going on, Strong, abandoned by our tacklers, ran across the goal. Newman saw him and passed to him. Strong to Newman to Strong! Who would be foolish enough to dream up such a play? But in this particular situation, it worked. The Giants led 21–16.

We took the kick and pushed the ball, mostly with Nagurski plunges, to the Giants' 34. Once again Nagurski took the ball and started to drive ahead but stopped short and tossed to Bill Hewitt. Hewitt was surrounded but Karr was clear. Hewitt lateraled to Karr.

175

Strong tried to stop Karr but Ronzani blocked him so hard that Strong crashed into the bleachers. Karr scored unmolested and the conversion put us ahead 23–21.

The thrills were not yet over. The Giants' Newman threw a long pass to Burnett. Mel was there running beside Burnett, ready to block or to take a lateral. Only Red Grange was in their way. Red knew if he made the usual tackle, Burnett would lateral to Mel and we would lose the game. So Grange, the great Red Grange, made a new kind of tackle. He flung his arms around Burnett in a bear hug, clamping Burnett's arms to his side. It saved the game.

Nagurski said the game was the happiest he ever played. He spoke for us all. We held our championship. In two seasons, we had lost only three games. We scored 329 points to our opponents' 147.

If figures can prove anything these statistics must indicate that:

1. The rules which grew out of our indoor game had opened up football, and,
2. Our modern T-Formation with man-in-motion was the most successful strategy in football.

Even so, very few coaches and players yet saw the lessons. They still continued with the wings and boxes. That was fine with me.

The Bears acquired Beattie Feathers in 1934. He and Nagurski made a powerful pair, Nagurski opening the way and Beattie following closely. One day we made a good punt return but officials said Bronk held. The kick was negated and we were penalized 15 yards. In a couple of minutes the other team scored. After the kickoff Bronk said in the huddle, "That was all my fault. Give me the ball." He got it and went straight through the center and up the middle so fast that he crashed into the dugout. Some people will today show you a crack in the south wall at Wrigley Field they say was made by his helmeted head. He was knocked out. When he came to, he is supposed to have said, "Man, somebody really hit me!"

Bronk is easygoing. He doesn't anger easily. Sometimes in tight conditions, a colleague would say, "Coach doesn't think you have any guts." They'd rile him and he'd go like hell. He needed that extra incentive to reach his potential.

It has been said Bronk tackled a Model T parked on the sidelines and it had to be towed to the garage to get a new fender. And another day he tackled a policeman's horse. The horse had to go to the boneyard. Bronk does not deny the stories but insists he is opposed to mistreatment of horses.

Red Grange has a term for Bronk: "The greatest football player of all time." That is hard to dispute.

Before a Green Bay game Luke Johnsos had a premonition something strange was about to happen. He told his wife, "Rosemary, it is going to be tough today. When I come home, don't say a word. Just give me a drink and let me relax."

We led 14–3 with only a minute and a half to go. We fumbled. Green Bay recovered and with one pass they scored. They kicked off to us. On the very first play, Bernie Masterson, our quarterback, tried to hand off the ball and fumbled. Again Green Bay recovered and, again, one pass gave them a touchdown. With only two plays they beat us 17–14! Damnedest thing I'd ever seen. All our quarterback had to do was get the ball and lie on it for three plays. But no, he had to hand it off. Over the years we have had historic meets with Green Bay.

When Luke went home, Rosemary said, "May I ask just one question? During that last minute and a half, are you sure you had eleven men on the field?"

Over the years, I had pondered the comparative abilities of college and professional teams. An opportunity to match undergraduates and post-graduates arose in 1934 when the city of Chicago extended the World's Fair into a second year and Mayor Ed Kelly asked Arch Ward, sports editor of the *Chicago Tribune*, to try to arrange a unique sporting event. At about the same time I asked Ward about the possibility of bringing together the Bears and a college all-star team. Arch put the two propositions together. He organized a poll by the *Tribune* and thirty other papers to select a twenty-seven–man collegiate team and a coach. The game drew 79,432, the largest crowd to attend any sporting event that year. Before the game, everyone joined in singing the National Anthem, a feature that became a Bears tradition. The game was scoreless. Profits were given to the United, Catholic and Jewish charities.

The game became an annual event, with the current professional champion representing the League. At first some college coaches who opposed professional football refused to participate but soon they coveted the opportunity to coach the All-Stars for two weeks and bring them into Soldier Field. Similarly some professional team owners were hesitant to part with rookies during their own training season but Art Rooney and I convinced the League the game was good for professional football. By 1976, when the game was killed by insurance and other costly regulations, the game had raised nearly $4 million for the *Chicago Tribune* charities.

178

As to the comparative abilities of under- and post-graduate players, League teams won thirty-one games, lost nine and tied two.

The year of 1934 was terrific, a great year. For the first time we won every League game, all thirteen, 1.000 percent. We earned 286 points to our opponents' 86. We beat the Giants twice, 27–7 and 10–9, but because of the oddities of scheduling, at that time, the Giants emerged as top team in the Eastern division. Of course, we were top in the Western. The championship match was scheduled for the Polo Grounds in New York.

For days rain had fallen. The field was a lake. On Saturday we practiced in the mud. That night, a north-easter swept into New York. When I went to Mass, the thermometer showed 9 degrees. Street puddles had turned to ice. But the sky was clear and as the day passed the warm sun melted the ice. When we arrived at the field, the turf was spongy, with a thin topping of water.

The Giants scored on a field goal. Then Bronko began moving. He crossed the goal and Manders converted. Manders was on his way to seventy-two conversions in a row. We next got the ball on our 43. Nagurski plunges led us to the 9. Manders kicked. We led 10–3. We picked up a fumble on the 6 and Nagurski ran the ball over but the referee said a Bear was too eager, brought back the ball and penalized us 5 yards. Manders tried for a field goal and, for the first time in memory, missed. Soon Nagurski scored again but again the referee called back the ball and penalized us, this time 15 yards for holding. Manders kicked and, I could hardly believe it, missed. We went off for the half safely ahead 10–3 despite the bad breaks which had cost us a couple of touchdowns. We had dominated the field. As Mel Hein said later, "Nagurski was three-yarding us to death."

When we came out, the shadows cast by the bleachers were creeping onto the field. It got awfully cold. In the shadows the ground was freezing, not into ridges but into a slick sheet. Three or four Giants came out wearing tennis shoes! During the first half, a Giants' emissary had broken into lockers at Manhattan College and taken nine pairs of tennis shoes, all he could find.

Strong, the kicker, was wearing tennis shoes. His kick squirted sideways, out of bounds. We laughed. He kicked again.

The ball sailed into the end zone. We stopped laughing. We started to drive up the field as we had in the first half. We were at the sunny end but even there icy patches were starting to form. My men slipped and slid and upended. One by one Giants changed into tennis shoes.

I shouted to step on their feet. That didn't work either.

Late in the third quarter we recovered a fumble, Manders kicked and widened our lead to 13–3.

We changed ends. The shadow now covered all of our end of the field. I wish I could forget the fourth quarter.

"We were helpless," Nagurski recalls. "We had to mince about. We were down more than we were up."

"Some players took off their shoes," Johnsos says. "That helped a little but not much. I kept my shoes on. I had holes in my socks. We just flipflopped around. The Giants could go anywhere they wished. The game ended 30–13."

It was a freakish way to lose but it was legal and it cost us the championship!

At training camp the next fall, a big box arrived COD addressed to me. It was filled with tennis shoes. Must have been a hundred pairs, all worn, with holes in the soles. I never did learn who sent it. But I swore that no Bear ever would go to another game without two pairs of tennis shoes in his equipment bag.

Later we met the Giants again in Los Angeles for an exhibition game. With no ice, we won 21–0.

Unbeknownst to me, in the stands that day was Will Rogers, the wise homespun philosopher. Every day a few paragraphs of Rogers' wit and wisdom appeared in papers throughout the country. He wrote of many things, exhibiting a deep understanding. The day after the game he wrote:

> I never thought the time would come when I thought I would be able to advise the colleges how to run their businesses, but in California Sunday we saw our first real professional football game played and 25,000 people came away raving about it—especially the rules under which they play, where you can pass from everywhere, anytime.
>
> Now, as football is not only the backbone but the gravy of college existence, you fellows better open up your game, for this pro-game was just made for an audience. No penalty every minute to make an audience sore, nobody getting hurt every play, referees not in the way of the players.
>
> Colleges have developed yelling but the pros have developed the game. Now you colleges wake up. I don't want you to close your doors.

I could not celebrate the victory. For some time Red Grange had been talking about retiring from active play. He was thirty-one. He had been giving 100 percent for eight seasons in professional football and eight years in college and high school before that.

As the game was ending, we had the ball on our 20.

181

In the huddle Brummy said, "I'm giving the ball to Red for the last time. Boys, let's give him some help. Red, when you reach the end zone, put the ball down between the posts and head for the bench."

The boys opened a great hole. Red went through. The boys knocked down the secondary. Red had a clear field ahead.

"My feet got heavier and heavier," Grange says. "I was caught from behind on their 39 by a 230-pound tackle. I just couldn't make it."

Red put down the ball and walked to the bench. It was the end of an era. If I could rewrite just one play in all my experience, that would be it. I'd like Red to have gone off in a torrent of cheers.

The player draft was inaugurated in 1935. My first draft choice was a tackle, Joe Stydahar, known as Jumbo Joe, 6 feet 4, a solid 245 pounds. He came from West Virginia, where Brumbaugh had coached and Bill Karr had played. They recommended him highly. I found Joe Stydahar to be a very special man. His contributions to the Bears and to the League became monumental. More important was his character and loyalty. He was ferocious and courageous on the football field but off the field he was gentle and kind and loyal, asking, "Is there anything I can do to help?" He asked the fundamental questions: Does God have a place in our lives? Do the Ten Commandments regulate our actions, our decisions, our relationships with others? Joe knew what is good and right in life.

In the last round, all players known to me had been chosen. I saw a name I liked: Danny Fortmann. It had a good sound. I said, "I'll take Danny Fortmann." He turned out to be a medical student, a Phi Beta Kappa and a great player.

In 1935, the Bears first collided with Don Hutson, an Alabama end signed by Green Bay. On the very first play Hutson took off like a rocket. Beattie Feathers, our safety, let him go by. He considered Hutson was already out of passing range. Hutson kept on running. He didn't even turn around. The ball came over his shoulder. Hutson pulled it down and ran to the goal. The game was less than 20 seconds old and the score was 7–0. There the score stayed. But for a decade Hutson roamed the football fields, pulling down impossible passes and helping Green Bay lead the division in three of the next four years and win two national championships.

We slipped in 1935, winning only half of our twelve games. We did little better the next year, winning nine. In 1937, we could have drafted a string of a Texan named Sammy Baugh. He played halfback but was one of the best passers ever to come into football. Instead we drafted Ray Buivid, from Marquette. We acquired a powerful back from Northwestern, George Wilson, who was converted to an end and became important in our winning nine while losing one and tying one, good enough to bring us into the championship game against Washington and Sammy Baugh. We lost 21–28.

We were an aggressive team. In thirty-six League games during three years, we had made 636 points against 328 for our opponents. Another consoling 1937 statistic was that 155,000 people watched the Bears play. What we would have achieved had we had Baugh!

In 1938 we signed three excellent players: fullbacks Gary Famiglietti of Boston and Joe Maniaci of Fordham

183

and halfback Bob Swisher of Northwestern; but we slipped again, winning six and losing five.

Only once before, in 1929, had our win-loss performance been worse. But even in 1938 we made 194 points to our opponents' 148. We were fierce against the Redskins, winning 31–7.

I traded Eggs Manske to the Philadelphia Eagles, depriving Luke Johnsos of his running partner. They had been very successful lateraling to each other. In our next game at Philadelphia, Eggs took an Eagles' pass and was well on his way to a touchdown. Luke was near but couldn't catch Eggs. He called out, "Lateral, Eggs, lateral," just as he had in the former days. Eggs didn't even look around. Luke's voice told him Luke was in the proper position, four steps to the side, two behind. Eggs tossed the ball. Luke caught it, stopped, turned around, and ran for a touchdown.

In an exhibition game out West, the boys decided to help a guy just out of college, Cotton Warburton, who was being stopped cold by the Bears. The fellas let Cotton go for a long run to make him look good. After the game I told my players: "Every player must perform. If he can't, that's the way it is." I imposed a $50 fine, each.

By 1939 the League limit on players was raised to thirty. What a wealth of material we brought in—Sid Luckman; Bill Osmanski; Bob Snyder; Ray Bray; John Siegal; Aldo Forte; and, in 1940, the magnificent Bulldog Turner, who was to be our center for twelve years; Lee Artoe; Harry Clark; Bob Nowaskey; Ed Kolman; and two halfbacks, George McAfee and Scooter Ray McLean.

Luke Johnsos made a rich discovery that let us make the most of our Monsters. "A coach has the worst seat in the stadium," Luke explained.

184

If you go to the Folies Bergère in Paris, sit in the front row, but at a football game, sit high so you can see the teams deploy. One day when playing Brooklyn, I went up to about the fortieth row. I saw a defense that looked crazy. I came down and told Coach the middle was wide open. Coach ordered a receiver to circle back behind the defense line. The quarterback threw him a pass and he went all the way for a touchdown. I went back up into the stands, taking a couple of freshmen to run messages. They were too slow. After the game Halas said: "We'll put in a phone from you to the bench." So was born the Spy in the Sky.

Other coaches learned of our system and demanded phones. I put in a phone for George Preston Marshall but somehow our band stationed itself behind the Redskin bench that day and George Preston Marshall couldn't make out the messages. When the Giants came to play, their phone went dead. We promised an investigation. The telephone company reported the line had been cut at a street junction box. They said a youth had been seen opening the manhole cover and going down into the pit. Of course, the Giants claimed the youth was my son Mugs. Football does breed suspicion.

CHAPTER TWELVE

73–0!

WHEN THE 1940 SEASON OPENED, I felt we were fit for anything or anybody.

We beat the Packers 41–10, George McAfee running a punt 93 yards and Ray Nolting returning a kickoff 97 yards.

We thought the Cardinals would be a pushover—they lost all but one game the previous year. Lo and behold, they beat us 21–7.

We made 30 points against the Giants in the first half, including a 53-yard field goal by Lee Artoe, while holding them to nothing. Then Eddie Miller threw 19 good passes for 252 yards. We won, 37–21.

We went to Detroit. As the first half was ending Harry Clark was tackled within 1 foot of a touchdown. A Detroit man was slow in getting up from him to kill time. Eggs Manske, who had rejoined us, jerked the Detroit staller away. A referee accused Eggs of roughness and penalized us 15 yards. We lost 17–14. I fined Eggs $50 for roughness but everyone contributed—me too.

We ended the season 8–3, best in the West. Washington was best in the East.

How we yearned to get at the Redskins. We had a score to settle. Three weeks earlier we were losing to the Redskins 7–3. With less than a minute to play, McAfee took a pass and reached the 1-yard line. To stop the clock, he pretended to be hurt—we had already used up our quota of time outs. The officials penalized us 5 yards. The clock gave us an option of one running play or two passing plays. With 6 yards to go, Sid Luckman made the sensible choice to pass.

The Redskins spaced themselves widely. The pass failed. Ten seconds! Sid took the ball and faded back. Bill Osmanski scampered around the defense and into the end zone. He was clear. Sid saw him and threw.

"There I was, hands out, just waiting for the ball," Osmanski recalls. "Sid's pass was perfect. Someone, identified to me later as Frank Filchock, grabbed me from behind and pulled my arms tight against my sides. The ball hit my chest and flopped to the ground. The gun went off. I shouted a protest to the referee. Mr. Halas came running."

I was furious! I was ready to tear the referee limb from limb. I knew his ruling of no interference must stand, but I wanted to make my feelings known. He popped into a dugout. All I could do was shout abuse after him. I probably used all of the words I had learned on the Chicago streets and in ball parks and training camps and maybe even made up a few new ones.

187

George Preston Marshall heard of my protests.

"The Bears are a bunch of crybabies," he said. "They can't take defeat. They are a first-half club. They are quitters. They are the world's greatest crybabies."

His comments were reported coast to coast. The words burned into my mind. I did not let the players forget them. You can understand why the game for the championship took on special importance.

Marshall sent me a telegram: "Congratulations. I hope I will have the pleasure of beating your ears off next Sunday and every year to come. Justice is triumphant. We should play for the championship every year. Game will be sold out by Tuesday night."

The game received tremendous press buildup. The 36,034 tickets were snapped up for $102,280, the most ever taken in at Griffith. Reports of scalping were so prevalent that the Washington police brought in 20 men from surrounding forces to help some 120 local cops. They arrested eight scalpers. Mutual Network bought broadcast rights for $2,500. In those days that was good money. More important than that, it brought the game to millions who had never seen a big-league professional football game.

An estimated 150 sportswriters came to see the most effective passing team—the Redskins—versus the most efficient running team—the Bears. In the mood of the early war era, they described the game as a battle between bombers and tanks. The more literate writers saw competition between ponderous power and superlative speed.

The Bear-Redskin rivalry had been sharp. The Skins had defeated us 28–21 for the 1937 championship. The next year we beat them 31–7 in a League game. We didn't meet in 1939.

188

For two weeks we prepared rigorously. We watched the 7–3 game on film a hundred times. We scouted Washington's last two games and gratefully noticed the defense was unaltered.

Clark Shaughnessy called from Stanford to ask if he could help. I accepted as I had only two assistants. He came on Thursday before the game. We discussed for hours which of our plays might be most effective against the Washington defense. We stayed up all night to review again the game movies. We chose about twenty plays. We selected other plays to fit every conceivable pertinent defense Washington might adopt.

I was totally confident of our T-Formation with man-in-motion. Clark was having great success with it at Stanford. The previous season Stanford had not won a game. With the T, they were top in the West and had been chosen to play in the Rose Bowl against Nebraska, where Biff Jones was still preaching the virtue of the wing and the box. Biff was coming to our game. He said he wanted to see how Washington struck down our T. He believed those uninformed persons who claimed that Washington had conceived a strategy which could demolish our T. I invited Clark to come to Washington with us but he had to return to Stanford to prepare for the Rose Bowl game.

We took thirty-three players to Washington. George Musso weighed 270. Writers said Osmanski could pick up a grand piano and run with it. Bulldog Turner was "chosen at random from a rock pile."

Special trains brought 1,499 Bears' fans.

The Redskin star was Sammy Baugh, widely accepted as the most effective passer yet. I heard he had developed his astounding accuracy as a youth by throwing the ball through a tire swinging from a tree. To the fans and the press he was Slinging Sam, but to the teammates he was Fighting Legs. His mates said he would never quit until the game was over.

Writers quoted 7–5 odds on the Bears. They reasoned the Redskins could score with Baugh but we could score with several men.

"I'll never forget the train ride to Washington," Osmanski recalls. "Everyone had his play book out."

"The buildup was like preparation for a war," Sid adds. "We were going to fight and we were going to win. You could feel the emotion, the stress and strain."

"When we came into the dressing room," Osmanski resumes, "we saw that Mr. Halas had pinned the clippings to the wall. When we were ready to go out, he pointed to the clippings and said, 'That's what the people in Washington are saying about you gentlemen. I know you are the greatest football team ever. Now go out and show the world.' We almost broke down the door."

I held Sid back. I gave him three plays. "I want you to call these first," I said. "They will show you whether the Redskins are staying with the defense they used in the last game against us. If they are, you will attack it as we have worked out in the past two weeks."

To the press I said I thought we would win but a championship playoff is anybody's game. If a team is good enough to get into a playoff, it is good enough to win.

The Washington coach, Ray Flaherty, was asked if the Redskins would repeat their earlier victory. He replied, "I don't know." Ray was an honest man.

George Preston Marshall said: "We have whipped them before and we will whip them again."

The Bears won the toss and elected to receive. The Skins kicked to the 5. Our Ray Nolting ran the ball back to the 25. A good start.

Now came the test. Would the Redskins stay with their proven 5-3-3 defense? My first play, a fake reverse with man-in-motion, could start giving the answer. Sid handed the ball to McAfee. The defense reshaped just as it had three weeks earlier. McAfee made 7 yards.

I was delighted. I knew we could collect enough points to win the championship. Our adjusted plays could go time and again through the weaknesses we had detected in the Washington defense.

"I called Coach's second play, an off-tackle play," Sid relates. "McAfee went in motion to the right. I took the ball. Osmanski went hard to the left. I pitched the ball to him. The line opened the hole but a Redskin backer was coming in fast. He got his hands on Osmanski. Osmanski straight-armed him aside and swung to the outside. Osmanski was through."

The Skins' secondary defense, Ed Justice and Jimmy Johnston, were closing fast on a collision course with Osmanski at about the 35. George Wilson threw himself at Justice and knocked Justice into Johnston. All three went down. Osmanski ran the 68 yards untouched.

"Wilson's block was the most ferocious I have ever seen," Luckman says. "He absolutely obliterated both safety men. I signaled the Coach that the Redskins were in the old defense and he could sit back and relax. From then on I did everything he had asked me to do."

Automatic Jack Manders kicked the conversion. Only 55 seconds gone and we were ahead 7–0. I could see this was going to be a great day for the Bears.

Krause took our kickoff on the 4 and ran through our entire forward and secondary defenses. He made 56 yards before Osmanski, our speedy Bullet Bill, brought him down. Son of a gun, the Redskins were also hot. In a few more plays they were on our 28. It was time for

191

Sammy Baugh, Ol' Slinging Sam, to start operations. Charley Malone slipped past our secondary and waited on the 4-yard line. Not a Bear was within reach. It was a sure touchdown if Baugh saw him and if his aim was true. He did, and it was. But the ball went straight through Malone's hands. Perhaps the sun blinded him momentarily. Whatever the cause, thank you, oh thank you! The Redskins tried to pick up a field goal but the kick was bad.

It was our ball on the 20. In seventeen plays, all on the ground, including a beautiful 27-yard run by Osmanski, we were within 1 foot of the goal. Our adjusted plays had the Redskins totally confused. They didn't know where the runner was going. Luckman, carrying the ball for the first time, burrowed through the line for the final foot. The kick was good. 14–0. Eleven minutes gone.

Washington tried to catch up. Baugh threw pass after pass after pass. All failed. His punt was partly blocked. We got the ball on the 42.

I sent Maniaci in for Osmanski and told Luckman to run a special play in which both guards pulled back, the right halfback shifted toward the center and the left halfback went to the right, drawing the secondary in that direction.

Luckman lateraled the ball to Maniaci, the fullback, who took off fast on a wide run to the left behind the right halfback. The left guard went through the line and knocked down the defensive halfback, while the right halfback hit the left end and knocked him into the linebacker. The way was clear. Maniaci ran all 42 yards without a hand touching him. That is the way a play should work when everyone does his job.

192

Martinovich kicked the goal. Suddenly it was 21–0, with 2 minutes 15 seconds remaining in the first quarter.

Baugh left the game. Filchock's passes were no more successful. The Redskins did get one opportunity when a Luckman lateral to Nolting was fumbled, but Nolting recovered for a 14-yard loss.

The breaks were still with us.

In the second quarter, we collected our first interception but lost the ball on a fumble.

Suddenly, Washington's air game began to click. Three passes brought the Redskins from their 19 to our 18. We went into a five-man line. Four passes in a row failed.

The ball went back and forth until Nolting intercepted a Redskins' pass and, a minute later, Luckman threw to Kavanaugh in the end zone and Snyder kicked the goal. 28–0.

Baugh came back into the game. He passed to our 44 and called time out to stop the clock, taking a 5-yard penalty. It was all or nothing. Baugh faded back and back, taking his time, letting the receivers range far. A Bear got his hand on Baugh, but he still threw long and hard and straight to the 5-yard line where Charley Malone was again waiting. Our Snyder and McLean were also there. McLean jumped highest and knocked the ball down. Another time out. Another 5-yard penalty. Time for one more play before the half. Baugh threw again, short and hard. Osmanski intercepted the ball on our 3-yard line. The half ended with everyone on their feet roaring.

Normally, 28–0 at half time would be considered a safe lead, but not against a team with a man like Baugh. In the dressing room, I pointed to new clippings. I told the players, "They also say we're a first-half club." I don't know what Marshall told the Redskins but they came out fired up for the second half—perhaps too fired up. On the first play they were penalized for holding. On the second, Baugh threw a ball to one of our ends, Hampton Pool, who had floated out to the 15 following their left halfback. Pool ran the ball back for a touchdown. Plasman kicked. 35–0. Fifty seconds gone.

The Redskins soon found themselves fourth down and 20 to go on their own 34. Son of a gun; if they didn't try another pass! They were desperate! The ball fell to earth. We got the ball within scoring distance. Luckman called a quick opening play. The left end and left halfback went to the left to draw the linebackers. The guard and tackle opened a good hole in the line. Nolting went through. He feinted Baugh out of his way. The goal was open. It was a simple play. When a quick opener works, it works very well because only a few people are concerned. This time it worked perfectly. Plasman's kick was wide. 41–0.

Soon McAfee intercepted a long pass and ran it back for a touchdown. Stydahar got his turn kicking. He did well. 48–0. Nolting was sent off for swinging a fist.

Bulldog Turner intercepted a short pass on the 20 and scored. Maniaci tried a kick. It was blocked. 54–0.

"Sixty, sixty," the crowd chanted. There were 2 minutes left in the third quarter.

Washington sent in a new backfield.

To start the fourth quarter, I sent in a West Virginia rookie, Harry Clark, to help carry the ball. The Redskins were losing their tempers. One slugged a Bear. The 15-yard penalty brought us to their 43. The quarterback called a reverse. Clark started to the left as though making way for the left halfback who was following close behind with the ball. But after three or four steps, Clark sharply reversed. The halfback flipped him the ball and off Clark went to the right. The defense was totally out of place and Clark made it to the goal behind beautiful blocking. Famiglietti tried a kick. It was wide. 60–0.

"Seventy, seventy!" the crowd chanted.

Eleven minutes remained. On our bench a player said, "This is ridiculous, making them look so bad. Take it easy." He was shouted down.

The Redskins gave us the next score. Filchock missed a pass from center. Jack Torrence recovered on the 2 and Famiglietti pushed over for the tenth touchdown. The referee ran to me. He said he had been supplied with nine balls and eight had been lost on kicks into the stands. If we kicked again, the game would end. I told Saul Sherman, the quarterback at the moment, to pass for the extra point. He threw to Maniaci across the goal. 67–0.

The Redskins persisted in passing. A Bear, Chet Chesney, got his fingers on a pass but couldn't hold it and the ball bounced into the waiting arms of Maniaci, who reached the Redskins' 41 with Chesney blocking. Ten plays brought us our eleventh touchdown.

"Eighty, eighty," the crowd chanted.

Bob Snyder passed toward Maniaci for the extra point but the pass was knocked down. We had to be content with 73–0.

All thirty-three Bears saw action in the game. Ten players scored a touchdown. One had made two. We used so many kickers that one sportswriter said he was waiting for us to bring on Mrs. O'Leary's cow. He declared the hoof that had kicked over a lamp and started Chicago's great fire could have lofted the ball over the goal post.

195

"A game like that is hard to forget," Sid says. "Of all games, I treasure it the most."

Osmanski walked off the field with Baugh. "Don't feel bad, Sam," Osmanski said. "Think what would have happened if Charley Malone had caught the first long pass. A completion might have made a lot of difference."

"Bill, this is the most humiliating game of my entire life," Baugh replied. "If Malone had caught that pass, the score would have been 73–7."

Later Baugh, near tears, repeated the 73–7 statement to the press. You'll find it all in the accounts of the game.

Statistics bore out the score: Yards gained rushing, Bears, 372, Redskins, 31 (net 3). We passed 8 times. Six were good for 120 yards. Washington passed 49 times and completed 21 for 229 yards but we intercepted 8 and ran 5 back for touchdowns.

George Preston Marshall was angry and declared: "Some of those guys quit! We've got to make a few changes." Later, after he cooled off, Marshall said, "Maybe they didn't lose their courage. Maybe they just lost their heads." And still later when he sailed into a party with all the shine of a newly risen sun, he said: "I don't remember a thing."

Headline writers had a problem finding the most accurate words. They used "slaughter," "massacre," "stampede," "overwhelmed," "ripped," "crushed," "scalped." They said we sent the Redskins to the cleaners and took candy from a baby. One historically minded writer said the defeat was the biggest rout since the British sacked Washington and another, searching for a similar catastrophe, recalled Wellington's defeat of Napoleon at Waterloo. A third said the contest evened accounts for Custer's Last Stand.

196

A writer said he had come to boo the Bears but ended up roaring his approval. A gentleman with a faulty crystal ball who had predicted an easy Washington victory said he was now prepared for anything, such as snow on the Fourth of July or Wendell Willkie in the White House.

One writer reported the Bears had not been gentle playmates. How true! Charley Malone left the game with three broken ribs and a bruised kidney after tackling McAfee. Bob McChesney rebroke a broken fist. Max Krause hobbled away with a bad knee. Dick Todd was knocked out by a bang on the head the first time he carried the ball. Our Bears were a bit sore, but all came off the field on their own feet.

A writer who took note of the time we had devoted to devising plays and working out strategy to overcome the Redskin defenses wrote: "Coach Halas comes pretty close to being the number one football genius in the land. The carriers were on their way before they got the ball. The Redskins didn't know where the Bears would strike next."

A writer taking a broad view said: "The Bears did everything right. The Redskins did everything wrong."

Similarly Max Krause said, "They had a good day. We had a bad one."

One gentleman of the press who sought more to explain than exclaim said: "The Bears have a knack of getting aroused. Maybe they really were mad."

That man, I felt, was coming close to the truth. To win a closely contested game, players must have mental heat, a great desire. On that day the Bears had it.

Musso put it this way: "We wanted revenge and we got it."

197

The New York Times' Arthur Daley began his report simply: "The weather was perfect. So were the Bears."

Washington's Coach Flaherty said: "It's just one of those things."

Tuffy Leemans said: "No team on earth could have beaten the Bears today. I've never seen a hotter club. Once a fire has started, there's no way to put it out. I don't know how to explain it."

Tim Mara said: "I'm glad the Giants were not out there today."

I said: "We were just the hottest club in the world today. It's one of those things that will never happen again."

As soon as I could decently depart, I went to the hotel, shut myself in my room, got down on my knees and said a prayer of thanks.

We rode the train to Los Angeles for an exhibition game against a group of professional stars. Some of the opponents told our boys the Bears had erred deeply in beating the Redskins so badly and they were going to bring us down to earth. I missed the game. My appendix flared up. I found myself in the hospital.

Luke took over running the team. As the boys were about to go out onto the field, Luke said, "Coach wants to talk to you." Everyone was puzzled. I had rigged a phone from my bed. I said,

> Men, I feel pretty good. I'll be all right. Men, this is a very, very important game. I have received hundreds of telegrams. I wish I could read them all to you. There is one I do want you to hear. It is from Mayor

Kelly. He says: "The Bears are great. All of Chicago is proud of you." But, men, we won't be great if we don't win this game. So let's go out there and get them.

Bill Osmanski told me later, "Half of the guys were crying. The game was rough. We won 21–7. We won it for Coach George Halas."

Clark invited me to sit on the Stanford bench for the Rose Bowl game. I was feeling pretty good by then and did try to get out of bed, but the pain stopped me. Stanford won. Our astonishing championship victory and now the Stanford win made everyone in football aware of the benefits made available by the modern T-Formation with man-in-motion, the strategy Ralph Jones had conceived ten years earlier, the strategy that for a decade made the Bears the most successful professional team.

At West Point, Coach Earl "Red" Blake telephoned his good friend, Lou Little, at Columbia to ask if Lou could arrange for Sid Luckman to go to West Point and teach the Pointers the modern T with man-in-motion. Red had been Sid's high school coach. Lou relayed the message. Sid said he would be delighted, but he must get my permission. I said, "By all means. Go there and help them. Give Red every bit of information you can. Don't keep any secrets." Sid proposed he call our strategy the Halas Formation, just as other formations were named for their originators. I said, "No, if my name were attached to our modern T, some coaches might be reticent in adopting it." I said I did not want any hindrance attached to our T.

For ten weeks during spring training Sid worked with the West Point staff. Later Pittsburgh, Maryland,

199

Holy Cross and his own alma mater Columbia asked for his help, which he willingly gave. In 1946, Frank Lahey asked Sid to come to Notre Dame to help perfect their use of the modern T. For several years Sid devoted many weeks each spring to Notre Dame.

Greasy Neale adopted another learning approach. He obtained newsreel film of Bears' games and spent most of the winter studying them.

Before the decade ended, the modern T with man-in-motion was the basis for all offensive play in football.

The autumn of 1941 was most enjoyable. We had a great team. We were the Monsters of the Midway. I picked up a Stanford halfback, Hugh Gallarneau; a fullback, Norm Standlee; and, to be safe in the backfield, added Frank Martin from Alabama, Lewis Hamity from Chicago, and Bill Glenn of Eastern Illinois. To the line I added Bernard Hughes, a center from Oregon, and Harold Lahar, a guard from Oklahoma.

We were powerful and smart. Green Bay also had a formidable team. They had been runners up in 1940. As usual in those years, our League season opened in Green Bay. We beat the Packers narrowly, 25–17. In the next four games we scored 184 points, more than we made in entire seasons before our modern T with man-in-motion gave us new scoring abilities. Then Green Bay came to Chicago. They were unbeaten. They produced a defense we had never seen before, putting seven men in the line. They went ahead 16–0. At halftime I gave Sid some new plays that might overcome their strategy. We scored two touchdowns. With a minute and a half to play, we were on their 25-yard line. Sid called a pass. A Packer end,

Harry Jacunski, hit Sid from the blind side and knocked the ball from his hands. Green Bay recovered. The game was over, lost 16–14. "I should have called for a field goal by our Automatic Jack Manders," Sid recalls. "That would have won the game 17–16."

We beat the Rams 31–13, the Redskins 35–21, the Lions 24–7, the Eagles 49–14. The Packers also rolled over their opponents. We both went into December and the final game unbeaten except by each other. I saw another championship and, after that, another, and another, and another. We were the Monsters of the Midway. We had the men, the skill, the mentality. Chicago had the fever.

CHAPTER THIRTEEN

Time Out
for the Navy

.

OUR FINAL GAME of the 1941 season was again with the Cardinals. The outcome was hardly in doubt. We had crushed them 53–7 early in the season. In ten games we had scored 362 points, almost half again as many as during the 1940 championship season. Injuries could not hurt us; our reserves could play a hard game against the starters.

The Cardinals put up a good fight. At half time the game was close. Then over the loudspeakers came a voice: "Ladies and gentlemen: The Japanese have bombed Pearl Harbor." Everyone was stunned. I didn't know what to do. We decided the game should go on. Very few people left. George McAfee broke free and made a beautiful run up the center of the field for a touchdown, winning the game. The final score was 34–24. Our ten-won one-lost record tied us for top place in the conference with the Packers. The playoff and championship games were just ahead.

But the Japanese attack brought to the fore a commitment I had made to myself at the end of World War I. I had gone into the navy as a volunteer and asked for sea duty but the navy had assigned me to the sports program at the Great Lakes Naval Training Station north of Chicago, playing on the base football, baseball and basketball teams and helping to coach football. On discharge I pledged myself that if another war came I would get myself where the action was.

The time had come to make good that commitment. I went to Great Lakes and asked to be sent to sea. The commander, an old friend, Captain T. DeWitt Carr, said I was too old. I was forty-six. I argued, "I'll send your name to Washington," he said. "Maybe someone will pick you up."

I returned to the Bears. In the playoff we beat the Packers 33–14. The Giants came to Chicago for the championship game. We won, solidly, 37–9.

Almost a year passed before a navy punch-card machine seeking a former officer with an engineering degree turned up my card. The navy was building a large base at Norman, Oklahoma, to train aircraft mechanics. The navy reactivated me as a lieutenant commander. My sword was presented during the half time of a game with Detroit, on November 1. We won 16–0. We had met six opponents and soundly whipped them all, scoring 193 points to their 70. The power and mental heat of 1940 and 1941 surged on.

I inducted my son Mugs into the navy, turned over the administration to Ralph Brizzolara, by then vice-president of a steel company, and Frances Osborne, my wonderful secretary from Stanford University who had been recommended to me by Clark Shaughnessy, and

203

made Luke Johnsos and Hunk Anderson co-coaches, with Hunk, a two-fisted guy, responsible for defense and Luke for offense. "The division could have caused trouble, but didn't," Luke recalls. "Neither of us told the other what to do. The team played both ways."

At Norman, I found myself third in command with many duties. I would not have chosen the assignment. The duty I wanted was in the Pacific, fighting the Japs. I hoped an early transfer could be arranged.

My Bears roared on without me, overcoming the Dodgers 35–0, Green Bay 38–7, Detroit Lions 42–0, Cleveland Rams 47–0 and the Cardinals 21–7. For the second time in twenty-two years, my Bears were unbeaten and untied. Percentage 1.000. Our scores totaled 376 to our opponents' 84. We had won eighteen League and playoff games in a row. We punted only thirty-four times all season. The Washington Redskins won the Eastern title. The championship game was scheduled for Washington. The Norman chief of staff and I arranged leave and hitchhiked on military planes to Washington. We lost, 14–6.

"We were beginning to think of ourselves as unbeatable," Sid Luckman recalls. "Coach Halas would never have allowed that. He always told us we must go into every game prepared to meet a superior team. We did not work as before. The inevitable occurred. We ceased being the champions."

During the Christmas holiday, Min and Virginia visited me. Three years earlier I had insisted Gin attend Drexel Institute of Technology in Philadelphia where my brother, Walter, was coaching. I knew he could look after her. Gin had enrolled in a business management course so, on graduation, she could take her place in the

Bears' office. At the start of her senior year she had become engaged to a University of Pennsylvania senior, Ed McCaskey. He was in the ROTC and expected to enter the army as an officer on graduation. He came to Chicago and asked permission to marry Gin. I gave it. They set the wedding for December 18. By then I was at Norman. I told them I could not get leave. They cancelled the wedding.

At Norman I suggested Gin date a junior officer. She declined. "I think that was the first time I ever refused my father," Gin says. "I did feel badly but I am certain I did right." Min went home and Gin returned to Drexel. "Ed and I began resenting having to wait," Virginia says.

I was twenty; Ed was going to war. We ran away to Maryland. We called on Ed's father in Baltimore and then went to a nun's chapel where a priest married us on February 2, 1943, Dad's forty-eighth birthday. In the spring Ed entered army officers' school at Fort Benning, Georgia, Mother came to my graduation. I went to live with Ed's mother in Lancaster. Ed received his commission in December just as Michael, first of our eleven children, was born. Ed was assigned to Camp Blanding, Florida. We rented a furnished house there. When Ed went to Europe, I returned to his mother. I did not see my father until after the war.

Meanwhile, a crisis developed in League affairs. A powerful Hollywood group led by Don Ameche, the actor, and supported by Arch Ward, the *Chicago Tribune*'s sports editor, applied for the Buffalo franchise and permission to move the team later to Los Angeles. I had promised Charlie Bidwill I would back him when Los Angeles opened. I got leave to attend the League meeting. I told Arch I could not go back on my promise to Charlie. The League did not approve the application. Arch was furious. His anger was to prove costly.

We owners had our own arguments. At one point George Preston Marshall said, "George, you're too old to fight a war. Why don't you take off the uniform and let a younger guy do the job?" I went through the roof. Rooney recalls, "I thought Halas would kill Marshall."

Norman quickly developed into a very busy base, with 20,000 sailors and 2,000 Waves learning almost instantly how to repair and maintain planes. Each month we held a parade. I, with sword drawn, led the march past the reviewing stand.

Captain Carr was transferred from Great Lakes to the headquarters of the Seventh Fleet in Brisbane, Australia. Brisbane was also General MacArthur's headquarters. The Seventh Fleet was the general's naval arm in leap-frogging up the New Guinea coast toward the Philippines and Japan. Carr asked for me. Gene Tunney, a special advisor to the chief of naval personnel, supported the request, saying that as the navy's forces expanded, more attention must be paid to physical fitness and recreation. "I was informed you wanted service in the Pacific," he added, in a note to me.

I boarded a troop transport, the *Robert L. Howze*, in San Francisco and after twenty-one days arrived at Milne Bay, a supply base on the southeastern coast of New Guinea, and then flew on to Brisbane. I was made Welfare and Recreation officer for the Seventh Fleet. I would have preferred a place on a warship but, looking back, I can see my years with the Bears did make me more useful in the duty the navy allocated to me. A staff officer, Rudy Custer, was assigned to me. He was most efficient. I tagged him for postwar service to my Bears.

I looked into services provided on ships and at shore stations and found them almost nonexistent. Movies were the most popular shipboard recreation but only large ships had films and most were old. Sailors awarded a day ashore hit the beach with beer, pop and perhaps a baseball and bat. A USO show was a rare event. The navy planned a major base at Manus, one of the newly captured Admiralty Islands, but no orders for equipment or personnel had been written.

I scrounged films and shows from the army, bought sports equipment in Australia, drafted Seabees into building baseball diamonds, volleyball courts, pop and beer gardens. I was surprised to find more sailors drank pop than beer. Soon we had shore recreation centers for 4,000 at Biak, 40,000 at Manus. Admiral Kincaid, the Seventh Fleet commander, presented me with a citation ribbon for "contributing to high morale."

General MacArthur sent for me. "Bob Hope is in Sydney," he said. "You know him well. Please escort him on his tour of forward areas."

I flew to Sydney. Hope's Pacific flight had been eventful. An engine had failed and the crew had dumped baggage to stay above the water. Hope brought comedian Jerry Colonna; Frances Langford, a singer whom I was to serve manfully, carrying her piggyback along muddy roads; Patty Thomas, a dancer; Tony Romano, who played the guitar; and Barney Dean, a comedian.

Bob's troupe gave shows at army and navy hospitals in Sydney. Lord Wakehurst, the governor, and Lady Wakehurst gave a reception. Then we all flew 2,000 miles in a DC-3 bucket-seat two-engine plane to Hollandia halfway up the north coast of New Guinea where MacArthur was setting up his advance headquarters preparatory to the invasion of the Philippines. Bob Hope's troupe gave thirty-one shows in ten days before 185,000 servicemen. Hollandia, Wakde, Toem—the Japs were only 600 yards away—Owi, Noemfoor, Woendi, Aitape, Ndrilo, Lambrum Point, Ponam, Pitylu—how these names bring back memories of exhilarating hours.

At Noemfoor, Lt. Henry McLemore, a sportswriter, invited me to ride his PT boat on a midnight rendezvous with friendly natives. We darted up the coast at 50 knots for four or five hours until we were in enemy territory. I tried to sleep but the roar of the powerful engines, the crash of the water against the thin shell of the PT boat and the thrill of the adventure kept my eyes open. As we neared a native village where our important passenger, a Mr. Black, hoped to meet with the head man and learn about Japanese movements, we cut the engines and waited. A sailor with sharp ears whispered he thought he heard the soft paddling of a canoe. I could hear nothing.

"They're coming," Mr. Black said. "Commander, will you remain aft?" I heard the canoe bump softly against the side of our PT boat. I saw Mr. Black help three dark figures aboard. They sat on the deck and talked. I couldn't restrain my curiosity. I wriggled forward on my stomach until I could hear their voices, but they used a language strange to me. After about 45 minutes, our visitors slipped over the side. Paddles sloshed gently in the water.

We moved slowly along the shore until we saw some huts. The gunners raked them with our 50-caliber machine guns and 40-mm cannon. Then we roared at top speed out to sea and headed home. We arrived at dawn.

208

I asked Mr. Black why we had used our guns. He said the natives had told him the Japs had taken over the village. Mr. Black seemed happy. I assumed the natives had told him much about Japanese movements on the far tip of New Guinea.

Madang was the troupe's last stop. Everyone was worn out but the troupe gave an encore for 4,000 Aussie soldiers clearing the jungle about 50 miles up the coast. The Aussies had not seen a girl's face for years.

On October 23 MacArthur made good his promise to return to the Philippines.

I was promoted to commander. I flew to Leyte and set up shop near Tacloban airstrip to start developing a recreational center for 60,000 sailors. On the third night, three tracer shells floated into the sky. A Jap plane dropped six or eight small bombs along the coral runway. A night fighter swept up to take him on. The Jap came again and dropped another stick of bombs. The gas dump exploded, lighting the sky. One after another, nineteen B-24 bombers blew up. I think the Jap got away.

One night three sailors, with nothing to occupy them at an isolated shore station, saw several local girls pass. The sailors followed them. They did not return. Later we found their bodies, the heads chopped off. The incident supported my contention that men being assembled for the big push ahead must be kept busy and sport had a vital role.

Joe E. Brown, the comedian, toured our ships and shore stations. After the war he came to many Bears' games. We never lost when he sat on our bench.

At Christmas the navy commander in Hollandia, Captain Albert L. King, gave a dinner for Irving Berlin, who was bringing out his show, "This Is the Army." I had lived with All-American football selections. I asked

Berlin: "What are your greatest songs?" He listed: "Alexander's Ragtime Band," "God Bless America," "White Christmas," "Easter Parade," "A Pretty Girl Is Like a Melody," "Say It with Music," and "Always." He said he had written "Easter Parade" in 1917 with the words, "Smile and Show Your Dimple." It got nowhere. He changed the words in 1933 and it became a classic.

The combined forces invaded Luzon in January and entered Manila. The Seventh Fleet's job was over.

The assistant secretary of the navy came to Manila and recommended me to Admiral Nimitz as Welfare and Recreation Officer for the Pacific Fleet and the Pacific Ocean areas. I arrived at Pearl Harbor on May 7. Soon I submitted recommendations to Commodore B.L. Austin, later an admiral. They came back negative. I sent more. Negative. More. Negative. I wrote Austin stressing that as men were assembled for the invasion of Japan, it would be of paramount importance they be kept fit and busy.

Austin replied: "Be ready to fly to Manus at 0800 to report to Admiral Nimitz." I told my convictions to the admiral. He ordered I was to have recreation centers on Okinawa for 30,000 men, more and better movies for all ships, more time on the armed forces radio, more amateur shows, more USO shows, more ice cream machines, a pop bottling plant, our own picture magazine.

I sought suitable recreation sites. Seabees promised centers would be ready by December 1. I flew to Pearl Harbor and on to Washington to cut red tape.

The atom bomb was dropped; the war ended. I thanked God. The invasion of Japan would have taken many, many lives, American and Japanese. Now that horror was not necessary.

210

I was eligible for discharge but Admiral Nimitz asked me to stay on to see that the movement of men and freed prisoners back to the United States—the magic carpet—was as smooth and quick as possible. When the push was over, Nimitz asked if I would like to join the assistant secretary of the navy on a tour of the forward areas in the Pacific and in western Europe. I did not see how I could accomplish much. I told the admiral if the trip were regarded as a reward, I would prefer to see my Bears in action. Admiral Nimitz understood my priorities for pleasure. He presented me with the Bronze Star citing "outstanding ability and initiative in organizing and administering all recreation policies, and installing and operating adequate recreation facilities in the Pacific Ocean area."

Later I was made a captain in the reserve. Rudy Custer, on his discharge, came to the Bears as business manager.

I arrived home after thirty-nine months in time to see my Bears' last two games. It had been a terrible season. My Bears had won only one of eight games. I saw my team tear through the Steelers 28–7 and our old rivals, the Cardinals, 28–20, and send fans home hopeful for the new year.

I found the Bears were quite different from the team I had left three years earlier. Luke Johnsos had kept me informed, somewhat. When we won, he sent a cable. When we lost, he wrote a letter. I think sometimes he put the letter in a bottle and dropped it into Lake Michigan. The cables caused excitement. To save space on the wire he sent the game result as a series of letters and numbers. A suspicious naval intelligence officer thought he caught a spy sending a military secret.

Johnsos recalls:

The war crowded us out of our training camp at St. John's Military Academy at Delafield. Ralph Brizzolara and George's brother Walter arranged with Father John Lefko for St. Joseph's College in Rensselaer, Indiana, to take us in. The college raised cattle so we had the pleasure of eating steak. The toughest thing for me about fall training was telling kids they were not good enough. Mr. Halas used to soften the news with a check for two or three hundred. All we could give them was a handshake. I shoved the job onto Hunk. He'd call in three or four players and say, "You're fired."

We all needed second jobs. I had a sweet wife and two kids and I needed my job at the Zellerback Paper Company. Hunk had a job with a steel company in Detroit. He would come to Chicago Tuesday night and go back Sunday night.

The war cleaned out the colleges. We needed players. Bronko Nagurski had left the Bears in 1938 for big time wrestling. I phoned him. "Bronk," I said, "how about coming back? We'll play you at tackle."

"Oh Luke, no," he said. "I'm not in shape."

"Playing tackle you just stand there and push them around," I said. "You owe it to the Bears, Bronk. Why don't you come back? Just for one year." He came.

We started well in 1943. We tied Green Bay 21–21. We romped 48–21 over the amalgamated Philadelphia–Pittsburgh club and, listen to this, on November 14, 1943, we beat the Giants, 56–7! That was Sid Luckman day in New York. Fans gave him $1,000 in war bonds. So did the Bears. His mother came. Sid threw six touchdown passes. We thought Sid had done enough and sent in a substitute but the team sent the substitute back to the bench. Sid threw another pass. His passes that day totaled 433 yards, a record.

In eight games we made 261 points to our opponents' 112. Then the Redskins beat us 21–7. However, if we could beat the Cardinals in the final game we would still win the Western title. For the Cardinal game, a lot of snow was on the ground. Snow, like mud, is a great equalizer. In the third quarter, we were behind 24–21. Luke told Bronk, "Why don't you go in and see what you can do? We're going no place this way."

Bronk went in. In the huddle he had some words with Bulldog Turner. Then: 4 yards; 6 yards; 4 yards. That's the way Bronk went, with Bulldog opening the way. Then we became stuck. It was the fourth and 4. Sid again gave the ball to Bronk. He drove ahead for a first down. In gratitude, Sid threw the winning touchdown pass. To make sure, we added another touchdown. We won 35–24.

In the dressing room Luke asked Bulldog what Bronk had said to him in the huddle. "Damnedest pep talk I ever heard in my life," Bulldog said. "He told me, 'If you don't want to block for me, all right, but just get out of my way or I'll break your back!' "

In the East, the Redskins again won their division title. We went to Washington for another championship game the day after Christmas, 1943. Everyone expected a passing duel between Sid Luckman and Sammy Baugh. The real contest turned out to be on the ground. Baugh punted early in the game. Sid took the ball and ran, knees high, through the Redskins until only Sammy Baugh was between him and the goal. Sammy dived at Sid. A knee hit Sammy in the head and knocked him out.

213

Sammy was carried off. He returned later but was never at his best, while Sid was masterful. He passed thirty times; twenty-three were good for 508 yards and five touchdowns. We made another 194 yards on the ground. We won 41–21. Players shared $68,679.50, the biggest pool up to that time.

"Hunk and I felt pretty good," Johnsos recalls. "We had gone through the year without Halas. We had lost Artoe, Gallarneau, Stydahar and others. Yet we achieved a championship. Sid was named Most Valuable Player in the League."

"I can honestly tell you we won all those games and the championship because Coach Halas was still there," recalls Luckman. "His vision, his character, his personality were with us."

Then the roof fell in. Johnsos recalls:

We lost 19 of our 28 players to the armed forces. Bulldog Turner joined the air force, was sent to Colorado Springs, played on the service team there and was named to the All-Service squad. McAfee went into the navy. Fortmann joined the navy and was put on a hospital ship in the Pacific. Luckman joined the merchant marine in Washington. For a while Admiral Land let him come to Chicago on weekends to play but then he was assigned to a tanker carrying gasoline to Europe, a risky job. During the Normandy invasion, he was on a transport ferrying troops from Britain to France. Osmanski went into the navy.

Osmanski was sent to marine corps base at Camp Pendleton, California. The San Diego Bombers offered him $1,000 to play one game. "I said I couldn't play

214

under my own name," he says. "That was OK with them; what name should they use? A marine wife at the base had a new baby boy. The father had played football. He was on Guadalcanal. His name was Scott. The baby had been christened Mike but was called "Red." I played as Mike 'Red' Scott and made a couple of touchdowns. The wife sent a clipping to her husband. He got a big kick going around saying, 'What do you know! My son is only two weeks old and he scored two touchdowns.' "

"We tried to get replacements," Johnsos recalls.

We held tryouts at Cubs Park and signed up anybody who could run around the field twice. We had players forty years old, fifty years old. We had a very poor ball club. But people were making a lot of money and audiences held up fairly well. We drew 267,000, only 35,000 fewer than in 1940. We had a 44,000 turnout for Green Bay. Pittsburgh drew only 9,000 but by then it was December and cold.

Through much of the war I watched a boy at Northwestern, Otto Graham. He did not drink or smoke. He was a real religious boy. He was good at basketball, played center field on the baseball team and quarterbacked the Varsity. I figured he would be great with our T. Hunk agreed. So did Ralph. We made him our number one 1944 draft choice.

We tied Detroit for second place in the Western division. We flipped a coin to see which would take his draft turn first. Detroit won and, can you believe it, Freddie Mandel picked Otto Graham. Freddie, who didn't know if a football was stuffed or pumped! His business was department stores. He had bought the Detroit team from Richards. Before Otto could play with Detroit, the navy grabbed him and sent him to Great Lakes, where Paul Brown was coaching. After the war, Paul—and Otto—went to Cleveland. Otto had twelve great years. The Browns won all of

215

their championships until their League expired in four years. The Browns came into our League, made it to the championship game six years and won three times. If only that coin had come up tails!

In 1944 we were top of the division in points—258—but won only six games, lost three and tied one. 1945 was awful. We won three and lost seven. Bears had never performed so poorly. George didn't have much to come home to.

Fans had found football a good way to forget the war for a few hours and attendance, instead of falling off as I had anticipated, held up. Expenses had gone up but for three years Ralph Brizzolara was able to produce sizable profits—$11,816 for the 1942 season on income of $398,748, $12,802 for 1943, $19,157 for 1944. In 1945 fans fell off with our performance and Ralph had to squeeze pennies to end with a surplus of $87.03. I was eager for our veterans to come home from the war, for the Bears to recover their winning abilities, and for our fans to return to Wrigley Field.

During the war, Min had, without telling anyone, begun taking instruction from a Catholic priest. She wanted to be ready to carry out her pledge to herself that if I came home safely, she, baptized a Lutheran, would convert to Catholicism.

Mugs had an idea of her pledge. When he was home on leave, Min asked him to include in his prayers one for a special intention. Mugs thought she meant he should pray for me. He said he always did include me in his prayers. She said, no, she meant he should pray for an intention for her. Min selected a special day for her personal act—V-J day.

With great delight, Min showed me her savings account. We had capital for new ventures!

With the family together again, we exchanged the small Edgewater Beach apartment for a larger one. Mugs earned a business degree at Loyola, came to the Bears and lived at home until he married in 1963. Ed fought with Patton's Third Army in France and Belgium. He went through some bitter battles. He was stricken with hepatitis and spent months in French and British hospitals. The effects lingered for years. When he came home after the war, he and Virginia first lived in New York and then came to Chicago. Ed became a successful sales representative. His company asked him to move to Dayton. Virginia and Ed didn't want to leave Chicago. Ed joined the Bears as vice-president. By then, as Virginia said, everyone in the family had calmed down.

The war still was very much on my mind. I had been impressed by the way so many fine young men served valiantly to bring victory to our country. Our League teams had sent 638 players into the service. Twenty-one were killed. I wanted to do something to help men still in the service. I had seen how the military was excellent in supplying weapons but often, I felt, was remiss in caring for men off the battlefield.

I wondered if I could inaugurate an annual preseason game to raise money to help improve the recreational aspects of service life. I spoke to Ralph Cannon, sports editor of the *Chicago Herald-American*. He was enthusiastic. I presented the idea to the armed forces. A meeting was set with the chiefs of the three services. Cannon and I went to Washington. We were escorted into a conference room at the Pentagon. Precisely on the appointed minute, the door opened.

"Gentlemen, the chiefs of staff," an orderly said.

General Eisenhower strolled in casually, followed by Admiral Nimitz and General Ira Eaker of the air force. Nimitz greeted me and introduced me to General Eisenhower. Nimitz said, "I will be eternally grateful for what you did during the war." General Eisenhower said, "That's a great team you have." He picked up a football which had been brought in for picture-taking purposes and remarked it was more streamlined than the egg-shaped ball he had used at West Point.

"I was really a fullback," he said, "but I played halfback." He said he had learned to pass by throwing the ball end over end. A West Point player, V.E. Pritchard, had been one of the first to throw the ball in a spiral. "Army used the spiral against Navy in 1913," he recalled. "Army won 22 to 9 but the Navy said we were playing basketball."

He said he approved my proposal for an annual charity game. The others agreed. Documents were produced, read and signed. We lined up for a photograph. Eisenhower held the ball. He handed it to Nimitz who said, "We must be careful not to fumble the ball now."

Nimitz told me: "This game will help keep alive the spirit of cooperation between civilians and the military for many years to come."

General Eisenhower lingered behind. Cannon told the general he had been at West Point and visited Marty Maher, the gymnasium custodian. "When I hurt my leg," the general said, "Marty worked his head off trying to get me back into the game. Remember me to him."

I remarked to an aide about the ease with which the meeting had been arranged. "General Eisenhower," he said, "is the most accessible chief of staff Washington ever had. He never forgets he is serving a civilian public. He is a great general because he wins over everyone. But he can be like iron. If someone says, 'The general in command says,' General Eisenhower will break in with, 'I don't care what the general in command says. Tell me what the man who knows something about it says.' "

For the first Armed Forces game I assembled the greatest players of all time as guests:

Don Hutson, end, Alabama, 1934.
Wilbur Henry, tackle, Washington and Jefferson, 1919.
W.W. Heffelfinger, guard, Yale, 1889, 1890, 1891.
Bulldog Turner, center, Hardin-Simmons, 1939.
Jack Cannon, guard, Notre Dame, 1929.
Duke Slater, tackle, Iowa, 1922.
Gen. John Reed Kilpatrick, end, Yale, 1909, 1910.
Jim Thorpe, quarterback, Carlisle, 1912.
Willie Heston, halfback, Michigan, 1903, 1904.
Red Grange, halfback, Illinois, 1923, 1924, 1925.
Bronko Nagurski, fullback, Minnesota, 1929.

The game was played in Wrigley Field on September 1, 1946. It was between the Bears and the Giants. We won, 19–6. The game drew 32,367 and made $69,395.29 for our servicemen. It began a series that continued twenty-five years and produced $1,214,159 for the army, navy, marine corps and air force service funds.

Each year the game gained in popularity, prestige and profit. It opened the new season for colleges and professionals. It outgrew Wrigley Field. I moved it into huge Soldier Field. Military bands played. Drill teams marched. Choruses sang. One year Admiral Nimitz and Mrs. Nimitz came. Rain fell copiously but the admiral, in his dress white uniform, rode around the playing field in the open car.

All Chicago newspapers joined in sponsoring the games. No other sports event received such approbation and support in print. The games were one of the most satisfying experiences in my life.

Bronko Nagurski. It was said that Bronk tackled a Model T parked on the sidelines and it had to be towed to the garage for repairs. Anyway, Red Grange called Bronk "the greatest football player of all time." That is hard to dispute. (*left*)

Bill Hewitt laterals to Bill Karr for the winning touchdown in our 1933 championship game against the New York Giants. In two seasons we lost only three games. (*below*)

The first indoor game in pro football was played between the Bears and the Spartans on December 18, 1932, in Chicago Stadium. (*top*)

We were blessed by having three great quarterbacks on the team: (left-right) Johnny Lujack, Sid Luckman, and Bobby Layne. (*bottom*)

Sid Luckman passing for a touchdown against Detroit in 1946.

Mike Ditka intercepts a pass. (*right*)

The scene after our 73–0 championship victory over the Washington Redskins. (*below*)

Dick Butkus makes a bone crunching tackle. "I'll make this into a championship team all by myself," he told me. He was All-Pro four years running. (*opposite, top*)

I hold the headlines that say it all. (*opposite, below*)

Brian Piccolo. All I have to do is say his name. We all remember. (*far left*)

Gayle Sayers had rare ability supported by courage, enthusiasm and spirit. (*middle*)

Just before the end of our 1963 championship game with the New York Giants. It was Bears 14 and Giants 10, and I wanted us to hold on to the lead. (*above*)

Watching the Super Bowl XIII in Miami with Commissioner Pete Rozelle. "Isn't football a wonderful game?" (*Courtesy of Verno J. Biever*)

CHAPTER FOURTEEN

Number Two Is Not Good Enough

THE VETERANS CAME STREAMING BACK—
McAfee, Osmanski, Kavanaugh, Gallarneau, Turner,
Wilson, Luckman. With all that talent, I lacked enthusiasm for picking up new graduates from colleges.
However, I did not want to lose them to other teams in
our League. Unintentionally, the new American League
came to my rescue. I drafted collegiate players as usual
and let them go to the other league. As far as our League
was concerned, the players still belonged to me. I assumed that in a very short time the new league would
fold and the players would come back to the Bears at a
time when I would need them. In effect, I was putting
the new players on ice, keeping them fit for the time
when my veterans would begin retiring. But things did
not work out quite that way.   .

Having been in the service thirty-nine months, I
knew my veterans would be fed up with petty regula-

tions. When the spring training camp opened, I announced all rules were scrapped. Bears were men, responsible men, self-disciplined men, and would look after themselves.

At a meeting, I asked, "How do you fellas suggest we dress when travelling as a team?"

Someone said, "I think we should all wear shirts and jackets."

"Fine, gentlemen," I said. "We will all wear shirts and jackets. Anything else?"

Someone said, "A tie?" More a question than a fact.

"Thank you for the excellent suggestion," I said. "Is it agreed all wear ties?" More a fact than a question.

Silence.

"Fine," I said. "It is agreed we all wear shirts and ties and jackets. And I assume you gentlemen all insist that shoes be well shined."

Dr. Charlie Pechous, my old boyhood baseball chum, made a long visit to our new training camp. He was surprised to learn players were not given thorough physical examinations on arrival. We assumed a player who had done well in high school and college was physically fit. Charlie offered to look at my Bears. His examination became an annual routine, and other clubs followed our example.

The examinations turned up surprises. Charlie found a rookie with a rheumatic heart. I felt sorry for the kid. He needed the money badly. Charlie said he would approve the kid's playing for one year providing he could have frequent rest periods. Fortunately, or unfortunately, the rookie broke his ankle, ending his play for the season. The next year Charlie told him he should not play. The rookie said he knew all about the heart. He went West and played semi-pro.

We started our first postwar season strongly, rolling up 113 points in the first four games. We beat the Packers 30–7, the Cardinals 34–17 and the Eagles 21–14. We tied the Rams 28–28. Then the Giants beat us 14–0.

We staged a Sid Luckman day. Fans gave him a car and he gave the fans a 24–20 victory over the Redskins. We ended on top of our division and went to New York to meet the Giants for the championship.

Bert Bell, who had just been made our commissioner, heard that gamblers had tried to fix the point spread with two New York players, Frank Filchock and Merle Hapes. The pair had turned the gamblers down but Bell suspended Hapes for not reporting the bribe offer.

Early in the game Sid passed to Kavanaugh for a touchdown. Soon our linesmen hurried Filchock. His pass was bad. Dante Magnani got the ball and ran for a touchdown. In the second and third quarters, expert Filchock passes brought New York two touchdowns, leveling the score, 14–14. Late in the game, we were moving well, with McAfee doing most of the work around end. We reached the Giant 20. Sid noticed Giant backers were being suckered over to the strong side. He called time out and came to me at the bench.

"Now???" he asked.

I said, "Now!!!"

All season we had been practicing a play called "Bingo Keep It" in which Sid would run, a feat rarely assigned to our star passer. We had been hoping we could use it in a championship game.

Sid called the play. It began exactly as the previous ones. Sid took the ball, pivoted as though to hand the ball again to McAfee who was already driving to the left behind a row of blockers. The Giants went for him. Sid put the ball on his hip, drifted around the right end and made a touchdown. Nobody touched him.

"The easiest of my life," Sid reported. He said anybody could have scored.

As a reward, I let Sid play defense for a while. In return, Sid intercepted a pass. A field goal made the score 24–14.

For the seventh time we were champions. Jimmy Conzelman, the same Jimmy from our Staley days and now coach for the Cardinals, came to me and asked, "George, how did you do it? We had the better team."

I replied, "Read Shorty Ray's pamphlet. He recommends teams use 60 percent runs and 40 percent passes. I believe that advice won the championship."

We began 1947 badly, losing the first two games. Then we turned on our power and in the next eight games we scored 301 points. Then we dropped a game to the Rams, 17–14, but shared first place with the Cardinals, who had the best team in their history.

In their backfield they had Paul Christman, Charley Trippi, Pat Harder and Elmer Angsman. Conzelman was still coach. In the deciding game we kicked off. On the first play, the most successful Cardinal receiver that year, Mal Kutner, raced down the field. Our secondary went with him, creating a big gap. Babe Dimancheff entered the hole, took a pass from Christman and ran 80 yards for a touchdown. We never did catch up. We lost, 30–21. The Cardinals went on to beat the Philadelphia Eagles, 28–21, for the championship.

I regretted the Bears did not keep the championship

but I regretted more that my good friend and long-time supporter, Charlie Bidwill, did not live to see his Cardinals win their first championship. His wife, Vi, and sons were continuing with the team and I did congratulate them heartily on the long-sought success.

I also congratulated Greasy Neale on bringing the Eagles into the championship class. All through the previous winter, he had studied Bears' films I had given him at his request. From the films he had learned our modern T-Formation with man-in-motion. All season he drilled the strategy into the team. The Eagles' success was one more proof of the modern T's superiority.

It may have been that year that Sid Luckman did a good deed for Min. She had long plagued him to kick on an early down. I had told Sid never to do this; the quick kick can move the ball far down the field but it gives the ball to the other team. The yardage gained is not worth the loss of the ball.

But one day when the Bears were safely ahead, Sid felt a strong wind at his back and a stronger desire to please Min.

We were on the 8-yard line. Sid quick-kicked. The wind carried the ball about 75 yards. Everyone in the park heard Min shout: "That's my play! He did it for me!" After the game, Sid kissed Min and told her the kick was indeed for her. She said, "You must do it again." That he did not do.

In 1948, two spectacular quarterbacks came into the draft—Bobby Layne of Texas and Johnny Lujack of Notre

Dame. I did not want these potential stars to be put on ice. To bring them into the Bears immediately—against stiff competition from the other clubs—I paid Layne $22,000 and Lujack $18,000. I continued to start Sid on offense. I put Lujack on defense and kept Layne in reserve.

Into the line came George Connor. He had enrolled at Holy Cross in 1941, had gone to the navy and the Pacific, and had come back to Notre Dame. On graduation, the Giants drafted him but he told Mara he wanted to play only in Chicago, his home town. The Maras traded him to Boston. He told Boston he wanted to play only in Chicago. The message got through. He came to us, very mature, very fit, very experienced, most determined.

The 1948 opening game was again with the Packers, our most popular rival. We walloped them 45–7. We rampaged on, collecting 98 points against the Cardinals, the Rams and the Lions. Then we went to Philadelphia, where Greasy Neale was adding a powerful running game to the modern T. We lost, 12–7. We went into our final game with ten wins and one loss. As in 1947, only the Cardinals stood between us and a division title. It was a tight game, an excellent game apart from the final score: 24–21, for the Cardinals. Again the Cardinals won in the West, the Eagles in the East. The game for the championship was played in Philadelphia in a blizzard. Players disappeared into the swirling snow. Philadelphia won, 7–0, on a fumble.

We could have taken consolation in one fact: We had scored 375 points, topped only in '41 and '42. Our defense was also excellent, allowing only 151 points. Lujack had picked off nine passes.

During 1948, attendance at League games passed three million. My Bears were the most popular team, averaging 41,144. Washington drew 32,585; Pittsburgh 29,819; the Cardinals 28,054; Philadelphia 25,927; Los Angeles 25,590; the Giants 22,671. Poor Boston drew only 9,058. The League average was 25,420. That year the Bears' income passed a million dollars.

I was so confident we would have another championship in 1949 that I walked into my biggest blunder. Ted Collins needed a quarterback desperately. He pleaded with me to give him Bobby Layne. Ted was such a pleasant man. I happily passed hours listening to his stories. I agreed reluctantly. Ted also gave me $50,000 and two draft choices. I still had Luckman and Lujack. But within months Sid developed a thyroid condition and was out much of the 1949 season.

Our final game of the 1949 season was again with the Cardinals. We shattered them 52–21, but the Rams had beaten us twice and the Giants once. The Rams had won only eight games to our nine, but they had two ties so they won the division title. Neale's Eagles were tops in the East for the third year. They beat the Rams, 14–0, and again were champions.

Arch Ward's American League finally folded. I opened the Bears' door to welcome the players I had put on ice. Lo and behold, owners decided unanimously, apart from me, that each team could take in only three iced players. All other players would go into a pool to be drafted by teams in inverse order to the 1949 standings. I had outsmarted myself.

Now I really paid the piper.

My veterans were tiring. Sid was far from his best. Lujack was helping on offense supported by a rookie, George Blanda, who had a remarkable talent for kicking conversions. He was to produce a string of 156 conversion kicks over five years without a failure. We managed to tie the Rams 9–3 for the 1950 conference title but lost the playoff to them 24–14. For the fourth year in a row we were number two.

One by one my war veterans retired. Sid retired from play after the 1950 season. He had been important in achieving four championships and five division titles. He had completed 904 of 1,744 passes for 14,686 yards— eight miles. Sammy Baugh said Sid was the greatest passer of all time. "No," replied Sid, "Sammy was the greatest." Sammy was the better passer but Sid was the greatest all-around quarterback. Sid joined our coaching staff.

I also missed Bulldog Turner. He had provided so much excitement on and off the field. There is a story that one night Bulldog fell from a third-story window of a hotel. An awning broke the fall. As Bulldog brushed himself off, a policeman ran up. "What happened?" he asked. "I don't know," Bulldog is supposed to have replied. "I just got here myself."

Hunk Anderson, who had played with the Bears four years in the early twenties, and coached for eight after a very successful career at Notre Dame, left to devote full time to his steel company job. I brought in Clark Shaughnessy as defense coach.

My worst problem was at quarterback. It became intense when Lujack injured his throwing arm. I went from feast to famine almost overnight. In 1954 I was able to sign two good men, Ed Brown and Zeke Bratkowski. But after just one season, I lost Zeke to the military draft for two years.

I had better success with linesmen, picking up Bill Bishop, a fine tackle, and Bill George, a guard who developed into one of our best linebackers. He was sharp in a pinch. He could tell almost instantly where the play was going and put himself into position to stop the run or pass. I signed Bill McColl, 6 foot 4 and smart, a medical student who used his years with the Bears to complete his training as a surgeon. "Halas university," he called it. And on the tenth round of the 1955 draft I obtained Rick Casares, a powerful running back. What a boy! Other owners steered away from him because of an earlier injury. He was soon setting rushing records. Pain could not stop him, nor slow him. Colleges were turning out excellent Black players. I signed Eddie Macon.

At a Southern All-Star game, Clark Shaughnessy overheard two coaches talking about a small-college player, Harlon Hill, who had been ignored by the selectors but in their opinion was the best receiver in the South. Clark investigated Hill's performance at Florence State Teachers'. I signed Hill. He had an uncanny knack for pulling down impossible passes.

Our seven wins and five losses in 1951 dropped us to fourth place. We won only five games the next year and three in 1953, although in five of the eight losses we trailed by one touchdown or less. Our fans showed their displeasure. Receipts from home games declined from $730,554 in 1950 to $578,373 in 1953. I was able to cut our costs by merely $73,000. Only new money from television kept us in the black—and by only $354.44. The rebuilding began to produce results in 1954. Eight wins and four losses restored us to second place. We repeated in 1955.

An old naval friend, Admiral Dan Gallery, came to Chicago. Some years earlier he had written for *The Saturday Evening Post* a story about a football team's installing tiny radio receivers in helmets. I asked him if the story were true. "No," he said, "but the feat could be accomplished." I met with Paul Galvin, head of Motorola, and others. We buried a wire around the field to act as a transmitting aerial and put radios into the helmets of the quarterback and the defense captain. For three games I radioed instructions. The secret leaked. The League banned the operation.

My third decade as coach did not produce the glorious victories of the earlier years although we did achieve one championship and we did reach one playoff. Our win-loss record was the best in the division.

I had turned sixty. At the end of the 1955 season, I retired as head coach, and handed the head coaching job to Paddy Driscoll, my friend and colleague for forty years. I felt I owed him the satisfaction of being head coach before he ended his career. I told Paddy, privately, the job would be his for two years and then I would return.

I moved from the bench into the owner's box on the stadium rim. From there I saw many details I had missed from the worm's eye view of the bench. I made copious

230

notes. After each game I communicated suggestions to Paddy.

We lost the first game to Baltimore 28–21. At Green Bay, the Bears' kickoff sailed across the goal line. Usually the receiver would let such a mighty kick go and the ball would be brought out to the 20-yard line. But on this day the Packer back, Al Carmichael, threw away caution, took the ball 7 yards behind his own goal line and ran through our entire squad. No professional had ever run so far. Nevertheless, we won the game 37–21.

We put down the Colts 58–27 in a replay. We lost to the Lions and tied the Giants. Our 9–2–1 record brought the division title. Ed Brown led the League in passing, completing 57 percent. Forty-seven passes went to Harlon Hill. Casares rushed for 1,126 yards.

We flew to New York for another championship game. It was 1934 all over again except on this icy day we too wore tennis shoes. On game morning, Shaughnessy produced a new game plan. We lost the toss. Gene Filipski took our kickoff and ran it back 58 yards, leading to a Giant score. At the half, I was fidgety. I came down to the bench and fought a tough battle with myself not to interfere. We were beaten horribly, 47–7. The following year our defense reduced the opponents' points from 246 to 211 but our offense collapsed. In 1956 we had made 363 points. In 1957, the total was a paltry 203, the fewest since 1945. Our 5-won 7-lost record dropped us next to bottom. Amazingly, Green Bay was in the cellar, having won only three games, one of them against us.

I resumed the position of head coach, keeping Paddy as one of my assistants. Once again I needed to rebuild. This time I had a strong treasury. Bears' income that year passed a million and a half dollars and was rising by $100,000 or so a year. On the horizon glittered television's bags of gold. Shortage of cash had ceased to be a problem but the cascade of dollars was already changing attitudes and creating new problems.

The days of gold were ahead but already I was looking back on the lean years as the good old days.

CHAPTER FIFTEEN

My Promise Brings Trouble to All

WE OWNERS were a tight little group. We had gone through a lot together. We had helped one another. We had worked out a good system for composing schedules which provided competition and produced maximum attendance. We had developed rules to provide excitement for fans and protection for players. We had built a workable relationship with colleges. We had collected a good body of officials who knew the rules and made sure of fair play. We had held off gamblers and other nefarious interests. We had worked out a system of selecting players that gave weak clubs an extra opportunity to become strong. We had to the best of our abilities become professionals dedicated to the game of football.

As with most organizations, we perhaps were too unresponsive to newcomers wanting to join our League. After almost a quarter of a century, professional football was confined to ten cities. Several other cities were big enough to support a professional team. College football was strong coast to coast.

But we liked things the way they were. We did our best to keep things that way.

Looking back I can see our closed door was certain sooner or later to produce trouble for us.

I have related how early in the war Arch Ward asked me to support a franchise for Don Ameche in Buffalo to be moved later to Los Angeles and I told him I had promised to back Charlie Bidwill if and when a West Coast franchise appeared. The Buffalo franchise proposal came before the League. We turned it down.

Arch then set about organizing a new league. By November of 1944, he had assembled the United States Professional League with headquarters in Chicago. This league announced it would give franchises in eight cities: Chicago, Boston, Philadelphia, Washington, Akron, Cincinnati, Baltimore and—to my surprise—Honolulu. Also to my surprise, there was no mention of Los Angeles, the city which had started all the trouble. In Chicago, the promoters negotiated with the White Sox to use their park, ousting the Cardinals just as C.C. Pyle had done twenty years earlier.

A pro star, Cliff Battles, was being counted on to take one team. Other backers included Mike Sewell, manager of the championship St. Louis Browns baseball club; Lee Firestone, the tire man; and Dr. Samuel E. Lee, a surgeon well based in Chicago and Honolulu.

The group needed a big name just as we did when we formed our League in 1920. In our time, the biggest name was Jim Thorpe and we made him our president. In 1944, the biggest name in football was Red Grange. They made him their president. We replaced Thorpe after a year. Red stayed with the new league only a few months.

Grange said there was room for two leagues. He said the new league would not lead to a bidding race for players. He said the new league would build covered stadiums. The league was planned to start play in the autumn of 1945.

There were many problems. Play did not begin in 1945. The league reorganized as the All-American Football Conference. The prime mover was Ben Lindheimer, big in horse racing. He joined with Don Ameche, drew in Bing Crosby, Pat O'Brien and Louis B. Mayer, head of MGM movie studios. Together they had lots of money. They formed a Los Angeles club, the Dons.

Dan Topping, part owner of the New York Yankees baseball club and Yankee Stadium, held our franchise in Brooklyn and wanted to move the team into Yankee Stadium. But our New York franchise holder, the Mara family, said no. Dan joined the new conference and moved.

The strongest new team was set up in Cleveland by a businessman there, Mickey McBride. He was advised Paul Brown was the most promising coach outside professional football. Paul had begun making a name in the 1930's as coach of a high school team in the great old Ohio football town of Massillon. His team won six state championships. In one year the team made 477 points while allowing their rivals a total of 6. In 1941 he moved to Ohio State. The Associated Press said his 1942 team was the best in the land. Brown joined the navy and was sent to Great Lakes. A lot of good players had gone into the navy. He built a very strong team. It beat Notre Dame. On Sundays, he brought four or five players to watch the Bears. He wrote down every play and incorporated many into his game book. He became a master of our modern T-Formation with man-in-motion. McBride hired Brown for $25,000 a year plus 15 percent of any profits, a fabulous contract in those days. Brown took with him to Cleveland several of the best Great Lakes players. He imposed strict discipline. His players had to be neat and sharp. His teaching began with fundamentals—how to run, how to carry the ball, how to block, how to tackle. He drilled the men hard. He was ruthless in getting rid of anyone who did not measure up to his expectations. He organized the search for new players and the scouting of rival teams. McBride named the team after the coach.

McBride had another asset, a double-decked stadium with 83,000 seats. The city built it for the 1934 Olympics but the games had gone to Los Angeles. For twelve years the stadium had seen only an occasional event.

The new conference announced it would abide by our ban on signing collegians until their class graduated but it ignored our rule against taking players from another professional club. The bidding became high. Mara's payroll went from $100,000 in 1944 to $300,000 in 1947. In Chicago, a rich promoter offered Sid Luckman $25,000 a year for five years to become player-coach or just coach. He deposited $25,000 in a bank. Sid said no. He told me: "I was honored and flattered by the offer but my life is destined to be spent in football with you." In all things, Sid was loyal.

Three clubs offered a place to George McAfee but he came back to us on a three-year contract.

The Dons sought Johnsos. One day at the races,

Lindheimer asked Luke why he would not go to Los Angeles.

"Would you ask your horse trainer, Ben Jones, to coach a football team?" Luke asked.

"That would be ridiculous," Lindheimer said.

"Would you hire George Halas to train your horse Citation?"

"Of course not."

"Well, Mr. Lindheimer," Luke said, "you know the horse business but you don't know a thing about football. Why don't you stay in the horse business? The football game isn't ready for two leagues. You are going to lose your shirt."

A year later Lindheimer told Johnsos, "I wish I had listened to you. You would have saved me a million and a half dollars."

On our side, Dan Reeves asked the League in 1945 for permission to move his Cleveland team to Los Angeles. We turned him down. "If that is your final word," he said, "I'll sell the club." We selected another word—OK! How fortunate that was. Had we stayed with no, the West Coast would have become a monopoly of the new league. Californians took to pro football. Reeves' opening game with the Washington Redskins in Los Angeles drew 95,000.

Paul Brown's Browns won the American Conference championship in 1946. And 1947. And 1948. And 1949. His box office complained the uncontested victories were reducing attendance. Brown said he had just one objective—to win. If the fans didn't like it, they could go elsewhere.

By 1949 everyone was hurting from the bitter competition. Raiding was cutting into team morale. A team could carve the heart out of a player in the rival league by offering him a lot of money even though it had no intention of hiring him. The Philadelphia club was sold to a syndicate. The Chicago Rockets were sold, became the Hornets and then vanished. The Boston Yanks moved into New York as the Bulldogs.

In 1950, the American Football Conference folded. We took in Paul Brown's Cleveland Browns, the San Francisco '49ers and Baltimore.

Again we were a united League, with thirteen teams, coast to coast but with no club in the South. We organized ourselves into the National conference with seven teams, the Bears, Los Angeles, New York Yanks, Detroit, Green Bay, San Francisco and Baltimore, and the American Conference with six teams, Cleveland, Giants, Philadelphia, Pittsburgh, Cardinals and Washington. Los Angeles beat the Bears for our title while Cleveland beat the Giants. For the National Football League championship, Cleveland beat Los Angeles 30–28. Baltimore departed. We settled down at twelve and there we stayed for a decade.

CHAPTER SIXTEEN

Pot of Gold, or Time Bomb?

ONE MORNING EARLY IN 1947 I dropped in on Don Maxwell, by then city editor of the *Chicago Tribune*. I found him standing in front of his desk looking at a little black box, about 2 feet square, with a glass front on which fuzzy pictures were moving about.

"There it is, George," he said. "Television."

We watched the picture for a few minutes. Don asked, "What do you think of it, George?"

"The picture is so small, Don," I said. "What is it, about eight by ten inches?"

"Something like that."

"I don't think you could see much of a football game in a picture that small, Don," I said. "And the pictures are so fuzzy. They remind me of the early Doug Fairbanks movies I used to see at the Bijou Nickelodeon but those pictures were a lot bigger."

239

"You're right, George, but the television picture won't be like this very long. It will become larger and clearer. And before long it will be in color."

"How long, Don?"

Don said he couldn't even guess but he would bet that television would develop a lot faster than movies did. Television was starting with one big advantage. It had sound. Movies needed fifteen years to get sound.

"Will television ever be much more than a toy for grownups?" I asked.

"George," Don said, "that little box will change the American way of life. Think of this: You can point a camera at just about anything anywhere and deliver the picture instantly on a set miles away. In time you'll be able to deliver the picture into every home in America."

"That's a pretty impressive thought," I said.

"For spreading information, there never has been anything like it," Don said. "I wish I knew what effect it will have on newspapers. We have a lot of arguments around the shop whenever anyone mentions television. We agree it will have an impact. But whether for better or worse, no one knows. The argument here revolves largely about whether newspapers should join television or fight it."

"What do you think?"

"We had much the same argument when radio came in during the twenties. Colonel McCormick said the *Tribune* must get into radio. He had vision. Publishers who took the other tack soon regretted it. Today the colonel has the same approach to television. Our station, WGN, is gearing up for pictures."

We watched the picture a while longer.

"I can't see a football field shrunk to that size," I said.

Don looked at me, mockingly, teasingly, the way he did when he was about to spring a challenge.

"Well, George," he said, "what are you going to do about television?"

I confessed I had not given it a thought.

"You'd better, George," Don said. "Television is coming fast. We both had better try to treat it as a friend rather than an enemy or rival. We'd better get in on the act early and try to make television go our way as much as we can."

I began asking questions about television and, when passing a showroom with a set, pausing to look at the pictures.

One station, WBKB, was on the air in Chicago. It was owned by Balaban and Katz, the big Chicago movie chain aligned with Paramount Pictures. The Balabans were an eager family of seven boys and three girls.

The Balabans had opened some of the first movie houses in Chicago. By the late twenties they were erecting luxurious movie palaces. In the Depression, Paramount fell on hard times. The eldest brother, Barney, went to Hollywood, took over the Paramount presidency and turned the company around. A younger brother, John, ran the Chicago movie houses.

Britain had the first television in the thirties but used a mechanical process. In America, Dr. Vladimir Zworykin had invented the iconoscope tube and put television on the right technical track. In 1940, the federal government issued three permits for experimental stations. One went to Balaban and Katz. They hired a brilliant electronics man, Captain William Eddy. He had been in the American submarine service. An explosion in the mid-

241

thirties had almost deafened him and put him on the retired list.

Captain Eddy set up station W9XBK at 190 North State Street and soon began broadcasting the required one hour a day, although in all of Chicago there were fewer than twenty sets, bought by people willing to help test reception under various conditions.

Pearl Harbor put television on ice. Television is similar to radar. All military services needed radar. The navy inducted W9XBK's technicians. To keep the station on the air, Captain Eddy trained women. With approval of the Balabans, the captain set up a radar training school for the navy. The sailors lived at Navy Pier and studied at the station. The school became very important and turned out some very fine technicians. The navy promoted Eddy to commodore and gave the station the navy's E pennant for its excellent contribution to the war effort.

The wartime experience convinced the Balabans that television, thanks to electronic developments achieved by work on radar, was about to explode onto the unsuspecting public. The Balabans asked permission to turn W9XBK into a commercial station. The government, remembering the station's war record, quickly acceded. W9XBK became WBKB, property of Balaban and Katz Broadcasting, a subsidiary of Balaban and Katz and Paramount Pictures.

The Balabans exhibited faith. Few television sets had been made during the war. The first WBKB telecast went out to fewer than fifty receivers. But factories were setting up production lines and soon a thousand sets were being sold in Chicago every month. Most went to bars. Before long just about every bar had a sign, "TV INSIDE."

Eddy needed programs. He tried wrestling and found the sport could be televised. The action was confined to a small space. Wrestling proved acceptable to bar clients. Before long, the saloons were packed whenever wrestling was on the air. Suddenly, wrestling was big time.

Most of the first postwar sets had a 10-inch screen. The picture was fuzzy. It flared and faded. But people watched, almost in awe. The mesmerizing abilities of TV became apparent early. Before long, manufacturers offered plastic bags filled with cod liver oil which, when placed in front of the screen, magnified the picture. The bags added a yellow tone but everyone considered the advance fabulous.

In 1947, television was starting to enter the home. Eddy needed a wider range of programs. How about football? Eddy became interested in football just as I was becoming interested in television. I was beginning to look upon it as a help in telling people about the Bears, just as, for years, newspapers and radio had spread the word and built interest. We had been playing for more than a quarter of a century and I hoped every person in Chicago with any interest in sports knew about the Bears. But how about people in Minneapolis? In St. Louis? In Cedar Rapids? In Louisville? In Indianapolis? How about all those Notre Dame fans only 130 miles away in South Bend? Did they realize what a good game professional football had become? Tens of thousands of people in these cities within reach of Chicago went to college games every Saturday. I was confident our game was more exciting than the college game and if we could get the word through, quite a few college football fans

243

would start timing visits to Chicago to coincide with a Bears' game.

Eddy and I sought each other. With one voice, we asked each other, "How about putting the Bears on WBKB?"

He needed a ready-made program with popular appeal. The Bears needed publicity. Agreement was easy. WBKB would televise all six home games in 1947. It would pay the Bears $900 a game. It would pay? I couldn't believe it. The money was an unexpected bonus. It did help fade the dreadful prospect, which arose now and then, of bars being packed with Bears' fans watching the Bears play in an empty stadium. I set aside that worry, for the time being, by telling myself that by the time the season began, there would be only seven or eight thousand sets in the Chicago area. Anyway, as Don had said, television was coming fast and I had better see how it could be best fitted into the Bears' future.

The year 1947 was great in the back office. Our receipts almost doubled. Television may have helped, marginally. Salaries exploded but we ended well in the black.

The season proved financially satisfactory to WBKB also. Following the custom set in radio, the station sold the series to one sponsor, The Canadian Ace Brewing Company.

The station set up two cameras in Wrigley Field. They were big, awkward, slow to move and focus. On fast-moving plays, the action became fuzzy. Red Grange gave a play-by-play account and a popular radio announcer, Russ Davis, commented. The pattern is followed to this day. Sterling Quinlan handled the sound.

244

Eddy erected microwave relay towers on farms between Chicago and South Bend and on Saturdays he brought the Notre Dame game into Chicago.

I began to see the wisdom of Don Maxwell's forecast that television would change the American way of life. It was indeed a genie, capable of bringing benefits or disaster far beyond our vision. I determined to increase my effort to make television work for the Bears. The question was: Would new fans enticed by television into Wrigley Field outnumber present fans enticed into staying home to watch the game from the comfort of an easy chair? Thankfully, the size and quality of the picture did not make the easy chair the equal of a stadium seat for viewing a game.

I did not foresee television as a major producer of money for the Bears. Some money would come, yes, just as radio had brought a few dollars. My future actions would be governed by television's effect on the box office.

By mid-1948, so many sets were coming into Chicago homes that I lacked enthusiasm for having our games televised. However I did not want to break off a good working relationship with TV so I agreed that WBKB could televise our traditional final game with the Cardinals. The Pabst Brewing Company paid $5,000 as sponsor. For me the important fact was the game was carried into Milwaukee and Cleveland, sites of prospective ticket buyers, as well as into Buffalo and New York.

WGN began carrying pictures that year. On Thanksgiving Day it brought into Chicago the Cardinals' game in Detroit, thanks to Pabst Brewing Company's $5,000. We were not playing in Chicago that day so the telecast could not take any of our fans.

245

In 1949, only one Chicago game was televised, the meeting of the Bears and the Cardinals. The Standard Oil Company of Indiana, which had long supported Bears' radio broadcasts on a 25-station network, was the TV sponsor. Our share was $5,300.

During those three years we learned much about the technique of televising football games. Equipment improved immensely. Pictures were larger. Sets were proliferating. Other clubs were making a variety of arrangements with local television stations. Costs were rising so fast that the radio custom of sponsorship was becoming financially impossible. Stations began selling spot announcements.

The argument over television as friend or foe heightened. Nobody really knew. We were all operating without facts; 1950 was to be the year of decision.

I, a cautious man with no outside income to speak of, was most careful to preserve ticket sales. I was wary of helping provide Chicago fans with seats outside the gate. By so doing I was not enhancing my popularity. Critics said I was depriving the sick, the lame, the aged, child-laden mothers and others who could not easily come to Wrigley Field of the pleasure of seeing the Bears play. In time I was depriving them of the right to see a game. Critics even muttered I was unconstitutional.

Rudy Custer, our business manager, worked out a compromise. We filmed the Sunday games. On Monday Rudy and Bill Fay clipped the highlights and put them together for a half-hour show. The patched film was run on Tuesday night before WBKB cameras. Red Grange and Luke Johnsos adlibbed. "The Quarterback Show," we called it. Standard Oil paid the cost. I approved, totally.

In Los Angeles, Dan Reeves, owner of the Rams, took the opposite position. He signed with an LA station to televise all Rams games, home and away. Fortunately for him, Reeves did insert a provision that should the telecasts reduce the ticket sales, the TV sponsors would reimburse the Rams. We all watched. Attendance did drop, by one third. The sponsors paid the Rams $307,000 for lost ticket sales. The experiment told me I must do all I could to keep our games off Chicago screens and beam our games outward throughout the area Colonel McCormick liked to call Chicagoland. I could not rely on television to do this job. Television's prime objective would undoubtedly be to flood the rich Chicago market with football telecasts, something I did not want. I enlisted the Cardinals. I delegated Rudy Custer to the task.

Dumont was seeking a big place in television as a maker of sets and a supplier of network cables. I rented space on its cables to Minneapolis, Rock Island and Omaha every Sunday during the season, and to seven other cities—Bloomington and Indianapolis in Indiana, Columbus, Cincinnati and Dayton in Ohio, Louisville, Kentucky, and Nashville, Tennessee—on eight Sundays. WGN cameras picked up the game of whichever team was playing in Chicago, the Bears or the Cardinals. Dumont distributed the signals to the stations which sold local advertising to help pay line costs. It was quite an operation. We took a big gamble but Rudy worked hard and we finished with a loss of only $1,750. The Quarterback Show more than met the loss. Radio broadcasts earned $33,000.

I told Rudy he had worked wonders but next year he

247

would have to double them. He did. He signed fifteen stations. Standard Oil paid $30,000 for half of the commercial breaks. Dumont tried to form a national network to carry selected NFL games. The effort was premature.

ABC was waking up to the siren call of professional football and agreed to operate our network. It hoped to find a national sponsor but failed. Each station sold its own time. We made one innovation. In late September our network televised a game between the Cardinals and the Washington Redskins at Comiskey Park on a Monday night. Rudy's work yielded a cash profit for the season of $4,467.93 and prime exposure in the heartland of America.

ABC offered to extend the experiment for two years and pay $50,000 a year. Before we could say yes, fainthearts in ABC inserted a clause committing us to meet half of any losses. In New York, the Maras were building a network North into New England. In Washington, George Preston Marshall saw television as aiding his drive for fans in the South. The League had no southern team and Marshall was trying to project the Redskins as the hometown team for the entire South. He did well in the Carolinas and Georgia but when he tried to go farther he met us. At the time, the only cables into the South ran through Louisville and Jackson. We controlled both. I did not need a telephone to hear his roar of frustrated anger when we carried our games into Memphis, Nashville, Birmingham, Tampa and Miami. Our TV profit of $37,000 was very welcome because home attendance dropped radically and only television and radio money kept our income above a million dollars. Radio and television earned more for us than all pre-season games.

248

For the next year ABC doubled its offer to $100,000. I thought the sum huge until NBC paid that much to broadcast one game—the championship between Los Angeles and Cleveland in Los Angeles, coast to coast.

By the mid-fifties we had the biggest independent sports network in America. Running it was becoming a considerable task requiring increasingly refined expertise in several specialized fields. I was not disturbed, thus, when in 1956 CBS asked to take over the whole operation. CBS was trying to build a series of regional networks, each centered on a major city. Our network demonstrated the pulling power of professional football. We handed over. We were spared the work and worry, and were assured a radio and TV income of about $200,000 a year for several years. We still controlled the cables in and out of Chicago. Television could not move outside games into the city to compete with our own home games.

Television audiences rose into the millions. NBC estimated the 1958 championship game between the Giants and Baltimore was seen in 10,820,000 homes, indicating an audience of 30 million. The number boggled my mind. I found myself adding zeros to every kind of calculation. Peeking into the future, I glimpsed professional football on a scale I had not wildly contemplated as possible.

A new worry arose. I have written of the many times adversity brought benefits and of how prosperity, when that beautiful lady came along, brought problems. Television was bringing prosperity on a new scale and problems of similar size. Networks were able to play one club team against another, to our overall loss. In 1960 ten clubs were on CBS, two on NBC; the Browns had their

own network. Television was trying to dictate scheduling. Most monstrous, television money was enrich-
ing big-city clubs—the Bears, the Giants, the Rams—at
the expense of the small-city clubs. The League was
again on the road to disaster. Once again salvation lay in
sharing.

I spoke to the Maras, to Reeves and to Commissioner
Bert Bell. We proposed all clubs assign television rights
to the League, the League make all television contracts and revenue be shared equally.

Bert Bell died of a heart attack watching a game. We
chose Pete Rozelle, general manager of the Rams, as our
new commissioner. Our constitution gave the commissioner power to make League contracts. In 1961 the
League sold CBS the right to televise all regular League
games for $4,660,000 a year, or about $350,000 for each
club, but a judge ruled we violated the anti-trust laws
and voided the contract. Senator Dirksen and other farsighted men in Congress pushed through a bill legalizing
single network contracts. President John Kennedy
signed it into law. We began negotiations anew.

We set up a television committee with Art Modell as
chairman. He had been in television before he bought
the Cleveland team. In 1962 the League sold CBS the
rights to all regular season games for two years for
$4,650,000 a year, or about $350,000 for each team.

Television contracts opened a new financial era for
professional football. The value of franchises doubled,
tripled, quadrupled. The San Francisco franchise sold for
$19 million and was soon regarded a bargain. Owners
talked of $30 million, $40 million, as each new TV contract brought more money.

By the end of the seventies, each club was receiving about $5 million a year from TV, a sum equal to the average club's total ticket sales from a sold-out stadium for the season.

Television audiences grew—30 million, 40 million, 50 million for regular games; double that for Super Bowl games. Games spread to weekdays. Where was the saturation point?

Stadium audiences also grew. New clubs formed. New stadiums arose and new fans filled them until each autumn Sunday afternoon 800,000 fans were roaring for their teams. But for how long?

More than one owner has awakened shuddering from a nightmare in which he saw his team playing in an empty stadium.

Which is television? A bottomless pot of gold? Or a time bomb?

I daily ask myself the question. Time alone can tell.

CHAPTER SEVENTEEN

If You Live Long Enough, Everything Nice You Want to Happen, Will Happen

DURING THE YEARS I AM NOT COACHING, I remain a good observer. I make copious notes about defects in plays and measures which may be taken to bring out the best abilities of each player and to make cooperation among players more productive of victories.

When I returned to coaching in 1958, I started building the defense. I introduced the BUZ. The "B" stands for linebackers. The "U" tells them that they should move up close to the line before the snap as though they were going to help drive through the line. The "Z" tells them that when the play begins, they should back up and help the secondary defend against passes and it tells the defense ends that they should pick up the linebackers' normal assignments in defending against running attacks.

I introduced the red dog, white dog and blue dog defense calls. The call instructed one of the linebackers to get through the line and go for the quarterback in an effort to hurry him and make him throw an erratic pass which, hopefully, would be taken by our secondary, or at least fall harmlessly to the ground. "Red dog" gave the assignment to the right linebacker, "white dog" to the middle linebacker, and "blue dog" to the left linebacker. The tactic of using linebackers to rush the quarterback is now known as "blitz." Individual identification of the linebacker has disappeared.

I introduced the "RUBU." It was similar to the BUZ except that the instruction went to the rushers. RUBU wasn't a good word. We shortened it to "RUB."

Gradually we shifted from man-to-man defense, in which one or two men are assigned to each potential receiver or runner, to zone defense. We put four men on the line and supported them with two linebackers. The third linebacker and the four other backs were each assigned a zone in which they were responsible for stopping all offensive activity.

I sought strong linemen and linebackers. We picked up Guards James Cadile from San Jose State and Roger Davis from Syracuse; Tackle Bob Wetoska of Notre Dame; Center Mike Pyle from Yale; Ends Bo Farrington of Prairie View and Ed O'Bradovich from Illinois. Since 1952 Fred Williams of Arkansas had been going well at tackle. He had several years left. In 1957 we had acquired two good tackles, Bob Kilcullen of Texas Tech and Earl Leggett of Louisiana State. Doug Atkins, who came from Tennessee in 1955, was a giant, 6 feet 8, 255 pounds. He was tough and respected.

In 1959, for the first time since 1948, we held the opposing teams to fewer than 200 points and were on our way to leading the League in defense. But on offense we were thirteenth or fourteenth in a fourteen-team League.

253

We obtained some excellent men filled with desire and stamina—Charlie Bivins from Morris Brown; Rudy Bukich and Angelo Coia from Southern California; Johnny Morris from Santa Barbara; Richie Petitbon of Tulane; Ronnie Bull of Baylor. Rick Casares of Florida, signed in 1955, was acquiring the power and polish that would make him a record setter. William Galimore of Florida A and M, a 1957 rookie, became a regular. When Larry Morris of Georgia Tech joined Joe Fortunato and Bill George our linebacking wall was complete. In 1961 I acquired End Mike Ditka, a proper opposite number to Johnny Morris.

In 1958, we managed to climb into second place, with an 8–4 record, even though, for the first time since 1946, we were shut out. Baltimore did it to us. The next year was a repeat—second place, 8–4. I will barely mention 1960. Five won, six lost, one tied, our opponents scoring 299 to our 194. We were back on the track in 1961 with 8–6, increasing our scoring from the miserable 194 to a respectable 326. The year was made memorable by an interesting innovation produced by the San Francisco '49ers. They gave birth to a strategy called the shotgun. The quarterback placed himself 8 yards directly behind the center. The center bent over deeply and, with both hands, passed the ball to the quarterback. At the snap, the other backs and the ends scattered widely to receive a quick pass from the quarterback. The maneuver confused opponents. Four teams were felled by the shotgun. We were the next intended victim. I found an answer in Bill George, our enthusiastic linebacker. I moved him up directly opposite the center. As soon as the center passed the ball, Bill drove past him, one side or the other. Bill reached the quarterback only a second or two after the

254

ball. He smothered the quarterback time after time. We won the game 31–0. The following week the Steelers, using our defense, played the '49ers and also walloped them. The '49ers put their shotgun into the chest with other failed inventions.

By 1962, our game was improving on all sides. Midway through the season, on a Thursday, Clark Shaughnessy told me about a new defense he was going to use the following Sunday. As the signal was called, he was going to have the right tackle move over next to the left tackle. I said, "Clark, you cannot do that. The offense will see the hole, call a play on a quick count before you can adjust, and come roaring through." Clark walked out. I made his assistant, George Allen, head of defense. We also lost Galimore and Casares for several games due to injuries, but Bill Wade completed 225 passes, Ditka and Johnny Morris each taking 58. Wade's yardage, 3,172, transferred to him the record held by Sid Luckman. We won nine games and moved up into third place.

We entered 1963 feeling the touch of destiny. We overcame Green Bay, champions for the previous two years, 10–3, rolled over the Vikings 28–7, the Lions 37–21, and the Rams 52–14. We lost to the '49ers 20–14 and tied the Steelers and Vikings 17–17. We were the top of the League on defense. We allowed our rivals 144 points, half of the previous year's 287. No team managed more than three touchdowns. We made 301 points. All season we let only eight passes go for touchdowns while intercepting thirty-six, more than any other team that year. Our 11–1–2 record was best in the West, but merely a shiver ahead of the Packers' 11–2–1.

In the Eastern conference the Giants won eleven and took the division title for the sixth time in eight years, although they had gone on to win the championship only once, in 1956. By 1963 they were hungry. They were top of the League in offense, having gained 5,024 yards. In the air, their quarterback, Yelberton Abraham Tittle, was fantastic. He was excellent on the long pass, the bomb, and had developed the short pass, the screen, into a highly dangerous weapon. Of his 367 passes that season, 221 were completed for 3,145 yards. Quite a few sportswriters declared the Giants were a one-man team. The statement was nonsense. A star is a pleasant asset to possess, but no star can shine without support of the team. Of all sports, football most demands teamwork, in every second of play.

The championship game, several sportswriters declared, would be a demonstration of what happens when an unstoppable object meets an immovable wall. The game was scheduled for noon, Sunday, December 29, in Wrigley Field. Days before we covered the playing field with a layer of hay and a heavy tarpaulin. We placed aircraft hangar heaters around the field. The blasts of hot air billowed the tarp, thawing the earth below.

Sunday was bright and cold, far below freezing. We removed the tarp and raked away the hay. We found the ground quite spongy. But within an hour, the ground began to freeze. By play time, it was solid, ribbed, spiked ice rock.

Some fans came in face masks with holes cut for the eyes. Others were done up like doctors ready for an operation. Quite a few brought flasks filled with steaming coffee and, I presume, other warming beverages. The two mayors were there, Robert Wagner of New York and our own Richard Daley. By game time, the count was 45,802, not quite capacity. Another fifty million or so watched on television broadcast by 210 stations across America and 43 in Canada.

Others watched in auditoriums equipped for the day with closed circuit big-screen TV. McCormick Place in Chicago collected $21,128.52 in admissions, which was more than the total receipts for the Bears–Giants playoff in 1933. Television paid $900,000. Total receipts were about a million and a half. Professional football had truly come into big money, for better or for worse.

Our trainers, remembering the 1934 game in which the Giants beat us on ice by wearing tennis shoes, laid out six kinds of shoes.

We won the toss and elected to receive. Billy Martin, a 1962 rookie from Minnesota, took the ball just short of the goal. It slipped from his hands, bounced back to the goal line. He caught up with it. He picked it up. He stumbled. He started to run in a wide sweep. He was brought down on the 10.

We ran a few plays. Bill Wade completed a short pass. We were moving, not fast, but steadily. Then Wade fumbled and Erich Barnes recovered for the Giants on our 40.

We went into our defense position, five men on the line, three backing up the line and three in the secondary. We stayed basically with that formation all afternoon. It gave us ample opportunities to BUZ, RUB and Dog. How we needed them!

Tittle threw to Morrison for 12 yards. Four running plays brought the Giants to our 14. The pressure was really on. We sensed a bomb. Time to Dog. Larry Morris got through the line but Tittle threw when he was still a foot or so away. They crashed to the ground. Tittle winced. His left knee had twisted. The pass to Frank

257

Gifford was good. Gifford got away from Bennie McRae and scored. The Giants converted. After 7 minutes 22 seconds, the Giants led 7–0.

We took the kick, without any slip this time. We drove up the field. Our offense proved adequate. But Galimore fumbled. Dick Pesonen got the ball for the Giants on our 31. Tittle tried a bomb to Shofner who was waiting in the end zone. The pass was straight. Perhaps it was a bit too high. Perhaps the sun briefly got into Shofner's eyes. Shofner got his hands on the ball but it slipped through. Thank you. Thank you.

Tittle set up for a screen. We BUZzed. Larry Morris dropped back and when Tittle threw the short pass to Phil King, Larry was there. He gathered in the ball—the first interception of a Tittle pass all season. Larry wriggled free and headed for the goal. He ran and ran and ran. He never was very fast. After 61 yards he ran out of air. A Giant caught him on the 5.

Would the interception and the Shofner failure change the game? I firmly hoped so.

Ronnie Bull pushed for 3 yards and Wade plunged for the final 2. Robert Jencks converted. 7–7. We were back in the game and running strong. Leclerc kicked for us. Charlie Killett got the ball on the Giants' 5. It slid free. Our Charlie Bivins fell on it. Bears' fans went wild.

Thank you, oh thank you.

But the referee called back the kick. He said a Bear was offside. Ed Dove ran the next kick to the 38. After a few runs and a 36-yard pass, Tittle to Aaron Thomas, the Giants were on our 13.

Now was the moment of truth for our defense. For three plays the defense did hold. The Giants decided to settle for a field goal. They regained the lead, 10–7.

Six and a half minutes before the half, the Giants were again advancing ominously. Tittle drifted back to pass. Larry Morris red-dogged. He got through the line. He slipped. He continued ahead full force, bent double, steadying himself with his hands, advancing on all fours. Tittle also slipped and began to fall to the side. Although off balance, he threw the ball. A second later Morris struck Tittle's left knee with his shoulder. Both went down. Morris helped Tittle to his feet. When Tittle put weight on the left foot, pain shot through him. Teammates helped him from the field. Bears' fans cheered. That might not have been the sportsmanlike thing to do but I would not accuse them of being poor sportsmen. I put the cheers down to a feeling of relief that comes to everyone when a threat has passed.

It would have been easy and perhaps human for Tittle to blame the injury on Morris, even though Morris acted well within the rules. Instead, Tittle, gentleman Tittle, said he felt a twinge before he threw so he must have twisted the knee before Morris struck. It was just one of those things, Tittle said.

The Giants sent in Glynn Griffing, competent but no Tittle. Soon the Giants lost Phil King to a sprained ankle. We stopped the Giants' drive. We drove to within kicking distance but again failed.

During half time, I presume all 45,000 people wondered if Tittle would return to the game. To help pass the time, we staged a kicking competition. A snappy school band marched and some pretty girls in very short skirts pranced. The temperature had dropped to 7 degrees above zero, 25 degrees below freezing.

I had observed that Fred Williams, at tackle, was being blocked out of the play consistently by the Giants' center, Greg Larson, opening a gap through which Giants' backs had acquired quite a few yards. Our flanks had been well held by Morris and Joe Fortunato. I directed Williams to move out a bit. I hoped the new placement would shut the door.

A great roar from Giants' bleachers told me that Tittle was coming back.

We kicked. A few plays indicated the Tittle knee was bothersome. Tittle was favoring the left leg and not leaning into it when passing. In the first half he had completed only three of nine passes. I blamed the cold weather. I assumed his emergency stance would further reduce his control of the ball. Our Bill George picked up a Giants' fumble but the referee said the ball had been whistled dead. After the game, I studied the film. The fumble did come before the whistle.

The Giants resumed their drive. A Giant pulled in a Tittle pass with a beautiful one-handed catch and reached our 21. We held, got the ball and drove to within kicking distance but again failed.

Ed O'Bradovich noted that when the quarterback called a pass, the Giant opposite him would break off his blocking early and back up to protect Tittle. Ed smelled a screen pass coming up. The ball snapped. The Giant pressed forward. Ed stood his ground. The Giant backed up. Ed also backed up. Tittle threw a short pass. Ed was right there. He jumped. His fingers touched the ball. It went straight up. It came down into Ed's arms. We were in scoring position.

High in the stands, Luke Johnsos spoke over his phone to the bench. "Now is the time for the Ditka special," he said. I approved. While watching Giant films we had noted that Sam Huff chased our fullback, Jim

Patton remained close to our left half and Dick Pesonen shifted to the outside, creating a gap in the middle. We devised a play to put Ditka into the gap.

Joe drew Huff far off to the left; Patton stayed right; Ditka started wide to the right, drawing Pesonen, then sharply changed course and slanted into the open space. Wade threw him the ball. Ditka reached the 1-yard line. A plunge got nowhere so Wade made a springboard-like dive that carried him over a small mountain of Giants and Bears. Jencks converted. We went ahead 14–10.

Bears' fans indicated they were pleased.

Wade elected to keep the ball on the ground. Tittle took to the air.

We got through the rest of the third quarter. Once in the fourth, Petitbon did get his fingers on a Tittle pass but couldn't hold it. Petitbon picked up a loose Giants' ball on the 49. We advanced cautiously to the 34. Leclerc again tried for a field goal and again missed. The Giants ran and passed to our 36. Tittle bombed over our goal but Bennie McRay deflected it.

The minutes winced by. Each seemed to have at least a thousand seconds.

Now 120 seconds remain.

We have possession, safely, in midfield. Third down. Another plunge. Did we make it? In the mass of bodies, I can't see. No, 1 yard short. We kick. The Giants let the ball go into the end zone. They put it in play on the 20.

A pass carries them to the 42.

Sixty-three seconds.

Tittle screens. The ball goes into the ground. Tittle calls time out. His last. Speed is vital. No time to huddle. Line up. Pass. Line up. Pass. For me, pray.

Tittle passes. The throw is wide. But a Giant is there

261

and takes the ball. The referee rules the receiver had leaned over the sideline. The pass is no good.

Ten seconds.

Time for two more passes.

A bomb! It has to be a bomb!

The ball is snapped. Tittle fades. The possible receivers spread wide. Tittle falls back, and back, and back. He searches for the man who can win the game. He seems to have all the time in the world. Every Bear is out there waiting for the pass.

Shofner, empty-handed all day, crosses into the end zone. Tittle sees him and throws. It's high but wide. Shofner runs for it. But the ball settles into the arms of our Richie Petitbon. He half kneels. He cradles the ball tightly. He doesn't think of running. He is interested only in hanging onto the ball. He knows that will mean the ball game, and the championship.

I think I can safely say Bears' fans went wild. I felt pretty good myself. The game went through its final ticks with nobody watching. The referee walked the ball to the twenty. The center handed the ball to Wade. He fell on it. The game was over.

After seventeen years the Bears again were the champions.

Tittle strode off the field, bouncing his helmet against the hard ground in frustration. "It had to happen to me," he said. The game was his third championship try in three years. All efforts had fallen short.

Judged by statistics, the Giants should have won. On the ground we gained only 93 yards to the Giants' 128. Our longest run was for a mere 12 yards and our best pass advanced only 34 yards, hardly championship quality.

Surprisingly, in the air Bill Wade had kept pace with

Tittle, completing 10 of 28, to Tittle's 11 of 29. One statistic favored us and it was perhaps the most critical of all—we had intercepted five Tittle throws. Interceptions set up both of our touchdowns.

The Giants' dressing room, I heard, resembled a morgue. "Fourteen points and they win a championship," Sam Huff said. Shofner was almost in shock. Never before had he gone through a League game without taking at least one pass. "I don't know why," he said. "The field was okay. The pass that I dropped in the end zone was miserable, just plain miserable."

The New York sportswriter Red Smith composed a poem. A dirge:

> How doth the burly Giant
> Improve each shining hour
> In thermal drawers in Wrigley Field
> When Yelberton goes sour.

A *New York Times* writer commented: "Those who live by the sword risk getting cut."

The Giants' coach, Al Sherman, was asked if injuries cost the game. "You can't beat a team like the Bears with alibis," he answered.

Tittle repeated several times he injured his knee before Morris hit him.

When someone repeated in a low voice the old crack that Tittle was likely to fail under pressure, Sherman bristled.

"He was great on one leg," Sherman said. "Tittle is great, just great, one of the greatest."

When I walked into our dressing room, everything was tense. I looked around, raised my right fist high and shouted, "Go!" The boys broke loose.

263

Someone lit a cigar, saying he thought he would start celebrating right now. I admonished him to put it out. "No smoking in the clubhouse," I reminded.

The players sang our little victory ditty, dedicated after each good game to a player the others thought had given an outstanding performance. The ditty was always the same; only the name changed.

"Hooray for Halas. Hooray for Halas, for he's a @#$%¢&*" using the ditty's usual word which I prefer not to repeat outside the clubhouse.

Larry Morris had done a great job. He had harried Tittle. He had taken the Tittle pass that brought our first touchdown. Everybody patted Morris. Rudy Bukich made a little speech: "Morris' linebacking was the greatest I have ever seen." A sports magazine announced it would proclaim Morris the Most Valuable Player of the game and would give him a car.

Center Mike Pyle, when asked to explain why the Bears won, said: "We had become damned desirous." The questioners looked puzzled. Desirous? Desirous? "Well," said Pyle, "maybe there isn't any such word, but that's the way we felt."

O'Bradovich said he thought both sides had shown "good composure." He gave a little sermon. "To lose your temper and get into fights," he said, "is being selfish because you bring penalties to your team."

A reporter asked Wade if he felt any retribution from Giants' rushers after Tittle was helped from the field. "That's natural, isn't it?" he said. His bloody elbows testified to the times he had been put down throwing the ball.

It had been a clean game. Penalties totaled only 60 yards. Once Huff had piled onto Wade after Wade had been brought down. "Nice going, Sam," Wade said in reverse praise. Huff shrugged. "Well, don't run the ball so often, Bill," Huff said.

After another pileup, Ditka told Erich Barnes that Barnes was being unnecessarily rough with Johnny Morris. Barnes' fist found its way through Ditka's face mask. The referee was watching. He stepped off 15 precious yards against the Giants.

Petitbon, asked about his game-saving catch, said, "I accepted the ball gratefully."

Joe Fortunato, our co-captain, gave the game ball to defense coach George Allen. Allen had, indeed, done a wonderful job. Our defense in the game was outstanding.

The press expected me to say something for posterity. I choked up. I managed to say something like: "I have waited a long time. I guess today's game proves that if you live long enough, everything nice you want to happen, will happen."

They asked if I would retire as coach. I stalled. Someone saved me by reminding me I was due to coach the western pro team in the Pro Bowl and also the pro team against the All-Stars in the preseason exhibition the next August. "I guess I will have to hang on," I said. "Anyway, where could a sixty-eight-year-old find another job?"

For the game each Bear received $5,899.77; each Giant, $4,218.15.

Mayor Daley arranged a special meeting of the city council to honor the Bears. A band played. The fire department glee club sang. The Mayor gave us a 4-foot-high trophy dedicated to John Fitzgerald Kennedy. "The Bears," the Mayor said, "are the greatest football players in the world."

265

CHAPTER EIGHTEEN

Two into One Must Go

AFTER THE COLLAPSE of Arch Ward's All-American Conference in·1950, the prospect for professional football was good. League membership settled down at twelve, a workable number, providing two divisions leading to playoffs and a championship. Planes made travel to our new West Coast clubs easy.

The Bears were playing to a full house each Sunday in Wrigley Field. Newspapers and radio were giving us a good coverage. Television was expanding; for good or evil we yet did not know. Universities were providing an abundance of excellent players. The player draft was again working well. Bear player payroll, after rising from about $125,000 in 1946 to more than $300,000 in 1950, was turning down slightly. In 1946, Bear income was just over $400,000. In 1950, it passed a million and our profit that year was a happy $37,224. After thirty years, professional football was becoming a middle-sized, year-

266

round business. I still encouraged players and my assistants to develop outside careers to enlarge their savings and to lead to happy lives after their football years ended.

The prospect of big money from television brightened. Promoters and enthusiasts took new interest. The League was again vulnerable. Apart from Los Angeles and San Francisco, the League was confined to the New York–Chicago industrial belt. Cities were growing fast in the sun belt, in the mountain states, in the Northwest. For generations, Minnesota had been a collegiate powerhouse but Minnesota fans still had to go out of the state to see professional football.

The League considered expansion but lacked the required unanimity. The Maras solidly opposed creation of new teams. I liked the League the way it was but I argued that football would spread into new cities and past experience had shown the best course would be to have the growth come within the League.

In Texas, Lamar Hunt was moving into sports. He tried to buy the Chicago Cardinals. Charlie Bidwill's widow, Vi, would not sell. Hunt started along the dangerous, costly road pioneered by Pyle and Ward. He announced he would start a team in Dallas, the Texans, and organize a new league. He was a formidable rival. His oil money gave him a rare ability to absorb losses for a long time and to support other teams.

Suddenly, we old-timers decided the League must grow. We gave a franchise to Clint Murchison, Jr., and Bedford Wynne for Dallas. They called the club the Dallas Cowboys. Tex Schramm became manager of the Cowboys with Tom Landry as his coach. Play would begin in 1960 in direct competition to Hunt's Texans. We

267

convinced the organizers of a team in Minnesota, the Vikings, that they should come with us, and begin play in 1961. We gave both teams extra draft choices and veterans from our own teams. The League authorized Vi Bidwill to move the Cardinals into St. Louis, a virgin area.

Hunt found organizers in five open cities—Denver, Houston, Buffalo, Boston and Oakland—as well as in New York, Los Angeles and Dallas where the new teams would directly compete with NFL teams. They called themselves the American Football League and hired Joe Foss, a World War II marine corps flying ace and former governor of South Dakota, as their commissioner.

The battle was on. It was fought most fiercely in the selection of new players. The AFL organized a draft of collegians in direct competition to ours. They signed undergraduates. Signing became wild. Carroll Rosenbloom recalled:

> You can't believe what went on. Scouts would take to a hotel room kids who didn't know what it was to have 50 dollars, spread $5,000 in hundred dollar bills on the bed and say, "You sign and the money is yours." It wasn't hard to get a signature. Then another recruiter would come along and say, "Look, we'll give you $6,000 to come with us." The kid would sign and keep the earlier $5,000. Recruiters were making bums out of nice kids.
>
> They would also go after our players, especially the quarterbacks. They would hold a secret draft among themselves to decide who would go for whom. I don't blame them. They were trying to get stars. The new clubs would not make money but, soon, neither would we. Salaries were escalating. We could see

268

even bigger jumps ahead. A lot of poor players were getting a great deal of money they did not deserve.

At first, we told ourselves the new teams would be second raters and not able to draw fans. Boston, Buffalo and Denver were weak but the new team in Houston was good from the start. Houston won the AFL championship while our new Dallas team won not one game. We took comfort in attendance figures—78 NFL games drew more than three million; 56 AFL games just over 900,000. But one development rang the alarm—ABC signed to televise the AFL games. That should have told us the new league would not fade away in bankruptcy.

Lawyers entered the act. The Rams accused Houston of taking halfback Billy Cannon, who was already under contract to the Rams. The court ruled Cannon was legally free to go. Encouraged, the AFL went to court claiming that our draft system and our League-wide television contract were conspiracies. They lost. In 1963, Hunt moved his Dallas team to Kansas City, Sonny Werblin became major owner of the AFL New York team, and the Los Angeles team moved into San Diego and was again AFL champion. In 1964, Sonny Werblin pulled a coup. His business was radio and television. He had been a top man for the Music Corporation of America and very close to David Sarnoff, of NBC. All Sonny had to do was say, "Look, I want a television contract for the AFL" and he would get it. NBC agreed to pay that league $36 million over five years. That was about $900,000 a year per club. Our CBS contract that year gave each NFL team just over a million.

From the start, Halas had been adamant for a united League. Sometimes he spoke so strongly I thought he must be crazy. Now we saw he was farsighted.

The League asked me to try to negotiate a merger.

A meeting was set up in New York with Sonny, Hunt and Ralph Wilson on Easter morning. Art Modell joined me.

I don't know what a National Football League franchise was worth then. Say 10 million. The AFL franchise had no value. I told the Hunt group the day they became members of the National Football League, their franchises would be worth the same as ours. It was hard for them to believe this, but later they found it to be true.

We did work out a merger which I could present to the League at its meeting at the Plaza the following week. The AFL agreed to come up with $12 million.

On the appointed meeting day, I was about to leave for the Plaza when Sonny came on the phone. He said the AFL couldn't raise the $12 million.

"Sonny," I said, "if you can't get the money, you can't have a merger."

Our owners were furious. We decided Pete should go to Atlanta where the AFL was seeking a team. Pete arranged for a national polling outfit to conduct an opinion test. Of course, the Atlanta public preferred our League. We expanded into Atlanta.

The bidding for new players became wild. In 1966, owners of the two leagues spent $7 million to sign draft choices. This could not go on.

The AFL resumed negotiations. This time there were Hunt, Wilson and Sullivan. With me were Modell and Tex Schramm. Pete Rozelle acted as arbitrator.

Late in the evening we came to an agreement. All nine AFL teams would come into our League, making twenty-six after New Orleans and Cincinnati were formed. Pete would be the commissioner. We would have one draft. We would divide into two conferences, National and American, each with a president. The conference winners would meet in a Super

Bowl, a world series of football. The AFL teams would pay $18 million for franchises, each contributing equally. Of this, $10 million would go to our New York Giants and $8 million to our San Francisco '49ers because an AFL team would come into each of their territories. From the two new franchise payments, three NFL teams would be given $3 million each to move into the American conference.

We were hungry. Joe Kennedy, whom I had known for many, many years, and I had started a restaurant, La Caravelle. It had become famous when Jack ran for the presidency. It was considered the best restaurant in town. We found Bobby Kennedy, who was attorney general, his wife Ethel, Arthur Schlesinger and others at the table usually saved for Joe and me. Bobby knew a lot about football and football people. When he saw the AFL and NFL people together with Pete he asked, "What's going on?" I said we had been holding a meeting. He said, "This looks like an anti-trust conspiracy." Later Bobby sent over a menu on which he had written accusations against the National Football League and the American League. Actually, Bobby wanted a merger. He was a great football fan.

We celebrated with champagne. Ralph Wilson said Sonny had phoned him the previous day and told him the AFL didn't have to give the NFL money to get the merger. Ralph replied, "Sonny, you are a nice fellow, a really nice fellow. I think you are bright, very bright. But we could have had the merger for $12 million. Now it's going to cost us $18 million. Sonny, I cannot afford you."

After three years the new National Conference elected George Halas as its president. The American Conference chose Lamar Hunt.

One problem remained. No NFL team wanted to move, despite the $3 million. I said, "If we're going to be partners, we're going to be partners. If not, then all this is ludicrous and we shouldn't join at all." I said the Colts would move.

Minnesota offered to move but the AFL people wouldn't have it because it had started out with them and switched to us.

I asked Art Rooney if the Steelers would move. He said yes, if Modell and I would. Modell agreed, although it would mean giving up traditional rivalries. For years the Browns had met the Bears and the Giants twice every year. Now the teams meet only once or twice a decade.

We three thought we would meet weaker teams. We found to our horror that the South and West grew big and tough football players. The AFL teams had more young quarterbacks. They were on their way to dominating professional football.

The first Super Bowl was played in 1967. Our NFL Green Bay club beat Hunt's Kansas City club. The next year our Green Bay beat the AFL Oakland club. We prided in this proof of our superiority. In 1968 Baltimore was our winner, the New York Jets theirs.

Rosenbloom said:

We were favored to win by 16 points. I planned a big victory party. Teddy Kennedy and a couple of other senators were coming. I invited Vice President Spiro Agnew as a former governor of Maryland. I had fired the coach, Weeb Ewbank, thinking he had lost his hold on the club, and brought in Don Shula. We played so poorly it was a joke.

To my disgrace and horror, the Colts became the first NFL team to lose to an AFL club. The score was 7–16.

I went home. My wife was waiting. "Honey," she said, "a friend is in the den."

I said, "Georgia, I don't want to see anybody right now. I just don't want to talk to anybody. I want to pull myself together. Four or five hundred people are coming here tonight and I have to find a way not to go in."

Georgia said, "I think you'll want to see this person. I'll send in a couple of drinks and you will feel better."

I went into the den. I saw no one. I went into the bathroom. There was Ted Kennedy in the tub, soaking. He and his father had been to the game although the father had had a stroke. The father was furious that I had lost.

"Kind of rough, huh?" Teddy asked.

I said the loss was tough to take.

"Feeling sorry for yourself?"

"I sure as hell do. I am about ready to cry. I feel particularly sorry for my players."

Teddy said: "Carroll, I want to tell you something. Nobody died out there today. We lost Jack. We lost Bobby."

That brought everything back into perspective. But I went through the evening in a trance, trying to smile.

People outside football don't realize how emotional football is for people in football. We play only fourteen games. Winning each game is important. If you have ever been on a plane with a team coming home after a defeat, you have seen the despair and felt it.

What holds George Halas to football is the ecstasy of winning. It carries him through the agony of defeat. I know this doesn't make sense but it is true. Sometimes I think it's too bad every game can't end in a tie.

CHAPTER NINETEEN

A Dangerous Breach

THROUGH THE YEARS, some players on some teams were unhappy with financial arrangements and training conditions. Some did have legitimate grievances. Teams drew into training camps twice as many players as they would use. Each player, veteran or rookie, had to qualify for the team each year. In some clubs, men who did not make the team received nothing for coming to camp except board and room, return fare—and the experience.

Baseball players had formed an association to take up grievances with owners. By the 1950's quite a few football players thought they should have a similar organization. In 1956 such men formed the Professional Football Players association. Membership was voluntary. Dues were $25 a year.

The association asked the clubs to pay at least $50 to each player taking part in a pre-season game and all medical bills arising from injuries. This was OK with me as the Bears paid $100 for pre-season games. From the start I had paid medical bills. Thus Bears' enthusiasm for joining the association was scant and that disappeared when Bill Bishop, who many times had publicly called me a tightwad, told players I had picked up his wife's $5,000 hospital bill, Harlon Hill reported I had loaned him more than $20,000 to buy into a radio station and Bill McColl said his dealings with me had convinced him that I would never pay a nickel more than I thought a man was worth as a player but would pay thousands to a player for humanitarian reasons.

As time passed the association asked for a minimum salary of $5,000, at least $12 a day travelling expenses and a limit on the training period. The owners agreed to these minimums. They affected only a few players who did deserve help. The association also asked for recognition. That we did not give. We were determined not to share management decisions.

The association leaders were opposed to the player draft. They took the position, advocated by some players from the start, that the system limits a player's ability to negotiate. Over the years quite a few players have thought they could get more money in an open system with one team bidding against another. This may be true, but the draft has well served its prime purpose of building up weaker teams.

In Washington, the House of Representatives anti-trust committee was considering a measure which would give the League a degree of exemption from anti-trust laws similar to that enjoyed by professional baseball. The players association sent a committee to Washington to fight the measure. Bell and I were among witnesses for the League. The measure did not advance.

275

The association sought ways to put pressure on the League to secure recognition. It announced it would take the League to court on charges that the draft system was a violation of the anti-trust laws and demand $4.2 million damages. We recognized the association.

The association then turned its attention to medical insurance and pensions. We stalled. The association considered calling a strike but decided that would irritate the public. It considered joining an organized union but decided too many players would object. So it revived the threat of court. We owners looked around for sources of money to pay pensions and insurance. We reached a good compromise: The two second-place teams would play a post-season game in the Orange Bowl and the profits, along with some revenue from the *Chicago Tribune* All-Star game and from picture cards, would be used for player benefits. The first year the income barely covered insurance costs but in 1964 the fund received $1,197,500, enough to provide monthly pensions at sixty-five for current players with five or more years' service.

Members began asking why they should pay dues when nonmembers received equal benefits. There was talk of a mass walkout. I modified my position toward the association. I said I had nothing against the Bears' joining. The association responded by saying that if all clubs treated their players as I did the Bears, there would be no need for an association. In this new friendly air, the Bears voted to join the association, although individual membership continued to be voluntary.

The association remained a loosely knit organization. We met together once or twice a year and increased fringe benefits as money became available. The association avoided salary negotiations. Good players were acquiring agents—or perhaps it was the other way around. The best players and their agents thought they could pick up more money by negotiating individually than through group discussions. That was true in the early sixties when the new American Football League bid for players against an enlarged NFL. In 1966 the two leagues merged. Salaries levelled off. Active players urged that the association be strengthened and found wide support. The association turned itself into a full-fledged labor union, following procedures of the National Labor Relations Board.

In 1968 we negotiated our first two-year collective bargaining agreement with the union. It widened benefits. It was followed by a four-year agreement, with greater benefits. Then the union presented us with a long list of demands, fifty-seven by one count, ninety-two by another. Owners set up a management council to conduct the negotiations. Mara was chairman. Mugs, my son, was a member.

We owners still held to our old thinking that we had developed professional football and we knew what was good for professional football. The players, on their side, contended they must have representation.

The negotiations, while running the gamut of employer-employee relations, centered on two issues: the player draft and the player transfer system under which a player, after giving notice and playing a final year, could move to another club only if the new employer gave a player or a draft choice to the relinquishing club. If the two clubs could not agree on the award, the commissioner made an irrevocable decision. The players said the system retarded movement because the hiring club did not know when negotiating with the player what it would have to give to the relinquishing club.

277

The union wanted the draft and transfer system abolished.

"In no way," we owners said. "They are fundamental to the operation of professional football."

Meetings were long, noisy and unproductive of agreement. Mara told me that when meetings began to go badly awry, Mugs would say, "Let's get some sanity here."

The union went to court in Minneapolis asserting that the transfer system violated the anti-trust laws. The court had a fifty-five-day hearing. In Washington, a player, Yazoo Smith, had sued the Redskins and the NFL many years earlier challenging the player draft. The case was revived.

We sensed that the union thought it would win both suits and would gain more through the courts than it could in negotiations. We sensed that until the courts decided the cases, the union was not interested in reaching an agreement. It did, however, call a strike in 1974. Training camps opened as usual but almost all veterans stayed away. Clubs played pre-season games with teams composed heavily of rookies. The strike melted away. The next year the union called selective strikes. It did prevent an early game between the New England Patriots and the New York Jets but failed to stop a Denver–St. Louis game which was to be televised. Again the strike failed.

The court finally announced both the draft and the transfer system were illegal. We appealed. The union started a class action suit on behalf of all players who had been drafted or transferred, seeking damages that could have run into many, many millions. We owners began to realize that the old days were over and, much as we preferred the old ways, we must change. Similarly, the players began to see that full freedom is never possible. The time had come to negotiate.

New discussions led to a massive 101-page, five-year comprehensive labor agreement. The players accepted the draft and transfer system, with modifications. In return, we granted benefits to players which over five years would come to more than $100 million. The union pledged no strike; we pledged no lockout.

A dangerous breach had been sealed. But for how long? Soon the union and some owners were talking about possibly including in the next agreement a wage scale based on position, experience and special achievements. There was serious debate on either side.

During the negotiations, Mugs, who became president of the Chicago Bears in 1963, developed an excellent relationship with Jim Finks, formerly with the Minnesota Vikings. In 1974 Jim was brought in as executive vice president and general manager. I have left game strategy to the head coach, although it has been most difficult at times not to interfere.

I was asked not so long ago if, were I twenty-four now instead of sixty years ago, would I have my old eagerness to make a career in professional football. I said, as a player, yes. But as a coach, manager and owner, no. Football has largely turned from a personal sport into an impersonal business. The personal relations which meant so much to me are no longer so strong. Also the big developments in the game have been made. There are no new frontiers to conquer.

CHAPTER TWENTY

LAWYERS!

I HAVE ALWAYS BELIEVED that a man's word is his bond. When someone says he will do something, he must do it, regardless of subsequent developments. A contract endures, complete to its last comma, until the expiration date unless all concerned agree mutually to an alteration or termination. I see no difference between a spoken agreement and a written agreement. I believe that if a man breaks a contract, he debases himself. He destroys his most personal possession—the value of his word.

I have had two nightmarish episodes involving contracts. In one I asked for an injunction which would require George Allen to complete his contract as an assistant coach. In the second, Dick Butkus asked to be paid for four years after knee injuries ended his playing career and for aggravation to the knee brought by continued playing.

In both cases, I was widely depicted as a Scrooge. It was said I was preventing Allen, a smart young man who learned his football skills from the Bears, from achieving his ambition of becoming head coach for the Rams. With Butkus, it was said I was casting him aside after he had made middle linebacker a spectacular position.

Allen had come to me looking for a job. He had not had a distinguished career as a player or an assistant coach, but he did bring a neat three-ring binder filled with football player exercises. That did impress me. But I had no place for him. Six weeks later Frank Korch passed away. We had a position open for a man to scout players. I called George Allen, asked if he were interested to come and take over the Korch job. He came, scouted and assisted Clark Shaughnessy, the defensive coach. On March 1, 1959, we signed a three-year contract at $9,000 a year. I raised the pay yearly, to $12,000, to $14,000, to $16,000, to $17,000, each time with a new three-year contract.

At the end of 1965, Allen went to New Orleans to sign Randy Jackson. Three days after Christmas, Allen phoned saying the Los Angeles Rams had asked if he were interested in the job as head coach to succeed Harland Svare, who had just been fired by Dan Reeves following a terrible season. Allen asked if he could talk to Reeves. I said yes, but only to tell Reeves that he would not be available because two years remained on his latest contract.

The next day I called Reeves and chided him for calling Allen without my permission. He said he had not called Allen. He said Allen had called him on Christmas

Day, three days before Allen first spoke to me. Someone was not telling the whole truth or was mixed up. Reeves said he was very much interested in having Allen come to the Rams. He asked if the Rams decided on him would the Bears please release him? I said yes, after the 1966 season.

The following day Allen phoned to say Reeves had called him and asked if he could come to the Rams. I asked Allen to telephone Reeves and tell him he was not available now.

Allen asked, "Well, will I get a raise?"

I said we would talk about that when he came to Chicago on completion of the Jackson business. He had done well and I intended to give him a bonus.

Allen signed Jackson and returned to Chicago. He came into the office and asked if I would let him out of the contract. I said not before the end of the season. He said, "All right, I will stay with the Bears providing you will make me head coach when you retire."

I said I could not make that promise.

The next morning Allen said he was asking his lawyer if the contract were valid. The lawyer told him yes. Allen came in again and said if I would let him go to the Rams, he would come back in three or four years to be head coach for the Bears.

I found that ridiculous.

He said, all right, he would stay providing I gave him an option to buy 5 percent of the Bears' stock.

I found that even more ridiculous.

He took from his pocket a typed note of resignation.

I said I could not accept his resignation.

He put the paper on the desk and left. This is what Allen wrote:

January 8, 1966

Dear Coach Halas;

No man has ever owed more to another than I do to you for all you have done for me. No one has ever had a more agonizing experience in arriving at a decision than I have had in bringing myself to this final act of resignation.

The opportunity which has been offered to me to become head coach of the Los Angeles Rams is one I feel I must accept. The joy of realizing this ambition is marred only by the regret of leaving a team, and an association with you which has given me the most rewarding years of my life.

In accepting the challenge to take over the Rams, I do so with deep humility knowing that my opportunity has come about only because of my personal growth which has occurred under your leadership during the past eight years.

It is more than difficult to even imagine myself in competition with the Bears. Yet, I shall attempt to compete with you and with the other N.F.L. teams with the same spirit which you have so exemplified.

Most sincerely,
George H. Allen

The next morning, Sunday, he phoned that he had a reservation on a plane to California but would cancel it if I would agree to the option.

I saw no reason to alter my decision. Reeves telephoned saying he was going to sign Allen. Allen did fly to California. That night he phoned and said he would come back immediately if we would meet the Rams salary offer, generally reported to be $40,000. Allen said he must know at once because he was meeting Reeves in an hour. I said no. He asked what did I suggest? I said: "Come back to Chicago and fulfill your contract."

On the 10th of January, 1966, Reeves announced the Rams had signed Allen.

I felt my course of action was obvious and mandatory, as specified in the contract itself in paragraph four which states that if Allen walked out, the Bears had the right to ask for a court injunction to require him to stay. I asked our lawyer, Charles F. Short, Jr., to institute such a suit.

On the 12th of January, 1966, Judge Cornelius J. Harrington opened a hearing in the Circuit Court of Cook County, Illinois.

Allen had secured the service of Albert E. Jenner, Jr., an excellent lawyer.

I did not go to court. My lawyer called Allen to the witness stand.

SHORT: "Did you sign a contract with the Los Angeles Rams?"

ALLEN: "I have an agreement with the Rams."

SHORT: "When did you agree?"

ALLEN: "Tuesday after the New Year, January 4."

SHORT: "You agreed then?"

ALLEN: "Yes, by telephone, from my home in Deerfield."

Tuesday, January 4! I could not believe it. That was the day Allen returned to Chicago, the day before we met for the first time.

SHORT: "Did Mr. Halas ever give you a release in writing?"

ALLEN: "He did not."

SHORT: "Did you ask him?"

ALLEN: "I did not. I didn't know I had to."

Allen said he had never read the contract.

On cross examination Jenner asked:

"In your first conversation with Reeves, who called, you or Reeves?"

284

ALLEN: "I did, after I got permission from the Bears."

But Reeves had told me Allen called the Rams on Christmas Day, three days before Allen first spoke to me.

The hearing continued on January 19. I attended. The court was filled. Jenner asked the judge to submit the case to Rozelle.

Judge Harrington said:

> The court, after reviewing the pleadings and considering the evidence offered, has come to the conclusion that sufficient *prima facie* evidence has been offered to convince the court that a valid and binding contract of employment was entered into by the parties for a term of three years, which has been sanctioned and confirmed by reciprocal performance of the parties for a period of approximately one year. That the evidence indicates that respondent Allen breached the contract by negotiating for employment as head coach with persons representing the Los Angeles Rams without first receiving written permission, which was specifically required under his contract with the Chicago Bears, and it does appear that the respondent Allen further breached the contract in question by committing himself orally or in writing to be employed as head coach by the said Los Angeles Rams during the remaining term of his contract with the Chicago Bears. . . .

I rejoiced. "Valid and binding contract . . . Allen breached the contract by negotiating . . . Allen further breached the contract by committing himself . . ."

Those were the words I had expected to hear. They were the truth.

I approached the bench. I asked permission to address the court.

My lawyer was flabbergasted. He reached out for me. He told me to sit down.

285

"Charlie, I'll take care of this," I told him.

Jenner said he would oppose any statement by me unless I were under oath and he could have the opportunity of cross-examining me.

"I can't anticipate what the statement is going to be," Jenner said. "If a statement is made in this court and to this court, it is designed to influence the court. I do not mean by the word 'influence' to imply any devious intent on the part of . . . "

Judge Harrington interrupted.

"If the statement is not proper, counsel, the court will take cognizance of that . . . " he said.

To me, he added: "Take the witness stand, Mr. Halas."

I raised my hand and swore to tell the truth, the whole truth and nothing but the truth; my desire precisely.

"I am most pleased that Your Honor upholds the validity of the contract," I began.

"Objection," said Jenner. "If Your Honor pleases, it is immaterial and irrelevant whether Mr. Halas is pleased or isn't pleased."

Overruled.

"Your important ruling will uphold the integrity of National Football League clubs," I continued, "and will preserve the sanctity of contracts."

"Object!"

Overruled.

"Validity of contracts was the issue here and your ruling will prevent the breakdown of organized sports and all sports. George Allen was a minor issue here. The validity of the contract was the real issue."

I paused.

286

"Now," I said, "I want to drop this suit and give Allen his full release. He can go to Los Angeles and he goes with my blessing!"

Both lawyers were confused. Judge Harrington asked Short to present to the court my release of Allen in writing. He left the bench.

I had not planned my action nor discussed it with the lawyer. I did know from the start I wanted to preserve the validity of the contracts. I had intended to keep Allen through the season. But after learning what he said the first day in court, I wanted nothing more to do with George Allen.

I returned to my seat. Allen came over, bent low, thrust out his hand. "Thanks, Coach," he said.

I had to take the hand but there was no high regard in my eyes when I said: "George, a few of those statements you made on the stand I did not like. They weren't true, George."

In 1965 we drafted two great players, Gale Sayers, twice All-American at Kansas, and Dick Butkus, All-American at Illinois. Both had unusual running movements. I've never seen anyone run with Gale's agility. No one ever caught him from behind. Butkus was bow-legged. I learned later Butkus had knee injuries in high school and college. Both had rare abilities, supported by courage, desire and spirit.

Sayers came to Chicago to play in the pre-season All-Star game. He spent the day on the bench because of a knee injury a few days earlier. He came to our training camp.

"I was worried about having been benched," Sayers

287

recalls, "but Mr. Halas said, 'Gale, we're not going to judge you on what you did in the past. We're going to judge you on what you do starting today.'"

I made both Sayers and Butkus starters. Sayers became All-Pro the first year and repeated in 1966 and 1967. In 1968, he injured a knee.

"I lay in the hospital for weeks feeling sorry for myself," Sayers says. "Then I made up my mind I was going to come back. I did come back and was again a leading rusher. I proved you could come back from a knee injury."

Again he made All-Pro. His four-year contract expired. Sayers says:

It was for $25,000 a year, a good sum in those days. Each year Mr. Halas had given me a bonus, $10,000 the first year, $10,000 in the second plus another $10,000 because, he said, I had shaved off my mustache, $25,000 in the third and fourth years.

I thought I should be paid $100,000. I had no doubt that I would continue with the Bears. Mugs offered me $80,000 and said, "The only reason we are offering you this much is because you're a good friend of Father." That really upset me. I broke off the negotiations. Late next summer I heard Mr. Halas was going to England for a hip operation. I knew he was bothered by my not signing. I thought it would be helpful to him to clear this up. I went to see him. He said, "Gale, I've always been fair with you. If you sign the contract I will take care of you." I signed. I had a good year and again made All-Pro and at the end of it Mr. Halas gave me the other $20,000. Again he chose to treat old Gale right. In 1970 I was hurt again, in the other knee. I got into only two ball games but Mr. Halas paid me the $80,000.

There was a series of operations. In 1971 I played

in St. Louis to see how I could go. I felt my movement was good, but the pain was just too great. I told Abe Gibron, the new head coach, I'd had it. I saw Mr. Halas. The meeting was kind of emotional. He asked me if there was anything he could do. I told him there was nothing and I did appreciate everything he had done for me. He had encouraged me from the start to prepare for another career. I had taken an executive training course at Sears. I had become a stockbroker with Paine-Webber, the company which handles Mr. Halas' account. He had given me charge of it. By 1971 I was making speeches and other appearances. I was making more money outside football than in it. I saved. I was able to go to Kansas as assistant athletic director, which paid only $17,000 a year, without a drop in living style.

"Well," Mr. Halas said, "I do want to do something." He gave me a check for $50,000. Mr. Halas is a fine man.

Butkus reported during the 1966 season that his right knee had been sore since he was clipped from behind in an October game. After the season he went to Beverly Hills to see a prominent bone man, Dr. Daniel H. Levinthal, who examined him and reported torn ligaments but no damaged cartilage. He recommended no surgery.

Dick continued to play enthusiastically. He made All-Pro in 1967, 1968, 1969, and 1970. In 1971, his other knee was hurt. Dr. Ted Fox operated. The sutures festered. An allergy was blamed. Another operation was needed.

Dick played in 1972 and again made All-Pro. To save the knee he was excused from practice. As with all players, he was examined at the start of each week to determine his fitness. The doctors' decision was usually taken as final but for Butkus Gibron made an ex-

289

ception. He told Dick that only he, Dick, should determine when he was fit to play.

Butkus' contract was up for renewal after the 1972 season. In such a situation, it had become customary for players and clubs to agree to a series of one-year contracts, each becoming effective at the start of the new year. This allowed the club to pay a fair salary based on the current degree of performance for so long as the ability continued.

Dick said: "Give me what I am asking and I'll make this into a championship team all by myself. I can do it." That impressed me.

Three days before training camp began Butkus and I, both optimists, agreed on five one-year contracts at $115,000 a year, the highest salary figure paid by the Bears up to that time. The 1972 average for the Bears was about $30,000.

In the 1973 season the leg did trouble Butkus. He became known to other teams as a one-legged player. Fans noted he was not charging into the plays as in the past. He declared himself unfit for several games. Abe reported that Sundays on which Dick did not play were becoming a problem in the locker room. He sat there collecting $8,000 while others, getting much less, were going out on the field. This did not help team morale.

I encouraged Dick to see other doctors and send the bills to me. A Baltimore doctor, Edmond McDonnell, diagnosed arthritis and other ailments and forecast that the trouble would worsen and could lead to joint replacement.

In November, Mugs wrote Dick that unless he could play in 1974, he would not be paid.

In December Dick again saw Dr. Levinthal, who concluded:

> It is certainly impossible for Dick Butkus to play football with his present disability. It is also certain he will not improve sufficiently to participate in a contact sport with conservative treatment. It is evident his disability is progressive. I advise a high tibial osteotomy. The patient's desire will be a determining factor as to whether this patient will ever again be able to play any position in professional football.

Butkus decided to have a debridement done in Oklahoma City by Dr. Don O'Donoghue. I told him to do so, send all the bills to me and then undertake a rehabilitation program under our supervision with the hope he would be able to resume playing at some future date. During the rehabilitation, he would remain on the payroll at $115,000 a year. He had the operation.

He hired a prominent attorney, the late James A. Dooley, and filed a suit asking $1,600,000 from me, the Bears and Dr. Fox. He claimed that the Bears had "willfully and wantonly allowed high powered pain killers to be administered, interfering with natural processes of the human body and causing irreparable damage," and that the Bears forced him to play when he should not have done so, thereby furthering the damage to the knee. The lawyer also claimed that the five one-year contracts were in fact one contract for five years.

Dr. Fox carried malpractice insurance. Three-way discussions began between Dick's lawyer, my lawyer Don Reuben, and the insurance company's lawyer.

Butkus moved to Florida and became a representative of a body-building equipment company.

291

For two years, there was little progress in the suit.

In May of 1976, I told Butkus that if he would come to Chicago and act as a goodwill ambassador for the Bears I would pay him $115,000 a year for the four years remaining on the contracts after he ceased playing. Nothing came of my offer.

I became eager for a settlement; I thought the suit was disturbing the team. Dooley had become Democratic candidate for the Illinois Supreme Court and also appeared eager to settle. I heard that Butkus could use some money. Reuben advised a settlement.

Reuben asked a friend, Charles Swibel, if he happened to have a friend who was also a friend of Dooley and might arrange a meeting between Swibel, acting for me, and Dooley, acting for Butkus. Swibel did happen to be so blessed.

"A highly respected judge not involved in the case was a friend to both Jim and me," Swibel says.

He arranged an early breakfast meeting at the Drake. Halas told me I could go up to $600,000. I began at $200,000. Dooley began at I forget what. Eventually, I came up to $600,000 and he came down to $750,000. By then, the judge was long overdue in court. The judge asked if the insurance company might come up with the difference. The judge went to court. I went to see George. I said I thought I could nail it down for $650,000. Reuben was against going over $600,000.

I said, "George, you give me $650,000 and if I can get him down to $600,000, I'll keep the fifty thousand; if I have to go higher, I'll pay everything above $650,000." That broke the ice. We had another meeting and settled for $600,000. I did not keep the $50,000.

All mention of malpractice was eliminated. Dr. Fox's insurers paid $300,000 and the Bears paid $300,000.

There had been many predictions that if Butkus managed to collect a substantial sum, a host of players who retired because of injuries over the years would go to court suing clubs. That did not happen. Instead, clubs and the players' union reached a long-term agreement in which compensation for injuries is stipulated.

There were two happy aftermaths. Five years after Gale Sayers retired he became eligible for enshrinement in the Hall of Fame and was unanimously selected. Gale asked me to be his presenter. I did so, with love and joy. When the five-year waiting period ended for Dick Butkus, the nominators unanimously selected him for enshrinement in the Hall of Fame. Dick asked if I would be his presenter. I accepted with great pleasure. Dick Butkus is well worthy of such an honor. He had a rare ability. He played with dedication. He possessed the old zipperoo.

CHAPTER TWENTY-ONE

Pain Wears
Many Cloaks

ON THE FIRST DAY I played softball with my brothers under the street lights, I became acquainted with pain. I skinned a knee and bent a finger. As the years passed, injuries, minor and major, made pain part of my life. I developed considerable tolerance to pain. I assumed pain was part of the price of living required of me.

But the pain that began seizing my Min during the 1940's was something else. The trigeminal nerve on the left side of her face went wrong. The condition is called tic douloureux. The pain would grip her face, suddenly, without warning. Her eyes would well with tears. She would clench her hands. She would sit there, saying nothing, waiting for the pain to pass. She was brave. Doctors could offer her no worthwhile relief. Had I been she, I would have jumped out the window. I made certain none of our windows could be opened widely.

By 1947 the pain was coming so frequently that the renowned surgeon, Dr. Loyal Davis, proposed an operation in which the nerve is severed. Min agreed. The operation is done under local anesthesia. The patient sits upright to reduce the flow of blood to the head. The head is clamped securely to a frame to prevent any movement. A cloth is put over the patient, the upper part of the head protruding. The surgeon drills a hole in the skull and severs the nerve.

Two young doctors, John Bell and Dan Ruge, later Dr. Davis' partner, were assigned to help Dr. Davis. When they joined him in the operating room, Dr. Davis, who was very strict with young doctors, said, "All right, don't you fellas mess up this one the way you did the last one." From under the cloth came Min's voice, very plaintive, "Oh, please, boys, do help Dr. Davis!"

The operation did end the pain. The muscle tone of her face was undisturbed. The feeling in that side of the face, however, was gone. If something got into the eye, she would not feel it and infection could develop. To protect the eye, she had a little shield attached to her glasses. That marred her vision. She gave up driving.

She worked hard on recovery. She was such a good patient that Dr. Davis would ask her to talk to other persons with the same problem. He knew she would give a positive report.

Min resumed coming to our home games. She knew all of the players. They would say, "Good afternoon, Mrs. Halas," and she would say, "Hello, Jim," or "Joe," or "Charlie" or whoever he was, "have a good game." Always Min had been a rabid sports fan. But some time after the operation, she became so worked up at games that the doctor advised her not to attend. For a while, she

295

listened on the radio at home. He forbade that. Then she would keep looking at the clock to see how long she had to wait for the result. The doctor turned the clock to face the wall. Fred Nichols and other friends would phone her with the result. I felt it was very hard on Min to keep herself away from the games. I often pondered why the games affected her so strongly. Virginia came up with an explanation. She said her mother, a very orderly person, had really to be in control of surroundings and events. With football, she could not control the outcome.

Min did enjoy competition. Two sets of women friends organized a rotating, twice-weekly bridge game. Our friend and neighbor, Louise Lorenz, often came up for an evening canasta game.

As Virginia's eleven children came along, Min early made it clear she was not a built-in baby sitter. She used holidays as big family days. All the family would come to us for Fourth of July fireworks and for Thanksgiving and Christmas. When the family outgrew our apartment, we moved the feasts to a restaurant, and then to the McCaskey home.

Constant pain selected me for its next victim. Arthritis was freezing my hip joints. By the time of our 1963 championship team, I had resorted to using a golf cart in training periods and practices.

At games, I had to give up running along the sidelines, instructing officials, encouraging Bears, taunting our opponents—all activities which were part of the game and appreciated by our fans. Arthritis confined me to the bench area as no rule or official had ever been able to do. During most of the playing time, I knelt on one knee. I was fascinated to hear that rival coaches spent a lot of time watching me and trying to figure out what instructions my various kneeling positions were conveying to my men. After many years of my seeking opportunities, such conclusions were to be expected. I considered the coaches' interest a compliment. The pain became worse with each season, the mobility less. I could foresee the day when I might be immobile.

"I would see the pain in his face as he pulled on his stockings," Sid Luckman says. "I would ask, 'Coach, how are you feeling?' 'I feel great, I feel wonderful,' he would reply. 'Let's get out to practice. It's so important that we get out there. We've a job to do!'"

In time Dr. Jim Stack provided some relief at critical periods by inserting a five-inch-long needle through the groin into the hip. He felt around to find where the head of the femur fitted into the socket and injected painkiller directly into the joint. The injection would see me through the game.

One evening during our 1964 training camp period, Willie Galimore and Bo Farrington were absent when our eight o'clock chalk talk was due to begin. They had gone out for a couple of quick beers. I delayed the class for their return. Then came a dreadful phone call. The two Bears, hurrying back to camp, missed a sharp turn on the highway. Their car had crashed into a barn, killing both instantly. The men were popular with their team- mates and the staff. The tragedy blotted out enthusiasm carried over from our 1963 championship. For the Bears, the season was over before it began. We won just five of fourteen games; 1964 was a painful season.

In February of 1966, shortly before the month in Phoenix to which Min and I were looking forward, the League called a meeting in Miami. Min hated to fly. As the meeting was to be short, it wasn't worth a train trip.

She decided not to go. Mugs and I prepared to fly down. The Bears' trainer, Ed Rozy, and his wife Josephine helped get us off.

Josephine recalls:

It was the day before St. Valentine's. Mugs' little daughter Christine was dressed so prettily she looked like a Valentine. She was beginning to walk and she showed Coach and Mrs. Halas how well she could navigate. Mrs. Halas, in her busy, quick way, was packing Coach's bag. She gave baby a tender hug and kiss and handed her to me, saying, "You have more time than I, take care of her." With hugs and kisses, we said goodbye to Mrs. Halas. In the elevator Coach asked us to hold the door. He returned to the apartment door where Mrs. Halas stood smiling. He took her in his arms and hugged and kissed her several times. He rejoined us, saying, "Now let's get going." Perhaps the thought of St. Valentine made him return for the second farewell or there may have been something more. I don't know.

That evening, Marjorie Maxwell phoned and asked if Don's driver could pick up Min and bring her to the Maxwell home for dinner the next day. The Maxwells knew I was away. Min said no, thanks, she had to pack for the vacation in Phoenix. She still had errands to do. She had to pick up some dresses being altered. She was having a quick dinner with Louise Vetterick, Frances Osborne and Jean Doyle in Louise's apartment across the street. Marjorie probably was the last person to speak to Min.

The next evening in Miami we were at a restaurant with other League officials and Ralph and Florence Brizzolara. Mugs was called from the table. He returned, white. He asked Ralph and me to come to the office. There he said, "Father, Mother has passed away." Jerry Wolman had given him the message. Mugs had phoned the Chicago apartment. Frances Osborne and Don Maxwell were there. They confirmed the dreadful message.

When Min had not shown up at Louise Vetterick's apartment, her friends were surprised because Min was always so punctual. They thought she must have been delayed at the dress shop. After an hour, they did become worried. Louise phoned Dorothy Brown, who had an apartment at the Edgewater Beach, and asked her to go up to the Halas apartment and see if Min were all right. Dorothy found the morning *Tribune* still outside the door. She phoned the building manager. He opened the door. He called. No response. He walked from room to room. He found Min in bed. She had passed away during the night, in her sleep. Her face was composed. There was no sign of pain. Dr. Ted Fox, the Bears' doctor, said Min's heart had given out, although there never had been any evidence of a flaw.

Min! Dead! My own Min! My staunchest supporter. The Bears' most avid fan. I hardly heard the words "she died in her sleep," "she didn't suffer," "she was found in bed this evening without a sign of suffering."

Min sometimes had told me, "You are married to football." And I would reply, "You are exactly right, and the National Football League is my mistress." But now suddenly the world was a huge emptiness.

We slipped out of the restaurant as inconspicuously as possible. Ralph chartered a Lear Jet to get Mugs and me to Chicago quickly. I was dazed and silent. Raymond Lorenz, Virginia and Ed met us in Chicago. Everyone was numb with shock.

"I too had lost someone very close," Sid Luckman says. "I looked upon the Halas family as though they were mine. They asked me to be a pallbearer."

The next months were difficult. Daily, no, hourly, I realized how much Min had meant to me. The winter, spring and summer were each a century long. I welcomed the coming of the autumn training period when my Bears would absorb my waking hours. But the arthritis was steadily closing its grip. The cartilage had completely worn away in the joint. Bone was rubbing against bone. Two years crawled past.

Each winter I went as usual to the Arizona Biltmore in Phoenix for the month of February. There, in 1968, a woman told me she had found relief from arthritis in mud baths at a spa in Italy. I resolved to drop everything and devote my energies to challenging the growing disability. I arranged with the Italian spa for treatments in April. I announced I was retiring as coach and made Jim Dooley the Bears' head coach. I boarded a plane for Milan. With me went Ed Rozy. Neither of us had been to Europe. Before the flight I ordered his favorite dinner of ham hocks and sauerkraut. The 150-mile auto ride across northern Italy was wild. The driver went at least 90. He gestured with both hands and shouted at passing drivers.

The Grand Hotel Royal Orologio at Abano Therme was spacious, with gardens and a pool. Ancient Romans had soaked in mud there. Each morning for two weeks an attendant packed me in mud. At 11 A.M. Ed and I swam in a pool fed by hot springs. Then came cocktails and lunch. One afternoon we went to a casino. I hadn't thrown dice since my father early stopped that sport, except once briefly in Tijuana and again at the Nacional Hotel in Havana where I had gone with some friends on oil business. Castro staged a raffle. He invited one of our party—John Bowers. Castro told John, "Go home and put on a tux!" I never had linked Castro and a tux.

At the Italian casino, I broke even.

The mud treatment did ease the pain. Ed and I flew to Rome. Bishop Paul Marcinkus, a Vatican official from Cicero, Illinois, arranged an audience with Pope Paul. I found the audience a moving occasion. All my life my faith has meant much to me. Pope Paul was interested in football's role in the lives of young men. When he heard Ed was the Bears' trainer, he repeated several times, "Young men need good training!"

In a few weeks the effect of the spa wore off. I came to realize surgery was for me the only path to freedom from pain.

I went to the Mayo Clinic in Rochester, Minnesota. Surgeons recommended an operation. I would need crutches for a year. Then the second hip would be done, requiring one more year on crutches. A date was set for late autumn.

A great sorrow descended. Frances Osborne, my secretary who had done so much for the Bears ever since the days Ralph Brizzolara and she brought them through World War II, suffered a severe stroke. She could not speak very well. I spent hours by her bedside to try to help her realize she had my whole support in her effort to regain the mastery of her movement and speech. I often thought, as I spoke to her and pressed her good left hand, how there we were, both of us, with the problem of mobility. How were we going to get in shape again to push the Bears to the best of their potential? Frances did improve enough to go home and prepare to return to the office.

One day, a chemist, Dr. Sylvan M. Edison, whom I had not seen since we were at the university together fifty years earlier, dropped into my office. He too had been a victim of an arthritic hip. Three years earlier he had undergone a capping procedure and had been left with constant pain. Seeking permanent relief, he had gone to Britain for an operation developed by an English bone surgeon, John Charnley, in which the hip joint is totally replaced. Dr. Edison said he was out of bed after one week and walking with crutches on the eighth day. All arthritic pain was gone. I asked why the operation was not done in our country. "Because," he said, "the cement used by Charnley has not received the Federal Drug Administration's approval." When he added that the British operation required 55 minutes and the American one 4 hours, I was sold. But, being cautious, I asked our team doctor, Ted Fox, to investigate. He gave a favorable report, as did other doctors. I canceled the appointment at Mayo Clinic. Doctors Sid Shafer and Robert Ray arranged for me to go to the Wrightington Hospital near Wigan, some 200 miles northwest of London, in mid-November. Ed and Virginia flew with me to London and onward to Manchester.

In the hospital was a fellow Chicagoan, Milton Stein. He was seventy-nine, older than I, and was happily using a new hip. On Thanksgiving Day, which the English don't observe, Jennie, his very attractive wife, brought in turkey dinners.

The hospital had begun as a tuberculosis sanitarium. Most of the buildings were one-story, light and airy. Additions, made during World War II, rambled here and there. There had been no operating theater, not even a suitable room for conversation. Mr. Charnley—I learned British surgeons take pride in being called "mister" to distinguish themselves from physicians—chose a large room and installed in its center a structure he called his greenhouse. It consisted of three sheets of plate glass erected as a "U" and reaching from the ceiling to about four inches from the floor. The fourth side was closed with a plastic sheet split halfway up the middle sealable with a zip. A powerful purifying system directed a blast of air downward from the ceiling and out below the glass. The patient, feet forward, was wheeled into the greenhouse as far as his neck. The zip then was closed, leaving his head outside. Only two surgeons and two nurses were in the enclosure. Because the air was cool, they wore stocking caps, sweaters and gumboots under their sterilized garments. Masks covered their faces from the eyes downward and tubes carried their exhaust breath down along the leg to the floor. The only large cost was the air system. The interior of the glass cage could be sterilized easily. Trainee doctors could stand outside the glass only 2 feet away. Instruments could be passed in and out of the glasshouse cage through an open hatch— the stream of air made it a one-way passage for bacteria—out! At the time of my operation Charnley had not had one primary infection in 2,000 operations.

The operation is a big one but I had complete confidence when I met Mr. Charnley. He is a smallish, neat man, quiet with sure, quick movements.

I was rolled partly into his greenhouse. The anesthesiologist sat outside, beside my head. Of the operation, of course, I can say only what I was told later.

303

The surgeon made a long incision from above the hip down along the outside of the leg more than halfway to the knee. He cut off a section of the bone holding the muscle, freeing the femur which was pulled out of the socket and twisted outwards. The knob was sawed off, marrow scooped out. A 6-inch-long piece of stainless steel resembling a spike with a bent-over, ball-shaped head was pushed into the bone and sealed there with a cement, methyl methacrylate. The cement, when mixed, became extremely hot and had to be put into place quickly before it set.

The cup in the hip bone was enlarged and a semi-sphere of plastic resembling a thickened ping-pong ball cut in half was cemented into the cup. The leg bone was put back into place with the stainless-steel ball snapping into the plastic cup. The bit of bone with the muscle was wired into position. The wound was sewed up. Lo and behold, a new hip!

The first day I began moving my toes, ankles and feet. The next day nurses got me onto my feet. I used a walker for two days and then graduated to crutches. I went up and down the long hall, each time increasing the number of trips.

Twice I disturbed the night staff. In a nightmare, men chased me along a cliff. I screamed. Doctors and nurses came running. About three o'clock one Monday morning Mugs telephoned from Los Angeles to say we had beaten the Rams. Again I let out a whoop. Again doctors and nurses came rushing, wanting to know what had gone wrong. I introduced them to American football, which of course had grown out of their rugby. I found an interested audience.

Gin and Ed left. Their youngest child was six or

seven and Gin was eager to get home. Ed Rozy, my trainer and friend, took their place. Mugs and his wife came.

The doctor was delighted with my dedication to practice. I think he saw how a lifetime of discipline in sports helped me get moving again quickly.

I walked one day with Mr. Charnley to his laboratory. On benches along the wall was a series of stainless-steel spikes with different-sized balls, each moving back and forth in a plastic cup. The sizes, shapes and materials varied and so did the pressure holding the cup and spike together. It was here that Mr. Charnley had evolved the best materials and shapes. In a few days each joint received the wear and tear it would undergo in a human lifetime. I learned Mr. Charnley had a degree in engineering as well as in medicine.

Don and Marjorie Maxwell flew over. With them, from London, were *Chicago Tribune* foreign correspondents Gwen Morgan and Arthur Veysey. They all stayed at a small country inn some distance away, called "The Last Drop." A noose, not a beer glass, was on the signboard at the entrance, the inn standing on land once owned by England's last hangman.

From the Maxwells I had details of a Bears' game. During the night, they had fiddled the dials of a powerful radio until they heard the familiar voice of Sportscaster Jack Brickhouse. I think we lost.

John Bowers came. Joel Goldblatt called daily.

In three weeks I was ready to fly home. The arthritis pain was gone from the hip but I could still feel the wound. Mr. Charnley said I was moving better than many younger patients do in six weeks. "See you in six months," he added.

There are sixty steps between my apartment door

305

and the elevator. With the crutches I began playing a game. The first day I made two trips, the next day four, then eight, then sixteen, until I was making nearly one hundred trips a day.

I returned to Britain for the second operation the next May. The countryside was beautifully green and in flower. Maude and John Clarke came. Again Joel called daily.

Both operations were successful. My reappearance at Wrigley Field, walking, brought a great deal of publicity. Many people with the same affliction called—and still call me. I put everything aside, and still do, to tell them of my happy experiences. I wished doctors at Mayo's could soon perform the operation. Before leaving Mr. Charnley, I had asked him for copies of my x-ray pictures. I turned them over to Dr. William H. Bickel at Mayo Clinic. In time, when the United States approved the cement, the Mayo Clinic sent people to Charnley. The operation is now done throughout the world. The Clinic does thousands every year. I continue to try to convince sufferers this operation offers them a new life. Tens of thousands of arthritic hip victims have been relieved of the agonizing pain and have renewed active lives. In time Queen Elizabeth knighted Charnley. He is now Sir John. He deserves to be made a lord.

Another blow struck. Frances Osborne did return to the office part-time. She was making progress. One day, in a moment of depression, she jumped from a window of her apartment. I was stunned.

Old friends rallied around—Maxwell and Marge, Ed Lee, Colonel Crown, Joel Goldblatt. Every month or so a group of old friends took turns having a dinner—Federal Judge Abraham Lincoln Marovitz and his friend, Mickey

Curtin, Dr. James Callahan, who is now working on bone transplants, and Mrs. Callahan, Michael Notaro, who is in computers, and his friend, Ruth Sanford. They asked me to join them. I fear I was not a cheery companion. The Bears were having a terrible time. I had left Jim Dooley a strong team with two great players, Gale Sayers and Dick Butkus. The team broke even, winning seven and losing seven. Just before I had left for England for the first time, I watched Gale Sayers come around end against the '49ers. The play was directly in front of our bench. Clearly I saw George Seals miss a block on Kermit Alexander. I sensed disaster a second away! Alexander, off balance, slid underneath Seals. His helmet crashed into Gale's knee. Both went down. My heart sank. I knew Gale would not get up. I cried with him as he was carried off. He was such a magnificent person and a great player. What pained me so much was the type of man who had been hurt.

A worse disaster struck Gale's roommate, Brian Piccolo. He was not a star player but he was a star teammate. His good humor was ceaseless. Cancer seized him. We watched the dreaded disease slowly kill him. A book and a movie told his story and assisted his young wife and two small daughters in making a new life.

Gale is a tremendous individual. Gale, as recounted, rehabilitated himself following an operation. The next season he led the League in rushing—1,032 yards, but of fourteen games, my Bears won only one. Never in forty-nine years had the Bears been so bad. To deepen the anguish, the fault did not lie with the players. The problem was coaching. It took two more losing years before I replaced Dooley with Abe Gibron. In three years under Abe, the Bears won only eleven games. For me, the football seasons to which I once looked forward with joy had become long periods of agony. Life held little pleasure for me. No, I was not a cheery companion. Pain, I learned, wears many cloaks.

One evening Judge Abraham Lincoln Marovitz took me to the Empire Room at the Palmer House to hear Carol Channing. He thought her performance would cheer me. Carol saw me and began to say something about the Bears. Everybody booed. Then Carol said I was present and she wanted to make me a gift. The boos turned to cheers. People stood up and clapped. Carol gave me a ring. Young and old, men and women, came over to get my autograph.

One day in 1970 I asked my six friends if I could bring a guest. They agreed, eagerly. I telephoned Rita Hauk. Her husband, Roy, had died about six months earlier of cancer. Since the death of Colonel Hauk, Roy's father, the couple had run the White Bear Wholesale Laundry, in which I was still a partner. Since Roy's death, Rita had been managing the business.

"Rita," I said, "would I be out of place to ask you to have dinner with me and some friends this evening?"

She said, "George, I would be happy to come, and thank you very much."

Rita became a steady member of our group. We started calling ourselves the Super Eight. For several years I had received many invitations to social functions. I had been reluctant to accept. I did not wish to go by myself. Now, Rita accompanied me. Rita was French Canadian. She was small, very pretty, lively, full of humor. She carried sunshine with her. Everybody enjoyed her.

The laundry was becoming a burden to her. I helped

arrange a sale. One autumn, when our ticket office was in a mess, Rita volunteered to come in and help straighten out the accounts. She proved to be most efficient. I paid her the regular salary. All her life she had wanted a fur coat. She decided to splurge all her earnings. She asked our good friend Louise Lorenz, who lives in my building, about fur shops. Louise took her to the finest. Rita finally had her coat. She was pleased pink.

Over four years, I grew devoted to Rita. To revert to the language of my youth, I developed a real crush on her. We might have married, in time.

Then, on September 4, 1975, she did not meet me at the Tavern Club as arranged for dinner. She had been working hard directing the redecoration of my apartment. The job was almost finished. Louise asked her out for lunch. No, Rita said, she was tired. She would go to her apartment, rest, take a shower and meet me for dinner.

As the minutes passed, I became very alarmed. I phoned her apartment. There was no reply. I phoned the building manager. I asked her to open Rita's door. She went in. She called. No answer. She went from room to room. No Rita. She went into the bedroom. The dress Rita planned to wear that night was laid out on the bed. She went into the bathroom. There Rita lay, on the floor. As with Min, life had suddenly slipped away. As with Min, the doctors said Rita's heart had failed, although, as with Min, there had been no sign of any flaw.

I felt life was over for me. Old friends were disappearing. Don Maxwell slipped away while being driven to his office in the *Tribune* building. His companion, Tom Furlong, thought he was merely taking a nap, a Maxwell custom.

309

One day in 1977 I purposely took a walk past the Bears' waiting room to see a candidate who had come to ask our personnel manager, Jerry Vainisi, about a place as my secretary. The sight of this well-groomed woman pleased me. I wanted to hear her voice.

"Have you been helped?" I inquired, pausing.

"Yes, thank you," she replied. "I am waiting to see Mr. Vainisi."

I went into my office. I picked up the telephone.

"Hire her," I said.

That was the coming of Ruth Hughes, whose daily helpfulness and humor have again made life pleasant.

CHAPTER TWENTY-TWO

I Play to Win

I PLAY TO WIN. I always have played to win. I always shall play to win.

I speak no praise for the good loser, the man who says, "Well, I did my best." I am fortunate in having been a winner more often than a loser. I do not accept defeat. I have learned to live with defeat but each loss is an agony which remains with me for several days and is dissipated only by the growing prospect of a victory.

The agony is endurable because of the ecstasy that comes with victory. It might be thought that time would soften the agony and the ecstasy. But, no, the intensity is there today as firmly as the day I ran down the steps of our house to join my brothers in a game against the neighborhood rivals.

Football is a game of emotions. For me, that is the heart of its appeal. Yes, it is a game of skill and fitness and strategy, a game demanding brain and muscle, but it is also a game of emotions. The superior football player lives on a knife-edge as does the person hooked on gambling. A man betting on cards, on horses, on dice, on the wheel, even on sports, has little control over his fate. In football each movement is aimed at securing victory. I am fortunate to be hooked on football.

When in 1920, Mr. A.E. Staley asked me to produce a winning football team, I imposed two conditions: I must be able to seek the best players, and the team must practice daily. He saw the wisdom of my demands.

In searching for players over the past sixty years, I have looked for a fine combination of intelligence and natural ability. But the smartest and most agile player is useless unless he has also what I call the great desire, mental heat, the old zipperoo.

Over the years, I have put down my ideas about the paramount importance of mental attitude. This is the way I stated them in a 1962 manual sent to players coming to our training camp to try out for places on the Bears:

MENTAL ASPECTS OF FOOTBALL
The strength and character of the personnel determines the strength and success of the team. *This 1962 squad has great possibilities.* You may have speed, weight and ability, and all the physical qualifications that are essential to a great athlete. However, men are not machines, and so with the team. There must be some inherent force to drive you forward.

PRIDE AND TRADITION
We feel certain that anytime two teams are evenly matched, the team which has the greatest desire to win—will win. Usually the desire comes from a certain amount of pride in excelling in playing the game. *Nobody who ever gave his best regretted it.*

There are many factors involved in developing pride. Tradition of the entire organization and its contribution to professional football, of games won and lost, the number of championships won, and tradition of the former great players. It is an advantage to be a member of an organization with great tradition and it is a *responsibility* to uphold that tradition.

AGGRESSIVENESS
This is the most important single quality for a football player. At least 80 percent of the success of the football team is determined by the fight and spirit that they put into their play. The biggest and fastest material, superbly coached, would fail miserably without this indispensable characteristic.

This is the first quality a coach seeks in a man, for without it he cannot make a contribution to the team. As a candidate for the team it will be to your advantage to show aggressiveness the very moment you step out on the practice field. If you show that quality, you will be given every opportunity to become a football player.

CONCENTRATION
The player who has this quality will jump ahead the very first day of practice. Modern football systems are complicated in their method of offense and defense. Some men know the plays perfectly. Others go about learning them in a slip-shod manner. It is essential that every candidate know *every play precisely, exactly, immediately,* and without the slightest doubt as to how it should be executed.

DETERMINATION
Before it is possible to achieve anything, an objective must be set. Many people flounder about in life because they do not have a purpose, an objective toward which to work. Your objective is to make the team. Setting that objective is only one step—the other essential is to become determined to achieve it.

313

Each of you has a weakness in football technique. Do not be satisfied to continue on the same level of execution of the fundamentals. Become determined to overcome those weaknesses. Some men go through an entire season content to "fool around," cut-up, wisecrack, and as a result never contribute to the squad. This year let each of you take a personal pride in having serious determination of purpose to become the very best football player possible. You can achieve only that which you *will do*.

LEADERSHIP
Every organization must have leadership. In a football squad that leadership is in the captain, players, and the coaches. Many players resent criticism from the coaches and captain merely because they fail to understand the real reason for such criticism. We are all working for the common end—a championship football team for the Chicago Bears. It is *your team*. This means that all of us must pull together to do our best, to follow orders and plans which have been formulated.

Some football practice is monotonous and tiring. In the last two years we have attempted to avoid this and will try even more in 1962. Sometimes it becomes extremely fatiguing. However, it is all part of the game. Drill—Drill—and still more Drill are necessary in order to perfect the fundamentals. The mental satisfaction of winning the championship in 1962 will far outweigh any momentary discomfort of tedious drill. *When you leave the field physically fatigued but feeling mentally refreshed, you are on the right track.*

RELIABILITY
Reliability is one of your greatest single assets. It is the quality which every employer seeks. It is the quality which all men should cultivate.

314

CONFIDENCE
Every great athlete, every successful team, has this mental attitude. Confidence is belief in yourself and in your team that you can achieve victory by hard, intelligent fighting.

COOPERATION
Any man going out for football must bury his selfish interest. A football team is not the product of one player, one man, one group. The team is the product of every single candidate. It is your duty to yourself, to your friends, and to the team, to keep this thought foremost in mind at all times.

SUMMARY
Now that you have read this through, study yourself, and see if you have a full measure of all of these qualities. As a coach they are the things I would like to see in every candidate. These are the things which you should develop within yourself: Aggressiveness, Concentration, Determination, Obedience, Reliability and Harmonious Cooperation. They will broaden your personality. Apply them to your football. They will help make your associations and employment pleasant and successful.

I believe each person is an individual and must be treated accordingly. Something that turns one man on will turn another off. I am fortunate in that, somehow, I sense what makes a person go. I never said a harsh word to Red Grange or Sid Luckman or Gale Sayers. I spoke harshly to Bronko Nagurski just once, and regretted it ever after.

One season a young rookie did everything wrong. The more coaches rode him, the worse his performance became. I took him aside and said, "I think you are one of the strongest men I have ever seen. I bet you could move a house if you tried."

"You do?" he asked, his voice full of doubt.

I said, "Yes, if you try. Now go out there and move some houses." He tore onto the field. Nobody could stop him.

Doug Atkins was different. Paul Brown traded him to me because Doug resented discipline of any kind, and Brown was very much of a disciplinarian. One night a fan phoned that Doug was cutting up drunk in a bar. I drove over. Doug saw me enter and shouted a tumultuous river of profanities. I walked up to him and countered with a barrage that for volume and variety made his assault a peaceful brook compared to my Niagara. Doug put down his glass and came to camp. At 10 minutes before 9 in the morning, he was out there on the field with no trace of foggy-headedness or wobbly limbs. Doug became a powerful Bear. We became good friends.

"Halas," said Carroll Rosenbloom, "has to be the greatest motivator in the game. I offered him $100,000 to come out and talk to my Rams."

"About 1950," George Connor recalls, "Coach Halas needled me about how a great '49er fullback named Joe Perry would run all over me. Halas had me believing the game was a personal vendetta between Joe and me. I was 6 foot 3, 240, and I hit Perry so hard I broke the tape holding up my socks. Perry was knocked out."

"When I first saw Mr. Halas I was shocked," Gale Sayers says. "You don't think of someone seventy-three out there coaching. But he was first on and last off. To see this seventy-three-year-old man out there every day right through the season motivated me. He is the only person I could run for 100 percent on every play."

316

Connor says:

In one game, an Eagles' linebacker punched George
Gulyanics in the face. With malice George asked
Sid Luckman to call "46-fire-George." Sid said,
"Coach said we shouldn't use that play." George
said, "I want to get even with the linebacker who
socked me." Sid called time out and went to the
bench to speak to Coach Halas. Halas said, "George
will get killed but if he wants it, let him have it." Sid
called the play, in which the guard and George went
for the linebacker from opposite sides to clear the
way for McAfee, the carrier. They hit the guy so hard
they knocked him out. When he came to, he was missing his front teeth and there was McAfee safe across
the goal.

One day a player jumped on Bill Osmanski's brother
after he was down, breaking his back. Bill told the player
he did it deliberately. He replied, "That's part of football." Bulldog Turner overheard. On the next punt
Bulldog hit the guy so hard he was carried off.

Much earlier, while Bill was playing for Holy Cross,
his mother, a great fan, was hit by a car coming to a Holy
Cross game. Bill learned of the accident at the half. He
asked to go to the hospital. The coach said no. Bill's mind
was not on the game. He missed some tackles. With 6
minutes left, Holy Cross trailed 12–0. The coach called
Bill to the sidelines, pointed to the stands. There sat
Bill's mother. In the 6 minutes, Bill made two spectacular touchdown runs. Holy Cross won 14–12. That day
Bill had good cause for mental heat.

"Every player liked playing in the game Sunday,"
recalls Red Grange. "But practicing was different. One
Tuesday Johnny Sisk reported a knee had been hurt in

the game. There was no visible evidence, but Halas told him to sit out the practice. At the end, Johnny got into his car to drive home. There was a big bang and a lot of smoke. Johnny came out of that car like lightning and set a new 100-yard record in getting clear. It was only a smoke bomb. When Johnny came back, Halas said, 'All right, Johnny, five times around the field.' I never did know who set the smoke bomb, but Halas had heard all the alibis."

I do not underrate trivialities. Who outside football would place any value on winning the opening toss other than getting first possession of the ball? I can testify the toss is important. Both teams go onto the field full of confidence. The referee tosses the coin. One side wins. Suddenly fate is on their side. The other side suffers a loss even before the ball is kicked. I have seen several games between equally matched teams in which the team winning the toss makes a touchdown within a couple of minutes, and neither team scores again. Could the explanation be the slight shift in mental heat brought about by the toss? I believe this is true. That's why at Super Bowl XIII I gave my 1920 twenty-dollar gold piece to the toss losers.

A contest between equal teams is usually decided by the breaks. A team will fumble and the other will pick up the ball and score. Or a player will intercept a pass and score. Suddenly one team is high, the other low.

In the 1940 championship game, lady luck and the breaks were on our side. We won the toss. In three plays we had a touchdown. The Redskins drove back and dropped a long pass that would have evened the game. From then on, we could do nothing wrong; they could do nothing right. That was the game we won, 73–0.

When coaching, I did not stand stoically on the sidelines. No 40-yard line could confine me. I was up and down that field. When a Bear broke loose, I was running right there with him. Whenever a referee penalized my Bears I made my feelings known. I've been told some fans watched a play and then turned to see how I reacted. To some people I was being a showman. Perhaps so, but I was active on the sidelines because I had to be part of the game. My body was on the sidelines but my spirit was right there with my players, and they knew it, and the officials knew it.

There were side effects. One day a '49er fan took a kick at me. Mugs kicked back. Photographers got a great picture. It was printed coast-to-coast. The next Sunday we went to Los Angeles and played to 92,000 people. Another day I saw an opening for a specialty play. I called out, "26–40." The quarterback did not hear me but a great Pittsburgh linebacker, Cal Hubbard, did. Mockingly, he repeated my call. The quarterback did hear him. He called the play. We made a touchdown.

I did exchange comments with opposing players. Larry Brink of the Rams was one of my favorite conversationalists. He spoke with such enthusiasm and ingenuity that profanity became poetry. I replied to the best of my ability. We both enjoyed the verbal encounters. One day on a kickoff, he came charging down the sideline, watching the ball. As he passed, I felt a need to stretch my legs. He tripped. He tried to right himself but fell flat. He came back to speak to me. He did not apologize for hitting my legs. In time, I encouraged the Rams to trade Brink to me. One day when he was with the Bears he intercepted a pass and ran along the sideline for a touchdown. This time I ran along beside him, encouraging him. He did not need it, but he got it.

Teams visiting Wrigley Field constantly complained about lack of soap, towels, programs. They put it down to stinginess. But why not deprive visitors, if doing so upsets them? What better location for our band than directly behind George Preston Marshall, tootling in his ears? And if Curly Lambeau had trouble seeing the play from his specially allocated bench in a far corner, so much the better for my Bears. More to be impish, all this, than anything else, you understand.

I did outsmart myself one summer. I installed air conditioning in the Bears' dressing rooms for an important All-Star game, but none in the visitors'. Our players did enjoy the cool comfort during the half time that hot August night while the visitors sweated on the grass to escape their steaming rooms. But when play resumed, the Bears' muscles were cold and stiff. We lost the game.

Common sense suggests that every person be physically fit if he is to make the best of life. Common sense demands athletes be fit. Some athletes are content to seek fitness only during the playing season. My experience has led me to believe that fitness is best achieved day by day, week by week, year by year, all through life.

When I was young, fitness did not have to be diligently sought. Fitness was the result of everyday activities. Mothers were sensible cooks who had learned from their mothers how to feed the family with foods the healthy body requires. Exercise was part of daily life. Every kid had chores. We fetched and carried and ran errands. We went to school on our feet. After school and in summer, kids collected in vacant lots to play workup or kick the can. Always there were trees to climb, buildings under construction to test our nerve. As we grew older, part-time jobs built muscles. Bronko Nagurski plowed fields and chopped wood. Jim McMillen hauled ice blocks from frozen lakes until his hands bled. Ed Healey was a logger. Red Grange delivered ice. We all heaved and sweated and ran.

How different for young persons today! Junk food is no substitute for stew and soups that simmered all day. No longer does a boy carry coal or chop wood. We take our children to and from school in a bus and build indoor running tracks so they can, but rarely do, build firm bodies. Schools create elaborate sports programs, unfortunately designed not for participation by all students, but to develop the few super players. The great masses of students are moved from the playing fields to the bleachers. Nagurski ran 3 miles to town. Osmanski ran 2 miles to school. How many boys today can run a mile?

I have related how my early experiments with tobacco produced nausea. I have given thanks a million times. I do so again every time I talk to someone trying to give up smoking. From my high school days, coaches told me smoking would hinder my ability to run. As coach and owner I have passed on this wisdom. I have never allowed smoking in Bears' dressing rooms or classrooms or on the field.

I did not have early unhappy personal experiences with alcohol. Watching neighbors in Mother's saloon, I saw how alcohol in small amounts could add to the pleasure of social gatherings but when taken in excess produced terrible problems and much unhappiness. As an adult, I found alcohol has enlivened many social occasions for me and, in truth, I have laid one on more times than I like to remember. At training camps, the Bears provide no alcoholic drinks but I know I cannot keep alcohol from rooms. Nor do I place nearby taverns out of bounds although the probability of someone reporting whenever a player overdoes himself in a tavern is so great that some players accuse me of running a spy system. Actually, reports come from Bears' fans concerned that a player might be harming the team. I have one brake on too much drinking by Bears in season. Every player must report for workouts at 9 A.M. sharp. He is fined $5 for every minute he is late. Heavy workouts begin at once and any fogginess in the head or awkwardness in the body quickly reveals itself. When the day ends and I say goodnight, few players think of anything except going to bed.

On arriving at training camp each player is assigned a playing weight and checks in and out every day. The overweight player is given so many days to make the weight. If he fails, he is fined $5 a pound a day. If three days pass and he is still overweight, he hears a few choice words. The smart man keeps his weight all through his life. Red Grange and Sid Luckman have never varied by more than a few pounds. Keeping the correct weight is much easier than trying to recover it. With proper eating and exercise, weight is no problem. Being fit is fun, and adds years to a life.

In the seventies, drugs became a problem. Certain drugs do give a feeling of euphoria but I know of no evidence to support statements that drugs improve a player's performance. The truth is drugs merely make the player think he is playing better when he is playing worse.

In the old days, drugs were hard to obtain without a prescription. Players relied on the team doctor for all medical care. No player would think of buying drugs.

They did not have surplus money. Today, drugs can be bought illegally. Players have much money. Undoubtedly some players—no Bears, I hope—have developed private sources. Team owners have considered imposing tests on all players before each game. I would like to see such tests made. So far, the players' union has refused, saying the tests are an infringement on privacy.

A few years ago, the League hired the head of pharmacology at Cornell School of Medicine to set up a program to supervise administration of drugs by team doctors. Each team submits an inventory of its drugs. Each use of drugs is recorded. The League makes spot checks, by full-time investigators and representatives in all League cities. The League spends $100,000 a year trying to eliminate illegal use of drugs. We spend a lot of time and money running down rumors voiced in bars. Usually the rumor spreader is a pop-off artist bragging about his quote inside knowledge unquote.

Because I believe every person is different, I like continuity. That allows people to know one another. I do not believe in cutting and switching. Detroit has gone through fifteen coaches; the Cardinals had twenty-six in fifty-six years; the Oilers ten in seventeen years. For longevity I must cite myself. I have had forty wonderful years coaching, four periods of ten years each, separated by two two-year sabbaticals and thirty-nine months in the navy in World War II.

For Bears' victories after 1930, I must credit Ralph Jones, the intelligent Ralph Jones, who created our modern T-Formation with man-in-motion, the strategy now used by almost every team in the country.

Later, I had good support from Clark Shaughnessy as defense coach until he walked out in the middle of the season. Four months later he apologized. Subsequently he started a football business called "Football Projects" in which he created offenses and defenses for sale to college and professional teams. The business did not flourish. He gave it up. I heard of his situation and asked him to scout the Rams and '49ers and all Bear opponents visiting the West Coast. The usual fee for scouting was $100 a game but out of my respect for Clark I gave him $1,000 a game. We became good friends again. When he died he willed me a collection of his good plays and formations. One formation looks especially promising. I am holding it to turn it over to a Bear head coach who has established himself.

When I went to Decatur to build a winning football team for Mr. A.E. Staley, I knew from my experience at Illinois, Great Lakes and with the Hammond Professionals the names of excellent players needed to bring victory. Later, Mr. Walter Camp was helpful in listing his All-Americans each year. Coaches, fans and friends slipped me information, frequently wrong, about up-and-coming players.

Names fascinated me. I eagerly awaited the arrival of a rookie called Kill-'Em-Dead. He turned out to be big and strong but after the first scrimmage, he packed his shoes and went home.

For many years Frank Korch enabled me to acquire several top players, especially from small colleges. By the 1950's, we had two full-time scouts evaluating collegians. The player draft each year was becoming a major key to a team's future greatness. We needed all possible information. The task was bigger than one club could do properly. We joined with the Lions, Eagles and Steelers to form BLESTO. Its staff, operating out of the Steelers' stadium, gathers data on collegiate players throughout the country and distributes it to the four clubs. Other clubs have similar cooperative arrangements. Good scouting has helped bring the Bears our share of stars. Seventeen are in the Hall of Fame in Canton, Ohio: George Connor, Red Grange, Link Lyman, Joe Stydahar, Paddy Driscoll, Ed Healey, George McAfee, George Trafton, Danny Fortmann, Bill Hewitt, Bronko Nagurski, Bulldog Turner, Bill George, Sid Luckman, Gale Sayers, Dick Butkus, and me, as player, coach, manager, owner, and League member.

I find equal pleasure in another list of achievers—of the nineteen League players who became physicians or surgeons, nine are Bears—Joe Kopcha, Johnny Mohardt, Eddie Anderson, Danny Fortmann, Tony Ippolita, Jim Logan, Paul Podmajersky, Nick Sacrinty and Bill McColl. Two have become dentists, Bill Osmanski and John Siegal. I cannot count the number who have risen to important places in business. The qualities that make a winning player bring success throughout life.

Sixty years ago we knew little about opposing teams except by general reputation. As quality of play and competition improved, we needed to know our rivals' strategies, their strengths, their weaknesses. Team scouting became vital. I asked my brother, Walter, then assistant coach at Notre Dame, to attend games involving teams we would soon meet. He took on the task, partly for brotherly love, plus expenses. He bought a ticket, sat high in the stands and drew in his notebook offensive plays and defensive positions. He reported on skills of individual players. Each Monday we selected from our storehouse of 300 or so plays six or eight that would have the best chances of success, and defenses that would check the most dangerous attacks. Walter's reports won many games for the Bears.

325

Films earned an important place. We started using films to study performance of our own players. By running a bit of film over and over, by stopping it, we could detect flaws that escape the human eye during the excitement of a fast-moving play.

It was only a matter of time until teams began using movies to improve surveillance of rival teams. A dentist friend who made a hobby of home movies brought me many revealing films of opponents who did not suspect his presence. I shall take his secrets to the grave.

It was only a matter of time also until clubs began exchanging their own films. I would, say, send the Steelers a film of our game with the Lions, the Steelers' next opponent. In return, the Steelers would send me a film of their game with the Giants, our upcoming rival. The rules did not permit this kind of activity and some effort was made to stop it. But I argued that, knowing the amount of ingenuity existing within our League, no prohibition could be enforced totally, so why not make it legal and, going further, require that every team make its films available to all others on request. It was so agreed. The League asked that it too receive a copy to enable it to deepen its supervision of officiating. The result is a film merry-go-around every Monday.

One kind of information has a special importance. I would give a nice sum if every Saturday I could learn which plays our Sunday rival had selected from its repertory to use against us and modifications it was making in its defense. Acquiring such information requires originality. The '49ers called off practice one day because they suspected a Bear was watching from a helicopter hovering overhead. We didn't need a man in the sky that day. Our man was flat on his stomach, just beyond a canvas screen at the end of the field. One Saturday the Eagles magnanimously let us practice in their stadium. They even had two men painting a big sign saying "Welcome Bears." After some time, I noted the painters were making no progress but were writing things down on paper. I always made sure the old pre-electronic scoreboards were vacated for our practice. In Green Bay, windows of nearby houses were invariably occupied. "Bird watchers," the loyal householders insisted. Visiting coaches always asked me the identity of white-coated men visible in windows of the biology lab adjoining Stagg Field, their practice site. "Biologists," I said. "With binoculars?" they asked. For a Cleveland game I began practice at 5:30 A.M. so we could finish before Cleveland spies were awake.

One night before a big away game I assembled the players in the hotel conference room, locked the doors and ran through movies, pointing out weaknesses in our opponents and explaining how we would capitalize on them. I turned on the lights. "Any questions?" I asked.

A man at the back stood up and said, "Thanks, George. That was a mighty interesting hour," and walked out.

He was an assistant coach for tomorrow's foe. I did not discover how he had infiltrated our fortress. I would have given almost anything to learn the trick so we could work it on our subsequent guests.

Joe Stydahar liked to rent a room next to that of the visiting coach. He would sit for hours with a doctor's stethoscope pressed to the wall to tap the coach's instructions.

In the old days, coaches could not send in plays. Being a navy man, I knew something about wigwags but used them sparingly. Coach Greasy Neale evolved an elaborate wigwag system. I had an assistant record the position of Greasy's legs and arms on each play. In no time I had the code. I gave it to Bulldog Turner. He picked up the messages coming to the quarterback and adjusted our defenses. After a game, Neale said, "That Bulldog is the @#$%¢&* player I have ever seen! He seems to smell where our next play is coming from."

Joe Stydahar had a simpler system. He lip-read the quarterback's instructions in the huddle.

Bears have always been fortunate in having an army of dedicated fans. In Wrigley Field, the fans were at our elbow. The players could not make out all that was shouted but they knew when the fans were happy. Some players considered Wrigley Field was worth a touchdown. The baseball season became so long that we had to play all of our pre-season and two or three regular games out of town. That was unfair to our fans and hard on the players. After fifty years we moved to Soldier Field, an architectural gem dating back to early in this century. It is vast. We put the field in the south half and erected a temporary stand in the north end. There has been much talk about a new stadium. I even obtained an option on 22 acres near the loop but the proposition died. I do envy the clubs enjoying new stadiums which give comfort to fans and pride to players. But if I had to choose between loving fans and a luxurious stadium I would stay with the fans.

Fans love a winning club but victory can turn sour if it comes too early and too often. Carroll Rosenbloom recalled shortly before his tragic death:

I promised Baltimore a world championship in five years. We got one in six. More followed. We went to the Super Bowl. Suddenly the media turned on us. I invited the press to a lunch. I said, "Gentlemen, nobody seems to appreciate the Colts any more. I wish you would tell me what we have done wrong."

No one said a word.

I said, "Doesn't anyone have something to say? You all write for the papers or talk on radio or television. We're friends here. Nothing will be repeated. Say what you please. The Colts are looking for help."

A sports editor said: "You have gotten us used to wins."

I could not believe it.

I said, "Would you be happier if we lost?"

No one said no. No one said yes.

I said, "Gentlemen, thank you for coming. I wish you well."

I went home, taking my son. I said, "Steve, we can't stay here any longer. This town is satiated. They feel if you don't win the Super Bowl every year, you're due for trouble. I'm going to find a way to get out of Baltimore."

For many years, the media was most helpful. They sold their communities on professional football. They made heroes of players and coaches. We liked one another and helped one another and protected one another. Much of this changed in the late sixties and seventies. It became fashionable to stress the dark side, to play up discontents and misfits, to ridicule team spirit and fellowship. I miss the old happy days. I wish for a general revival of Ty Cobb's advice more than sixty years ago: "Kid, don't waste yourself being negative. Go for the positive."

Yes, go for the win!

The New Season Begins

THE BIG BLUE LINCOLN slides out of the under-ground garage in the Edgewater Beach Apartments at the top of Chicago's Gold Coast. It hurries along Lake Shore Drive, in and out of the shadows cast by the high-rise glass-faced apartment buildings. It scurries through Grant Park. The driver's large, strong hands, gnarled with rough usage and arthritis, grip the wheel firmly. He doesn't speak. Already, an hour before game time, he is tense. Soldier Field emerges from behind the Field Museum. The pedestrian overpasses from the sea of parking lots are already filled with fans hurrying to their seats. His Bears, his fabulous Bears, much praised when winning, much cursed when losing, much loved winning or losing, are starting the new season.

"This way, Papa Bear," a policeman shouts and leads the car among a forest of flagpoles to a private door.

People crowd around the car.

A man of about thirty, in working clothes, opens the door.

"Good luck, Papa Bear," he says.

"Thank you," the driver replies, slowly swinging his aching legs to the ground.

A young man holds out a photograph of Halas and a pen. "Very good picture," Halas says.

"I took it," the young man says. "I'll send one to you."

"That would be very kind," Halas says. He takes the picture and writes: "With all good wishes from the Bears, George Halas."

Other hands thrust forward programs, calling cards, parking tickets, envelopes, folded sheets of paper rummaged from pockets and purses. When the last paper is autographed, Halas pushes himself upright. He stamps each foot a couple of times and then sets off, lifting each foot springily. A friend offers an arm.

"Not now," he says. He doesn't want anyone to feel sorry for George Halas.

An elevator carries him slowly to the narrow ship-like corridor behind the press boxes. Reporters and broadcasters see Halas but don't come into the hall or shout greetings. They have learned that on game days, Halas has no time to chat. His mind is totally occupied. "A game is at stake," he always explains.

The owner's box is between the 40- and 50-yard lines. On a narrow shelf beneath the sliding windows are programs and fact sheets. A small TV set is alive with crowd shots. Five folding chairs are lined up against the shelf. A table holds a flask of coffee and an ice chest with a dozen cans of sugar-free pop.

331

His son Mugs and daughter Gin, her husband Ed, and Jim Finks come in. Gin kisses her father. The others say hello.

Finks says someone has phoned a warning that two bombs had been smuggled into the stadium and four Black men are going to kill Payton. "It's probably a phony," Finks adds.

"Probably, but we can't take any chances," Halas says. "All nuts are not in hospitals today."

A smiling man comes in. "How are things?" Halas asks.

"All right," the visitor says. "How are things with you?"

"Great, just great," Halas says.

They converse a moment and the visitor leaves.

"That's Bill Bidwill," Halas says. "He owns the Cardinals. I've known the family a long time. Fine people, the Bidwills."

Halas picks up a fact sheet, folds it carefully once, plain side out, then again, makes sure the edges are square and puts it on the shelf. He takes a pen from his coat and meticulously writes, "September 3, 1978. Bears vs. Cardinals."

He is ready. He sits back, arms folded, jaw thrust forward.

The Cardinals return the kickoff to the 24, go through center to the 33, slip around end to the 35 and a first down. They find another hole to the 39 and then to the 43. Halas fidgets. The Bears hold. The Cardinals kick. The teams move up and down the field. The Bears intercept a pass on the Cardinal 20.

"Let's go, gang," Halas says. "Now is the time."

The Bears kick a field goal. 3–0. Carefully. Halas writes a note.

A few plays later Avellini falls back to pass. A Cardinal brings him down for a 10-yard loss. Halas grunts. A second pass falls incomplete. Halas gets up and stamps around the little room. The quarter ends. Halas writes a note.

"Let's go, gang, let's go," Halas commands.

But it is the Cardinals who score. A field goal levels the game, 3–3. Halas sits mute.

Fifty-two seconds left of the first half. Avellini is again smothered for a loss.

"Block, you rumheads," Halas growls. "What's the matter with you? Goddammit." He throws his note paper on the floor.

The half ends.

Halas picks up the note paper and sits back, arms folded. No one speaks to him. A girl brings sandwiches. Gin pours sodas all around. Halas takes a bite from a sandwich, wraps it up again and puts it away. After sixty years he still is unable to eat before or during a game. A young man brings a sheet of statistics. Halas shuns it. He doesn't need a computer printout to tell him how the game is going.

The Cardinals kick off to start the second half.

"Come on, gang," Halas says. "The old zipperoo."

Payton runs to the 28, to the 33. Avellini passes. While the ball is still in flight, Halas announces, "It's good." It is good, to the 43. Payton crosses mid-field. Then he's brought down for a loss.

333

"Holy crying," Halas says. "Let's get blocking."

The Bears punt. Halas writes a note.

The Cardinals run and pass to the 45, to the 35, to the 29. "Red dog them," Halas orders. The Bears hold.

Two-twenty-two remains of the third quarter.

A Bear stops the Cardinal carrier and wrestles him back 8 yards. Bear fans roar.

"Attaboy, nice work," Halas says.

A Bear blocks a pass. Bear fans roar.

"Nice work," Halas repeats.

The Cardinals punt to the 48.

Forty-two seconds.

Payton gets to the 42, Harper to the 39. Third and one.

The quarter ends.

"Now is the time for the big drive," Halas says. "The big one. The old zipperoo."

Payton gets to the 36.

"All the way, kid, all the way," Halas says. "Come on, kid, you got to pick it up." Harper gets to the 33. Avellini passes to the 25.

Halas is on his feet.

He shouts. "Baybee, baybee. That's the way to go. Payton smells the goal line," he says. "Come on," he pleads.

The pass is bad. Halas sits. He writes a note.

Payton gets to the 10. The referees call a penalty against the Cardinals. First and goal, 5 yards away.

Payton finds a small hole and crosses the goal line. Halas jumps up, arms high. "Attaboy! Baybee, oh, baybee. Every time he smells that goal line, he goes."

Bears fans roar mightily.

334

The conversion is good. Bears 10, Cardinals 3. Twelve minutes remain.

The Cardinals return the kickoff to the 19. They pass to the 31.

"Red dog," Halas shouts.

The Cardinals try a bomb—a long, long, long pass to the goal. The receiver is clear. A Bear runs hard to catch him. The ball is overthrown. The receiver can't get it. No one can get it. But 1 yard from the goal, the Bear dives at the receiver and hits him.

The ball falls to earth. The Bear lies on the ground, pounding the fake turf with his fists. His interference gives the Cardinals the ball 1 yard short of their goal. "You stoop," Halas shouts. He writes a note.

The Cardinals score. The kick is good. 10–10. Time remaining: 7:56.

"The old zip, gang, the old zip," Halas says.

The Bears return the kick to the 33.

Payton gets to the 36, to the 49, across to the Cardinal 40.

On a fake reverse Harper reaches the 27. Harper goes to the 8, Payton to the 3. First down.

Halas grips the shelf so hard you can almost hear the wood crumble.

Payton slips but picks up a yard. Harper gets a yard. Time out. Avellini comes to the sidelines to talk with the coach. Halas asks Ed for a cup of coffee. Black.

"Quarterback sneak," Halas says. "Listen to the crowd. Don't disappoint them. Whack 'em with every-thing you've got. Nothing fancy, geez, nothing fancy."

Avellini takes the ball. Harper and Payton run to the right. Who has the ball? The Cards don't know. They tackle Avellini, then Payton, but Harper is still going. He has the ball. He's heading for a hole in the line. A Cardinal linebacker jams himself into the hole. Harper jumps high, over the linebacker's bent back, does a somersault in the air and comes down, head first, feet last. Touchdown!

Halas is up, arms high. "Attaboy, I tell you, that's a boy."

The band plays "Happy Days are Here Again."

Halas knocks over his coffee.

The kicker goes in. "Come on, kid," Halas says. "This is very important, very important." The kick is good. 17–10.

The clock shows 1:49.

"Everybody down hard," Halas says. It's an order. "Please," he adds, softly. It's a prayer.

The Cardinals throw away caution. They pass, pass, pass. They reach the 40.

"Smear 'em," Halas yells. "You've got to red dog them." The passer drops back and back and back. The receivers run far and wide. "Here's the big one," Halas says. There's a touch of fear in his voice. The pass comes. Twenty, thirty, forty yards. The ball spirals perfectly, high and far. Halas rises. He is stone cold. Two Cardinal receivers wait for the ball on the 10. Allan Ellis, the Bears' most effective defender, should have been there also but he went out earlier with a bad knee. The assignment was given to a rookie, Terry Schmidt.

Schmidt is there! He intercepts. Pandemonium!

"The rookie becomes the hero," Halas says.

Halas remains standing. Forgotten is the stick. Forgotten is the pain.

The roar of Bears' fans sounds like thunder.

The clock ticks off the final seconds.

"Four." "Three." "Two." "One." The thousands chant.

Nobody hears the gun.

"Yeah, yeah, yeah," Halas shouts. "That's a great win," he says. "That's showing the old spirit."

Gin hugs him. Father and daughter press cheek against cheek, giving strength, sharing pleasure.

"It's a tough way to make a buck," Finks says.

"But what a beautiful way," Halas replies. "Jim, that's a great win."

Mugs' new wife Pat comes in. She kisses Mugs and squeezes Halas' hand.

Halas leans against the wall. Nobody says anything. Finks leaves. Mugs and Pat leave. Then Ed and Virginia. Halas leans forward, resting against the shelf, looking onto the field. He watches fans laugh as they leave.

"I do believe we gave a lot of people pleasure today," he says, speaking to himself. "It's a great game, a great game."

Halas folds his note paper and puts it in his coat pocket. Perhaps he'll show it to the coach someday, but only if the coach asks.

The stadium empties. Gradually the tension goes out of Halas. His face softens. The jaw relaxes. The fingers loosen. When peace has been restored in the stadium and within himself, he moves slowly along the hall, down the elevator, out to his car. The sidewalk is empty, the police gone.

From nowhere, a girl of thirteen or so with tight, light curls comes up cautiously.

337

"Are you Mr. Halas?" she asks.

"Yes, dear," Halas replies. She holds out a program.

"Would you sign it, please?" she asks.

"Of course, dear," Halas says, "as soon as I get in the car."

The girl bounces up and down. She bends close to him. Almost in a whisper she says, "I prayed for the Bears last night."

"Thank you, my dear," Halas says. "I am certain it helped."

He takes his pen.

"What is your name?"

"Dora," she says.

Halas pauses, then writes: "To Dora, with thanks from the Bears. George Halas."

He returns the program. She reads it. She hugs it. She holds it at arm's length. She twirls. She clasps the program to her heart. She jumps up and down. She holds it out. She reads it again and again. She runs a few steps. She turns.

"This is the happiest moment in my life," she calls. And away she goes, dancing and prancing and swirling.

Halas watches, his eyes shining and moist.

"Can you believe it?" he asks. "Isn't football a wonderful game?"

Index

339